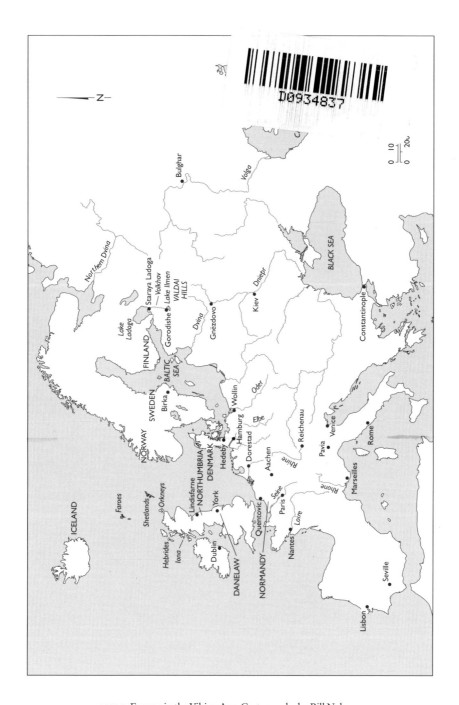

MAP 1. Europe in the Viking Age. Cartography by Bill Nelson.

THE AGE OF THE VIKINGS

PRINCETON UNIVERSITY PRESS

PRINCETON AND OXFORD

THE AGE OF THE
VIKINGS

ANDERS WINROTH

Copyright © 2014 by Princeton University Press
Published by Princeton University Press, 41 William
Street, Princeton, New Jersey 08540
In the United Kingdom: Princeton University Press, 6
Oxford Street, Woodstock, Oxfordshire OX20 1TW

press.princeton.edu

Jacket photograph © Kirsten Jensen Helgeland.
Jacket design by Faceout Studio.

Library of Congress Cataloging-in-Publication Data

Winroth, Anders.
The age of the Vikings / Anders Winroth.
pages cm
Includes bibliographical references and index.
ISBN 978-0-691-14985-1 (hardback : acid-free paper)
1. Vikings. 2. Civilization, Viking. I. Title.
DL65.W63 2014
948'.022—dc23
2014006488

British Library Cataloging-in-Publication Data is available

This book has been composed in Verdigris MVB Pro

Printed on acid-free paper. ∞

Printed in the United States of America

1 3 5 7 9 10 8 6 4 2

TILL MINA FÖRÄLDRAR

CONTENTS

THE AGE OF THE VIKINGS

CHAPTER I

INTRODUCTION

The Fury of the Northmen

FINALLY THE CHIEFTAIN TOOK HIS HIGH SEAT. THE WARRIOR band had waited eagerly on the benches around the great hall, warmed by the crackling fire, quaffing bountiful mead. The chieftain's servant girls had spent weeks this fall mixing honey and water, brewing barrels full for his famous party at Yule, the old Scandinavian festival of midwinter. Now the chieftain was there in his best clothes demanding to know why his famed warriors had been given such simple drink. Did they not deserve better hospitality after all they had accomplished in Frankland? Had they not hauled home barrels of the best Frankish wine from the rich cellar of that monastery last summer and paid dearly for their loot with their blood?

The appearance of the pitcher, its perfect regularity so unlike the clumsy local earthenware containers that most of them were used to, hushed the rowdy warriors in the vast hall. Tin foil in several horizontal lines and, between them, sequences of rhombuses decorated the pitcher, a glorious vessel for an exotic drink. The chieftain, served first, received a chalice with an artful decoration of blue glass in delicate strands after which the man in the seat of honor was handed a matching glass. The rest of them drank out of horns or simple mugs, but now everyone drank wine instead of mead to celebrate their bravery and their success when they had gone on Viking raids during the summer. Some of the warriors, recognizing the glassware bought by the chieftain when the band of warriors had visited the town of Hedeby on the way home from raiding, whispered that the blue-shimmering glasses were from a

FIG. I. This beautiful pitcher made on a fast-spinning potter's wheel was manufactured inside the Frankish Empire but found in a grave in Birka, Sweden. The pattern was made by attaching thin tin foil. Photo: Gunnel Jansson, courtesy of Statens Historiska Museum, Stockholm.

faraway kingdom called Egypt; the chieftain could have procured a good longship for what he had paid for them after hard negotiation.

Used to coarser drink, some of the warriors were unfamiliar with the taste of wine. What a great leader of men who so generously shared such luxuries! And he looked the part, too. His cape featured embroidered leopards and silver sequins, and it was trimmed with lustrous fox fur. He sported a silk cap on his head. An eiderdown pillow with a beautifully embroidered cover depicting a procession of people, horses, and wagons cushioned his seat, and by his side stood a ceremonial ax with rich decoration in silver-wire inlay depicting a fantastic animal. This was a real chieftain! Where did he get all these amazing things? Few of the warriors had ever been this close to such luxuries. They had never seen foxes as darkly glistening as these, nor had they experienced any textile that could shine this luminously.

Not everyone in the hall had sailed out last summer with this chieftain to seize opportunities in Frankland; many newcomers had come to the chieftain's celebration. They could be heard bragging about how they, next summer, would go with this chieftain to redden their swords with the blood of the Franks and the English, or why not the Moors in Spain? And they were going to gain undreamed-of riches.

This past summer, they had not been so fortunate. Of the three ships that had gone out under another chieftain, only one came back, and that was without their leader, who had fallen, it was rumored, when the Frisians had unexpectedly fought back. Nobody was really sure what had happened, for those who had returned were not eager to talk about it.

It was time for the food to be brought in, but first the gods must have their share. The chieftain cut the throat of the sacrificial animal and let the blood stream down on the floor, pouring some wine on top of it. The chieftain also held up a tiny gold foil between his fingers for everyone to admire. Those who sat closest could just make out an embossed picture of a couple embracing. The chieftain attached the foil to one of the posts supporting the roof. Not all of his warriors were sure exactly what this ritual implied, but they were certain it must be beneficial. The sacrificed lamb was taken out to be roasted, and the rest of the food was brought in, large chunks of roasted meat, cauldrons of boiled fish, and sweetmeats. The warriors feasted heartily and happily on all that was on offer. One certainly did not need to bring any packed food to the feasts of this illustrious chieftain!

Their bellies full of a glorious meal, everyone was leisurely cracking the hard shells of nuts to get to their sweet contents as dessert, but the chieftain himself and his closest men were having larger nuts that were easier to open, for their shells were softer and thinner. Were their contents more delicious, too? Few in the hall had ever tasted these foreign "welsh" nuts, or "walnuts." Some of them remembered seeing a single walnut when it had been put in the magnificent grave of the last great chieftain before this one.

That funeral had been something to behold: the dead man was given a huge, gorgeous ship with exquisite wood carvings, which was going to ferry him to the Afterworld. People were impressed that his son was willing to sacrifice such a grand vessel, although malicious tongues whispered that the ship was anyway not very seaworthy and had capsized twice, drowning the chieftain's brother. The son of the old chieftain had also sacrificed an unheard-of number of horses on the foreship. People talked at length of the sea of blood on the deck of the funeral boat before soil was thrown over the boat to form a mound, from which, as a reminder, the mast still protruded.

The skald stood up in the middle of the hall, and the warriors, by now boisterous, did not quite fall silent, but the hall became still enough that most people could hear him. He turned to the chieftain and declaimed: "Listen to my poesy, destroyer of the dark blue, I know how to compose." This skald was a good one, even a very good one; one could hear from his accent that he was an Icelander as, everyone knew, were all the best skalds. The warriors enjoyed the euphony of the verses he recited: the rhythm, the alliteration, the end rhyme, the slant rhyme, the assonances, but they did not quite understand every stanza. So unnatural was the word order, so complex the waft of rhyme, and so far-fetched the poetic circumlocutions. Dark blue . . . what exactly? Wound-swans? Meals of giants? But the verses clearly celebrated the achievements of last summer's Viking adventure. The warriors recognized individual words: Franks, fire, gold, horses, a raven. A warrior suddenly burst out, "We fed the raven well in Frankland!" when he suddenly realized that this was the solution to part of the riddle of one stanza. Everyone cheered, and the poet had to fall silent for a moment. In the ancient poetry of the Norse, to feed the raven (also poetically known as the wound-swan) meant to kill the enemy, providing a meal for beasts that feed on carrion. It was difficult for the drunken warriors to make out even such phrases, for the Icelander excelled not only in far-fetched expressions, but also in using unnatural word order and rare locutions. The beginning line had been easy enough, for the skald began, strategically, with expressions readily understandable. There could be no doubt, either, of the ending, for his gestures and inflections made it abundantly clear when he reached the grand peroration of his praise of the chieftain.

The chieftain rewarded the skald with a golden arm ring that he took from his own arm, and he lavished on the expectant warriors, for their bravery and loyalty, arm rings in gold and silver, swords with richly decorated pommels, clothes, helmets, chain mail, and shields. Even those who had just joined the chieftain received tokens of his new friendship, mostly weapons, each according to his standing and promise as a warrior.

At the end of the evening, everyone was happy. They had eaten and drunk to their satisfaction and beyond, listened to and half-understood what they were sure was great poetry, and they could proudly carry their new arm rings or swords that proclaimed to everyone that they were the valued friends of this great chieftain. This winter, a lot of men were spending months building a new, even more formidable ship for next summer's raiding season. Slave women and servant girls were spinning and weaving a great woolen sail, an investment of thousands and thousands of hours, but the sail would be worth it. The new vessel would not only sail faster but its greatness would also ensure that the chieftain's reputation spread even further, prompting even more warriors to volunteer to fill the rowers' benches.

Of course, he could easily afford any expense after all the silver and gold he had collected last summer; some he had simply taken in monasteries, churches, and homes; some had been paid out in return for his promise not to attack hapless Europeans; some had been his payment for men and women he had captured and sold as slaves. Life was good for this chieftain, who presided over a band of devoted warriors. They were all excited to go out and fight loyally for their chieftain, to the death if necessary. They were all looking forward to raiding again in Europe as soon as spring returned.

It all began in the great feasts in the halls of Norse chieftains. Viking raids started here, springing from the loyalties and friendships inspired by the drinking, eating, and gift giving. And in the halls it also ended with the distribution of the loot as gifts, laying the foundations for a new cycle of violence the next year. The warriors loved their generous chieftain who provided food and drink, entertainment, jewelry, and weapons. They were happy to give their allegiance and military prowess in return. Although the humiliation of Europe's powerful kingdoms, the sacking of the rich treasuries of monasteries, and the great battles between Vikings and Europeans may comprise the most spectacular and best-known events of the Viking Age, the real story of the time unfolded in the great halls of the North. They were the focal points of the early medieval geography of power in Scandinavia. Each hall was the centerpiece of its chieftain's honor, worth, and reputation, the focus of his world, the locus of his power.

The ancient king of the Danes, Hrothgar, resided in a most splendid hall, Heorot, at least in the imagination of the Viking Age *Beowulf* poet. When the Swedish warriors of the eponymous hero Beowulf approached Heorot in friendship, they were endlessly impressed by the tall and magnificent hall, famous throughout the world. Hrothgar had ordered it built so that his reputation would grow and remain forever great. The poet emphasized the glory and the excellence of Heorot, which gave Hrothgar bragging rights and a basis for his power. That was exactly the purpose of building a hall, a structure that impressed and a famed place to which warriors would flock to share in the hospitality and generosity of its chieftain.[1]

Chieftains built halls all over northern Europe, where archeologists have discovered the remnants of dozens, teaching us just how many warlords strove for power in early medieval Scandinavia. Each chieftain cherished his hall, built it as large and tall as he was able, had it decorated, if not with gold as in the imagined

Heorot, then at least with painted wood carvings, weapons, and other embellishments.

The halls of Scandinavian chieftains are the largest buildings known from the early Middle Ages in northern Europe. Measuring 48.5 by 11.5 meters, the hall at Lejre on the Danish island of Zealand was the greatest of them all. Beyond a few fragments of wood at the bottom of some postholes, nothing is preserved of the great building, the pride of its chieftain, except the imprint of its foundations in the Danish soil. That imprint is sufficient, however, for us to know the dimensions of the hall and to learn that it was solidly built: sturdy timber posts held up the roof, and the walls were six inches thick, made up of planks cut from ancient forests. A great hall should be a tall and impressive building. At Lejre, archeologists conclude that the roof reached at least 10 meters. It was held up by two rows of interior posts, and also by posts in the walls, which needed to be buttressed by twenty-two raking planks on each side, 1.5 meters apart. In the middle of the building, two sets of roof posts were omitted, creating a large interior space of some 9.5 square meters with the fire burning in the main hearth on one side.[2]

This open space was fundamental to the political power of the Lejre chieftain. His thronelike chair, or high seat, stood here, richly decorated with wood carvings and probably paint. Scandinavian artisans during the Viking Age were capable of splendid wood carving. Furniture found in a grave mound in Oseberg, Norway, displays, for example, exquisitely carved dragons, with large stylized eyes; the animals intertwine legs, creating a richly detailed interlaced pattern. Around the chieftain, his warriors would sit on what the *Beowulf* poet called "mead-benches," enjoying their leader's hospitality, certainly including much mead, but also more distinguished drinks, as well as food and entertainment. It was here that the Viking raiding bands first came together as communities of warriors under the leadership of the chieftain. Bonds of loyalty, fellowship, friendship, and blood brotherhood were established and oaths of solidarity were sworn. In the mead hall, throngs of Scandinavian warriors came together, drinking and feasting and generally having a good time. The generosity and wealth of the chieftain impressed them all deeply. As often happens when men drink together, they came away with a renewed sense of solidarity with one another and loyalty to their leader.

We will take the hall of the Viking leader as our starting point for exploring the history of the Viking Age, just as it was the starting point for Viking raids attacking Europe. Here, all strands of that history come together—politics, military prowess, trade, agriculture, exploration, religion, art, literature, and much else—and we will follow them from the hall out into the early medieval world, in some cases going very far indeed, to exotic places like al-Khwarezm in central Asia and Newfoundland in America, Seville in southwestern Spain, and the White Sea on the north shore of Russia. For the Vikings, experienced by Europeans as a kind of unqualified evil coming from the ends of the world in fulfillment of Biblical prophecies, were in fact deeply embedded in the texture of early medieval European society.

We continue to be fascinated by the Vikings and stories about their exploits. Ferocious barbarians in horned helmets with gleaming swords and sharp axes, descending on Lindisfarne, Hamburg, Paris, Seville, Nantes—almost everywhere—to slaughter, raid, rape, and generally wreak destruction, toppling kingdoms and laying waste to Europe; the Vikings pique our imagination. We picture them killing and maiming without regard for age, gender, or status in society. We imagine them as super-masculine heroes, practitioners of frenzied violence for its own sake, devotees of strange pagan religions that required bloody sacrifices necessitating horrendous torture. Just as we as a society continue to have a fraught and complex relationship to violence, we are both spellbound and repelled by the Vikings. While we may sympathize with and grieve for their helpless victims and feel put off by all the mindless slaying, we can scarcely help admiring the strength, courage, and virility of the Vikings.

But the Vikings also represent a more unambiguously positive image: we like to think of them as youthful, courageous, and exciting adventurers devoted to travel and exploration. We think of the Vikings as accomplished and fearless discoverers who sailed across the Atlantic five hundred years before Columbus. On the other side of Europe, they navigated the rivers of Russia and discovered overland trade routes to central Asia and the Arab Caliphate, connecting with China via the Silk Road. The new trade routes helped them make fortunes as traders and merchants.

Despite their propensity for violence, the reputation of the Vikings remains predominantly positive, and their image is constantly used in ever more inventive ways in metaphor and marketing. Viking-related trademarks promote herring, lutefisk, river cruises, computer games, kitchen interiors, power tools, and the NFL football team in Minnesota. A widely used computer communication standard borrows its name from a famous Viking king, while many musical bands—particularly those devoted to various shades of heavy metal, it appears—derive their name from Norse culture and lore. Viking-themed feature films, television dramas, and documentaries draw huge audiences, while college courses on Viking-related themes seldom fail to entice large crowds of students. Vikings sell and intrigue. They evoke an attractive blend of masculinity, strength, adventure, and northern heartiness.

Yet, do we truly know the real Vikings? Do we genuinely recognize who they were, what they did, and what they stood for? The modern cultural imagination captures only aspects of the Vikings, and what we think we know is skewed, exaggerated, or simply misunderstood. Their iconic horned helmets, for starters, never existed, or at least not before the premiere of Wagner's *Ring of the Nibelung* in 1876.[3] While we recycle myths, some of the most fascinating stories about the Vikings are seldom or never told.

The Vikings were violent, even ferociously so. They hunted slaves, killed, maimed, and plundered over much of Europe, including in Scandinavia itself, and it would serve no reasonable purpose to deny their thirst for blood. We need, however, to understand the context of and reasons for what they did. They were not simple mindless killing-machines. The Middle Ages were a violent time overall, and this was especially the case in the stateless societies of the early period. Violence played a pivotal role in the political economy of the time, even for purportedly civilized rulers like Emperor Charlemagne and early English kings, who operated within much the same violent framework as the Vikings, but if anything on a larger scale.[4]

Yet amid all the violence and warfare, the Viking Age was also a moment of great cultural, religious, and political achievement. Intense Scandinavian contacts with Europe unleashed not only the "fury of the Northmen" onto their European victims, but also a battery of European cultural and political influences on Scandinavia. The people of the European North responded in creative ways. Literature flourished, especially poetry of a complexity seldom rivaled. During the Viking Age, Scandinavians experienced a great boom in decorative art, much of it produced by artisans and craftsmen in the thriving trade towns of the region or at the courts of ambitious rulers. Some Viking Age Scandinavians embraced a newly fashionable religion, Christianity, while others fomented a resurgence of the old pagan religion. The Baltic and North seas saw unprecedented commercial activity precipitated by the new economic structures of the Eurasian continent after the rise of the Arab Caliphate. That trade and exchange, largely run by Scandinavians and other northern Europeans, brought not only untold riches to the Baltic regions, including enormous amounts of minted Arab silver ultimately deriving from the rich mines of Afghanistan, but also all kinds of exotic trade goods. Chieftains impressed people by drinking Rhenish wine from Egyptian glasses, by procuring the strongest steel in the world for their swords from central Asia and India, by wearing Chinese silk and Indian gems, and by offering those they counted as friends a share in all that wealth. The Viking raids were another source of riches, bringing to the North not only Western coins—more Anglo-Saxon pennies survive in Scandinavia than in the British Isles—but also other kinds of valuables, including jewelry, silk, gold and silver treasures from the church coffers of western Europe.

The wealth that Scandinavians accumulated was put to inventive use in the political economy of the region; chieftains who gained riches gave them away to inspire friendship and loyalty in those who gratefully received the gifts. Similarly, marriage alliances, blood brotherhoods, and godparentage were used to create and strengthen morally obliging ties of allegiance between warriors and their leaders. Each chieftain strove to build up as good and powerful a private army as possible. They therefore competed over who was most impressive, generous, eloquent, and well-connected, and over who could give the greatest gifts. Such competition involved open and violent warfare among rival chieftains, in a constantly shifting kaleidoscope of unstable political constellations. Some chieftains went under and some took their ambitions elsewhere, while others prevailed, accumulating more and more power, until, out of the turmoil, the three medieval kingdoms of Scandinavia crystalized around the year 1000.

Some Scandinavians moved away from their northern habitats into Russia, France, England, Scotland, and Ireland, taking with them not only their ambitions but also their language and customs. In doing so, they fundamentally changed the places where they settled. Other Scandinavians moved to Iceland, Greenland, and, if only briefly, Newfoundland, bringing Norse culture across the North Atlantic. Transatlantic migration, long-distance trade, and the Viking raids themselves would not have been possible without the sturdy, fast, and eminently seaworthy ships that Scandinavians learned to construct and equip with efficient sails just before the start of the Viking Age. The Norsemen were well aware of how important their ships were, and they created imaginative ideologies and mythologies around them.

The Age of the Vikings engages every major facet of Viking and Scandinavian endeavor from the end of the eighth century through the eleventh. This was when ordinary Europeans for the first time learned more than vague generalities about their neighbors to the north. They quickly came to fear them greatly, since Scandinavians discovered that wealth was to be easily gained by raiding along the coasts and rivers of the continent. The Viking longships provided an invaluable advantage: the ability to surprise the victims, who had no warning of the impending attack. The peoples of Europe were no strangers to indiscriminate violence in an epoch that always was violent, but when the enemy arrived overland, rumors of their approach spread fast. The Vikings also had a propensity for attacking monasteries and churches, which were soft and undefended targets but which Christian armies for the most part spared. Monks and clerics well-nigh monopolized early medieval literacy, so preserved chronicles and other literary works preserve their perspective, which understandably was utterly hostile to their attackers. The Vikings thus earned an unfavorable reputation as "a most vile people" and "a filthy race."[5] In contrast, I argue that their violence, seen in broad historical context, was no worse than that of others in a savage time, when heroes like Charlemagne (d. 814) killed and plundered on a much greater scale than the northern raiders.

During the Viking Age, Scandinavia pursued a distinct and different path from the rest of Europe. Art, literature, and religion developed in idiosyncratic ways, and Scandinavians opened trade routes that had never before been used, or at least not on the same scale. Many of them moved away to settle in places as different as Greenland and the interior of Russia, eastern England and northern France. Overall, the Viking Age was a dynamic and creative time when Scandinavia was bursting with energy. Multitudes of Norse men and women eagerly grasped the opportunities that had become available to them since the recent invention of the longship. The kingdoms of Europe also suffered through many periods of weakness and confusion, such as the Frankish civil war of 840–843 or the revolt of the English king's son Edmund in 1015, which made opportunities for Scandinavian enterprise much richer. In taking advantage of these opportunities, Scandinavians spurred political and social change, which in the long run enabled them to enter the mainstream of European history, though at the cost of losing some of what made their culture distinctive.

In *The Age of the Vikings*, I draw on an array of contemporary written, visual, and material sources, as well as abundant scholarship in history, archeology, literature, and neighboring disciplines, in order to recapture from a broad contextual perspective something of the excitement and innovation of that difficult period without glossing over its destructive heritage. The book is anchored in concrete and lively stories about the men and women who helped shape one of the most unique and interesting periods in history, the Viking Age.

The word "Viking" is rare in the Viking Age sources, but in modern times it has become a ubiquitous but ill-defined label. The original sense of the term is unclear, and there are many suggestions for etymological derivations.[6] In this book, I reserve the term "Vikings" for those northerners who in the early Middle Ages raided, plundered, and battled in Europe, in accordance with how the word is used in medieval texts. Otherwise, I refer to the inhabitants of Scandinavia as Scandinavians. The language they spoke is called Old Norse, so I have sometimes used the term "Norsemen."

CHAPTER 2

VIOLENCE IN A VIOLENT TIME

ALL AT ONCE, THE NORTHMEN SWARMED OUT OF THEIR BOATS. They scaled the city walls on ladders and spread throughout the city. They smashed, broke, and cut through doors and shutters; they plundered, looted, and ravaged as they desired; there was no one to defend the city of Nantes in what is now western France. The town was full of people, for it was St. John's Day, June 24, 843. Masses of people had come to celebrate the holiday from the surrounding countryside and even from distant cities. First to discover the approaching Vikings, the monks from the monastery Indre some nine kilometers away took their treasures and fled upstream along the Loire to Nantes to seek protection inside the city walls. Their flight was in vain; they were no safer in Nantes. Monks, clergy, and layfolk flocked to the sturdiest building in town, the magnificent ancient cathedral, dedicated to the apostles Peter and Paul, where Bishop Gohard, "an upright man filled with piety," organized them as best he could in the chaos. They barricaded the doors and anxiously waited. Resorting to their only remaining hope, they implored God for delivery and salvation. Bishop Gohard led his flock in prayer and liturgical invocations. It did not help.

The Vikings broke down the doors and knocked out the windows of the cathedral. They ran savagely into the sacred building, striking down everyone they encountered. They attacked the flock, cruelly murdering all the priests and laity except for those taken prisoner and hauled off to the ships. Legend claims that Bishop Gohard was at the altar saying mass when he was struck; he had reached the *Sursum corda*, "Lift up your hearts [to God]," from the preface of the Eucharistic liturgy. His exemplary behavior in the face of immediate danger earned him sainthood and martyrdom in the Catholic Church.

The Vikings killed some of the monks outside, others inside the building, but most of them were butchered like sacrificial animals on the sacred altar of the cathedral. Or so said a monk from Indre who witnessed the massacre and survived to tell the story. When he wrote down his memories many years later, he could not hold back an eruption of despair at the memory: "Who can disentangle all the pain and loss of that day? Who can hold back his tears when explaining what happened, when children hanging at their mothers' breasts got blood instead of milk, when the blood of my saintly brothers, shed by hostile swords, drenched the floor of the temple, when the sacred altars were besmeared with the blood of innocents?"

The Vikings plundered immense quantities of gold and silver, including the plate of the cathedral; they brought all the loot to their base on the island of Noirmoutier in the Loire estuary. They also hauled off many captives, some of whom were later released against ransom paid by "those who survived the massacre." A few days later, on June 29, the Vikings attacked the monastery of Indre, which they devastated and burned so thoroughly that it was never rebuilt.

This story of the massacre in Nantes, a great city close to the border between the independent principality Brittany and the Carolingian Empire, comes from the pen of an eyewitness. His account is unique because of its rich detail. The author was a learned man who wrote splendid Latin, sprinkled self-consciously with unusual words and rhetorical expressions. As we shall see, most other sources are couched in disappointingly vague and general terms. Thanks to this eyewitness, we can answer questions about the Nantes raid that we cannot even begin to address for other raids.[1]

How many Vikings attacked Nantes in June 843? We cannot know exactly. The eyewitness only tells us that the ships were "numerous"—he presumably did not have time to count—but a later chronicle claims that sixty-seven Viking ships sailed and were rowed up the Loire on that fateful midsummer day. Such numbers in medieval sources should normally be understood as more suggestive and symbolic than factual. But we would be safe to assume that it must have been a sizable group of several hundred warriors who descended on Nantes.

The Nantes eyewitness tells us, though not in so many words, that the Vikings were great opportunists. They attacked a month after the local Frankish army led by Count Rainald of Nantes had been crushed in battle with the Bretons under Prince Erispoe, on May 24. The count was the official appointed by the Carolingian king to administer and defend his region. Rainald had been count of Nantes since 841, but he was killed in the battle. The city lacked any military leader to organize its defenses, and the local army had been decimated, the eyewitness emphasizes. The Vikings clearly knew this and acted on their intelligence. How did they know? The eyewitness alleges that the treacherous villain Lambert, son of a previous count of Nantes, against whom the writer harbored some unspecified bitterness, led the Vikings through the dangerous labyrinth of sandbanks, marshes, and islands in the Loire estuary.

The truth is that the Vikings did not need any Frankish aristocrat to tell them that the count of Nantes was dead with most of his army and that the city was undefended. At the same time as some Scandinavians attacked and raided cities like Nantes, other Scandinavians participated in normal commerce and other intercourse in the Frankish Empire as well as elsewhere in Europe. Actually, many of the same people both raided and traded, as the opportunity arose. They would quickly get a whiff of important events.

The Vikings also knew when to strike. They waited a month after Rainald's defeat to attack. This was not only to collect the large force needed to attack a major center like Nantes; the Vikings of the early ninth century traveled in smaller groups of one or a few ships that, when a good reason emerged, such as the opportunity to attack an undefended city, would join with others to undertake a major enterprise. But the Vikings clearly wanted to attack on a major Christian feast day, in this case St. John's Day, when they knew that many people in their fineries would congregate in the main churches. The booty would be larger, both in gold and silver and in human captives who could either be held for ransom or sold as slaves. More booty would also be concentrated in a few places.

The Nantes eyewitness gives us the impression that the Vikings attacked suddenly and unexpectedly. Everything was fine, and then, all of a sudden, armed Vikings swarmed everywhere. It is not as if the good burghers of Nantes were not used to warfare; Brittany, still an independent duchy, was not far away, and border skirmishes were common. Even worse, for the previous three years the entire Frankish Empire had been torn apart by a fratricidal and very bloody civil war, in which the three surviving sons of Emperor Louis the Pious (d. 840) had fought about how to share the empire among them. The crucial difference with the Viking raid was speed; they appeared as if from nowhere, although, in fact, they came from the sea on their fast ships. The Carolingian armies of the civil war and the armies of the Bretons lumbered slowly across land, providing plenty of advance warning for civilians to hide themselves and their valuables before the armies' arrival. The Vikings appeared unheralded. Contemporaries noticed this feature in Viking tactics. The chronicler Prudentius noted, for example, in 837 that "the Northmen at this time fell on Frisia with their usual surprise attack."[2] The key word here is "usual"; Prudentius knew that the Vikings' preferred mode was warfare by incursion.

We begin to be able to discern the patterns of Viking tactics, first on the basis of the Nantes eyewitness report, but these patterns are confirmed by other sources: the Vikings preferred to attack suddenly and without warning when they knew that no organized military forces that might provide resistance were close and when they knew rich booty was to be had. To be successful under such circumstances did not require any particular bloodthirstiness or advanced weaponry or martial skills. As we shall see, the Vikings were, at least initially, amateurs at fighting, despite their reputation.

What did the Vikings want from Nantes? When one reads either what Prudentius reported in his chronicle about the raid or, in particular, the eyewitness account, the main impression is that the Vikings were homicidal maniacs who killed for pleasure. The eyewitness pulled out all the rhetorical stops to evoke the image of a

cathedral drenched in blood through the impious actions of a devilish people who sacrificed monks as the pagans of olden times sacrificed animals on their altars. Of course, from the perspective of the
victims, the loss of life was shocking, traumatic, and devastating.
That is why the sources often emphasize that the Vikings killed, and
killed in large numbers. If we read the sources a little more closely,
however, a more reasonable image emerges. The Nantes eyewitness
at one point says that "the heathens mowed down the *entire* multi-
tude of priest, clerics, and laity," but he immediately adds "except
those" that were hauled off into captivity. A few lines further down,
we find out that there also remained people in Nantes who had been
neither killed nor captured, for "many who survived the massacre"
paid ransom money for those captured. What we see is the writer
falling for the rhetorical temptation to say that the Vikings were so
bad that in their unquenchable blood lust they killed everyone, but
then having to admit that this was not actually what happened. It
is perfectly understandable that anyone who had lived through the
trauma of a Viking raid would like to portray the raiders as killing
machines and that all those people killed would loom large in their
memory, but we should not therefore draw the conclusion that the
Vikings were primarily interested in killing.

This is a lesson that we do well to bring with us when we are reading other, less elaborate sources that tell of the Vikings' exploits.
Sources from the Viking Age are full of violent Vikings and the
appalling destruction they wreaked. The great year-by-year accounts
(written in Old Irish, Old English, and medieval Latin) of current
events that were kept and updated at many royal courts and in many
monasteries and other Church institutions—works known to modern historians as the *Anglo-Saxon Chronicle*, the *Annals of St-Bertin*,
the *Annals of Ulster*, and other similar labels of convenience—dull
readers' senses with their repeated stories of Viking attacks. They
can become leaden reading, not just because of the repetition year
by year, but because the accounts of the Vikings are all so similar, so
stereotypical, and—most annoyingly—so devoid of detail.

In the annals that the cleric Prudentius semiofficially kept at the
palace of Emperor Louis the Pious in Aachen, and which he continued privately after the emperor's death in 840, a single sentence is

devoted to the sack of Nantes: "Northmen pirates attacked Nantes, slew the bishop and many clergy and lay people of both sexes, and sacked the city."[3] We know much more about this particular raid, thanks to the eyewitness report that has happened to survive. But for most Viking raids, the level of detail in the annals, similar to Prudentius's line about Nantes, is all we ever get: the Vikings show up, ravage, and kill many if not all, including such-and-such an important person. In 864, for example, another chronicler, Archbishop Hincmar of Reims, tells us, "the Northmen got to Clermont where they slew Stephen, son of Hugh, and a few of his men, and then returned unpunished to their ships." In 836, Prudentius writes about Viking attacks: "the Northmen again devastated Dorestad and Frisia." An annalist writing in Old Irish tells us that, in 844, "Dún Masc was plundered by the heathen [Vikings], and there were killed there Aed son of Dub da Crich, abbot of Tír dá Glas, and Cluain Eidnig, Ceithernach son of Cú Dínaisc, prior of Cell Dara, and many others." In 844, Prudentius writes, "The Northmen sailed up the Garonne as far as Toulouse, wreaking destruction everywhere, without meeting any opposition." In 873, we are told, "the Northmen, after ravaging various towns, razing fortresses to the ground, burning churches and monasteries and turning cultivated land into a desert, had for some time now been established in Angers." An Anglo-Saxon writer recounts that in 943, "Here [the Viking] Olaf broke down Tamworth and a great slaughter fell on either side, and the Danes had the victory and led much war-booty away with them. Wulfrun [a high-born Mercian lady] was seized there in the raid."[4]

The Vikings "lay waste," "raid," "slaughter," "ravage," "wreak destruction," and "devastate." The writers of annals and chronicles, trained in rhetoric, vary the words, but still do not tell us much about the details. How was the abbot of Tír dá Glas killed, and in what situation? Was he helping to defend his monastery, sword in hand, or was he saying mass in his monastery church when a band of Vikings lacking respect for Christianity cut him down (like Bishop Gohard in Nantes)? Was he hit by an ax, spear, or sword in the heat of battle, or was he captured and later executed when a suitable ransom did not materialize? Nobody tells us. The

Anglo-Saxon chronicler recounts that the Vikings in 994 "wreaked indescribable harm," and the curious modern reader is left to wonder exactly what the Vikings were doing and if they were more destructive in 994 than in their other raids. Or if it just seemed so to the particular chronicler who wrote down this notice because he had little previous experience of Vikings. When the sources talk, for example, about "the slaughter of men," as they often do, do they mean that the Vikings killed everyone (or every man?) that they saw when they ran from house to house or rather that the Vikings won pitched battles, killing everyone on the opposing side? The sources are unhelpful, leaving plenty of space for our imagination, but little concrete detail with which to reconstruct the violence of the Vikings.

If we are interested in finding out how the Vikings fought, what their tactics looked like, or why they fought, these sources do not provide much assistance. Neither do Frankish liturgical books that contain the kind of prayer said by Christians afraid of becoming the Vikings' next victims: "Save us, Lord, from the wild Northmen who lay waste our country. They strangle the crowd of old men and of youth and of virgin boys. Repel from us all evil."[5]

The medieval and modern reputation of the Vikings is also seasoned with the religious outlook and theological training of the people who wrote the preserved sources, almost all of whom were monks, priests, or bishops. We can see this already in the reaction that the first known Viking raid against a monastery stimulated in the theologian Alcuin (d. 804). In 793, a band of Vikings had plundered the island monastery of Lindisfarne in northeastern England, an important center for Christianity in Northumberland, one of the kingdoms in early medieval England. Alcuin, who was living in voluntary exile with King Charlemagne in the Frankish realm, wrote a poem and a series of consolatory letters to English acquaintances; he himself was English and had plenty of connections in England. Deploring "the tragic sufferings" of the monastic community, he chose scriptural language that was usually taken to allude to the Last Days. "Is this the beginning of the great suffering [which according to Christian belief would come before the end of the world] or the outcome of the sins of those who live there [in Lindisfarne]?" Alcuin suggested that the Viking raid should be given either an eschatological or a moral interpretation or, better, perhaps both combined. At the very least, "it has not happened by chance."[6]

We also find this kind of theological spin in the annals and chronicles. The writers of the *Anglo-Saxon Chronicle*, for example, usually refer to the Vikings as "the heathens." A source that provides more detailed insight into what the Vikings were doing even though it frames the story in religious terms is the *Translation of St. Germain of Paris*, which narrates events surrounding the Viking attack on Paris in 845. "Translation" refers to the moving of holy relics from one place to another. The author is anonymous but must have been a monk at the monastery of St. Germain-des-Près just outside the city. He wrote simple and straightforward Latin without the sophisticated rhetorical coloring of an intellectual like Alcuin or the Nantes eyewitness. Most of the text is devoted to miracles worked by the patron of his monastery, St. Germain, whose body usually rested in the monastery church, but which was moved farther inland at the news of the approaching Vikings. Considered its most valuable possessions, the relics of a church were also a source of power because they represented a powerful saint. In this case, St. Germain caused several of the Vikings, who "arrogantly were plundering and blaspheming God," to become violently ill, and he worked several other miracles, which are retold in detail. A pagan Northman inflated by pride, for example, entered the monastery church with a drawn sword and started to hack away at a marble pillar, striking it thirty times. The Northman's purpose is unclear. Perhaps the writer wished to portray the irrationality of a Viking acting in a manner that would destroy his own weapon. "Through the virtues of the Lord Germain," the right arm of this unwise Viking withered, so that he had no use of it again for the rest of his life.

The wondrous miracles of St. Germain make up the story that our author wished to tell, but in praising the acts of the saint, the writer also provided details about what the Vikings were up to. Without opposition, the Vikings had brought their ships up the Seine. In Rouen, the first major city on their way, they "did what

FIG. 2. The Vikings famously raided the Lindisfarne monastery in 793, and the monastic community fled to greater security inland. Monastic life was reestablished in Lindisfarne in the eleventh century but was suppressed in the sixteenth century, leaving the buildings to decay. Drawing and watercolor by Thomas Girtin, *St. Cuthbert's Holy Island* (1797). Photo courtesy of Yale Center for British Art.

they wanted, captured and killed people of both sexes, devastated monasteries, plundered and burned churches." Farther up the river, the Vikings met King Charles the Bald with the Frankish army, which had been divided into two contingents. The Vikings captured III men from one contingent and hanged them in plain sight of the other contingent, apparently on the other side of the river or on an island, "to insult and laugh at the king, his generals, and all the Christian people who were standing there." This atrocious spectacle had the desired effect on the morale of the Frankish army; the writer states that many Frankish soldiers deserted, taking flight "some through the valleys, others through the plains, yet others through the dense forests . . . , as I cannot write without plentiful tears." What makes this monk particularly indignant, to the point of crying, is that the Frankish army was well equipped, "provided with helmets, armor, shields and lances," while the people they fled from were "unequipped and almost unarmed, and very few."[7] Here, the monk of St. Germain tells us two things of particular interest. First, we learn that the Vikings were not averse to using psychological warfare to demoralize their opponents. Like the Mongols in later European history, they cultivated an image of ferocity, which served them well in achieving their goals.[8] Second, in comparison with the professionally equipped Frankish army, the Vikings were poorly armed and had little in the way of protective armor. This would change as the Viking Age wore on, but at this relatively early stage, the Vikings were fighting more as amateurs than professionals.

How did the Vikings actually fight? The best evidence comes from the graves of Viking warriors who were buried with their weapons. Scandinavian archeologists have found large numbers of weapons— swords, axes, spears, and arrows—in burials from the time.

In the Viking Age, no other weapon was as closely associated with fighting Northmen as the ax. The weapon had been quite unusual in Scandinavia before the Viking Age, when it became common. Many Scandinavians served the Byzantine emperor as mercenaries, and these "Varangians" were known in Constantinople as "the ax-bearing barbarians." They were the trusted elite soldiers of unquestionable loyalty in the Byzantine army, and the emperors were wont to use them for especially difficult assignments. Some members of the Varangian guard survived their service and returned home to Scandinavia, where some of them raised runestones to boast about their exploits. The Swedish warrior Ragnvald, for example, inscribed a huge boulder in southeastern Uppland in memory of his mother, Fastvi Onämnsdotter, and there he told everyone who could read runes that he "was in Greece, [where] he was the commander of the retinue."[9] In other words, he had held command in the Varangian guard of the Byzantine Empire, which Viking Age Scandinavians called "Greece." One man, now anonymous because damage to his runestone renders his name illegible, "fell in Greece" and may have been a less fortunate member of the same elite guard.[10]

FIG. 3. Axes and spears were less prestigious weapons than swords, but they were put to efficient use by Vikings and other medieval warriors. Photo courtesy of Riksantikvarieämbetet, Stockholm.

Varangian guards such as Ragnvald would have been trained to use an ax in addition to other weapons in battle. Scandinavian battle-axes were formidable and efficient weapons that could inflict great damage. In his praise poetry, the Norse poet Arnorr describes his patron, King Magnus of Norway and Denmark, wielding his ax in a battle at the southern border of Denmark: "The unsluggish ruler stormed forth with broad axe . . . the prince clenched both hands around the shaft. . . . Hel [the name of his ax] split pallid skulls."[11] The name of King Magnus's ax, "Hel," is also the name of the Norse goddess of death. Arnorr and Magnus, both Christians, would have associated the name with "Hell," perhaps a suitable label for such a hellishly efficient weapon. King Magnus had, according to later claims, inherited it from his father, the Norwegian patron saint Olav Haraldsson, and Hel is, thus, the very ax still portrayed in the Norwegian national coat of arms.

Fighting Scandinavians used many different types of axes, but warriors preferred the broadax, a formidable weapon with a wide edge and a thin blade. Such an ax weighed about a half kilogram, and the edge could be as long as thirty centimeters. It was kept sharp with a whetstone, always part of a Scandinavian fighter's equipment. In the hands of a well-trained warrior, a broadax could cut through chain mail and even helmets. Thus, Arnorr was not necessarily using poetic exaggeration when he said that King Magnus cleaved heads with his ax as if he were splitting firewood. The Norse poets talked about ax edges as "yawning iron mouths," which threateningly "gape against the enemy" or give lethal kisses. King Harald Hardruler (Hardrada; d. 1066) is believed to have composed a stanza in which he said that he could not remain king in Norway unless his main opponent, Einar, "kisses the thin mouth of the axe."[12] Sometime later, Einar was killed by the king's men, but no source tells us whether or not he was hewed down by an ax.

Not only the ax's sharp edge but also its butt could be used to inflict injury or death. In 1012, attempting to persuade the captive Archbishop Alfheah of Canterbury to allow himself to be ransomed with gold and silver from the treasury of his church and other churches, drunk Vikings first pelted him with animal bones and then "one of them struck him on the head with the butt of an axe." This killed the archbishop, who earned the crown of a martyr and soon became honored as St. Alphege, still the dedicatee of several English churches.[13]

Early medieval Scandinavians fought with other weapons in addition to the battle-ax. When archeologists excavate Viking Age warriors' graves, the variety of weapons is striking. Spears, arrows, and swords are common, and those are also the weapons that are mentioned in the most detailed contemporary battle narrative, the Old English poem *The Battle of Maldon*. The *Anglo-Saxon Chronicle* mentions, briefly and soberly, that "Ealdorman Byrhtnoth was killed at Maldon" in Essex on the eastern coast of England in 994. The poem eloquently celebrates Byrhtnoth's heroism and stiff upper lip in the face of defeat while providing details about how the battle played out (or at least how the poet imagines it). Spears were thrown, arrows shot, and the warriors fought with swords. The poet does not mention any axes, probably because he focuses on more prestigious weapons: swords and spears.

> The Vikings attacked first. After their battle cry,
> they loosed . . . from their hands the file-hardened spear,
> the sharp-ground lances to fly.

The Vikings at Maldon were in effect reenacting what they thought was the very first battle ever, which started when the warrior god par excellence, Odin, "shot a spear, hurled it over the troops; that was the first battle in the world," according to the old Scandinavian poem *Völuspá*.[14] Or perhaps it is more correct to say that the narrator of *Völuspá* describes the legendary first battle as starting in the way battles usually do, the way the battle of Maldon did. *The Battle of Maldon* continues:

> Bows were busied—shield met point.
> That rush of battle was bitter—warriors fell.
>
> —
>
> Even Byrhtnoth's kinsman, his sister's son,
> he with swords was fiercely hewn down.
> To the Vikings was given retribution.

I hear that Edward slew one
fiercely with his sword, not holding back his swing
so that a doomed warrior fell at his feet.

—

Then a sea-warrior [Viking] sent a southern spear
so that the warlord [Byrhtnoth] was wounded;
he then shoved so with his shield that the shaft burst

—

Enraged was that warrior [Byrhtnoth]. He stabbed angrily
the proud Viking who had given him the wound.
Wise was the warrior: he let his spear advance
through the neck of the youth, his hand guiding it
so that he reached the life of the sudden attacker.
Then he quickly shot another
so that the byrnie burst; he was wounded in the breast
through the rin g-lock[ed mail shirt]; at his heart stood
the poisoned point. The earl was the happier.

—

Then one of the warriors let a hand-dart [spear]
fly from his hand so that it, too, went forth
through the noble retainer of Ethelred [Byrhtnoth].
He who stood at his side, an ungrown youth,
a young man on the battlefield, Wulfstan's child Wulfmer the
      young,
who very boldly drew from the man [Byrhtnoth] the bloody
      spear,
and afterward let it, the hardened, go back.
The point went in, so that he lay on the ground,
he who had his lord [Byrhtnoth] so severely wounded.[15]

So far, the battle has mainly involved projectiles hurled from a
distance, probably between two armies lined up in battle formation. The spears are thrown back and forth, something the poet
emphasizes in focusing on the reactions of the English to the

FIG. 4. The Old English poem *The Battle of Maldon* tells of spears with sharpened points being thrown back and forth between Vikings and Anglo-Saxons during a battle in 991. Photo courtesy of Riksantikvarieämbetet, Stockholm.

invaders' aggression. A Viking throws a "southern" spear at Byrht-noth. By saying that the spear was "southern," the poet probably means that it was a spear from the equipment of the English that had already been hurled at the northerners, and one of them now threw it back, a practice common in premodern battles.[16] This enrages the earl, who throws it back. Since he is a wise and experienced warrior, he aims it so well that it hits the neck above the mail shirt of one of the Vikings, killing him. A second spear is hurled with such force that it penetrates the mail shirt of the Viking, hitting the heart. Then another Viking throws a spear again at Byrht-noth, wounding him severely, but a youth, probably an apprentice, pulls out the spear and throws it back, similarly felling the man who had injured Byrhtnoth. Thus, the poet portrays the fight as a series of reactions and counterreactions to previous actions, with increasingly higher stakes.

Byrhtnoth appears to be put out of commission, and one of the Vikings approaches in order to plunder him, "wishing to fetch wealth, his garment and rings, and the adorned sword."[17] This marks the beginning of the skirmish, when the battle lines break up and the soldiers engage in hand-to-hand combat. Here individual warriors might be able to gain trophies. As the leader of the English, the earl would have had the most costly equipment and adornments. Indeed, the poet alluded earlier to his sword having a golden hilt. But Byrhtnoth is still not defeated and he pulls his sword, "broad and bright-edged," striking the mail-shirt of the would-be plunderer. The Viking, however, quickly stops him by injuring his arm. Now Byrhtnoth can no longer stand upright; he falls, praying to God to grant his soul an easy passage and not allow any hellish enemies to injure it. But "then the heathen knaves hewed him." The verb chosen, used also for cutting wood, makes one think of axes, but the poet does not explicitly mention this weapon. The poet sets up an effective contrast between Byrhtnoth's pious wish for the preservation of his soul from devils and his inability to save his body from worldly (but heathen and thus devilish) enemies, the Vikings.

In this part of the poem, the poet depicts close combat in which a sword and possibly other suitable weapons were used. The immediate tactical goal of Byrhtnoth's Viking attacker is to disable his arm, rendering him defenseless. We may compare these battle tactics with what we know about the death of another warrior chieftain, a Norwegian man who was killed close to the year 900. In 1880, archeologists excavating a grave mound in Gokstad, Norway, found a splendid ship along with remnants of three smaller boats, twelve horses, six dogs, and parts of a human skeleton. The grave goods prove that the dead man was rich and powerful. The bones show that he was large, 181 ±3 centimeters tall, with strong muscles and thick bones. It is hard to know how old he was when he died, but the best guess is that he was in his forties. Several years before his death, he had fallen, or jumped, from a great height, injuring his left knee. As a consequence, he would have walked with a limp, perhaps using a cane.

With impressive grave goods, the Gokstad man must have been an important person, probably someone we should think of as a chieftain. He met a violent death. Both of his thigh bones and his left shin bone display several cut marks from at least two weapons. It is obvious that his opponent focused on immobilizing him by first injuring his legs, just as Byrhtnoth's Viking enemy aimed to deprive the earl of the use of his sword arm. The Gokstad man's right fibula (calf bone) had been cut straight through with an oblique blow from above, severing his foot. His left shin bone bore a cut, about four centimeters long, which was made with a thin-bladed weapon, more probably a sword than an ax. That blow alone would have caused him to fall to the ground. His right thigh bone carried a mark from a cut made by a knife or an arrow. The Gokstad man did not long survive these cuts; there are no signs of healing. The cut in his right thigh would likely have injured his femoral artery, which would quickly have drained him of blood and thus killed him, but he could also have sustained other fatal injuries that we do not know about, since we lack soft tissue evidence and only eight bones of his skeleton survived the thousand years he was buried.[18]

The Gokstad man was injured by a sword, and Byrhtnoth drew his sword. Swords are constantly celebrated in northern literature as the ultimate prestige weapon. Scandinavian court poets thank their patrons for swords, often swords that, like Byrhtnoth's, carried gold on the hilt. In the early eleventh century, King Olav Haraldsson of Norway gave his court poet Sigvat Thordarson a "gold-woven" sword with a "hilt-knob of silver." Thousands of Viking Age swords have been found by Scandinavian archeologists, and some of them have splendid hilts, decorated with gold, silver, and other valuable materials. For example, a tenth-century sword found in Dybäck in Scania, southern Sweden, has a silver hilt with the grip twined with gold thread. The silver hilt also carries engraved decorations depicting animals and geometric designs.

Swords were the weapons of the Viking Age North most associated with high status. This is why they are mentioned in poetry and in other literature much more often than more everyday weapons like axes. The very best swords came from inside the Frankish Empire. Even in faraway Baghdad, Arab writers praised the quality of Frankish swords. And so did Scandinavian poets. Sigvat in his *Viking Songs* says that the "Welsh [= foreign = probably Frankish] swords bite," when his hero, Olav Haraldsson, tries to take London. In fact, Frankish swords were so attractive to the Vikings that Frankish rulers prohibited their export on pain of death. Such prohibitions were futile, however, and the Vikings kept attacking the Franks with their own swords.[19]

The best swords of the time were made by Ulfberht. They had trademarks inscribed on their blades: "ULFBERH+T" or "ULFBERHT+," or a variant thereof. About one hundred such swords are known to have survived, but there may be many more, since hundreds of surviving Viking Age rusty sword blades have not yet been X-rayed to determine whether they have inscriptions. Modern metallurgical examinations have revealed that some of the Ulfberht swords were made of high-quality steel with unusually high carbon content. Such steel could not be produced during the Viking Age in Europe, with its primitive iron-melting technology, but must have been imported from somewhere in India, Persia, or central Asia, where different melting methods produced this kind of high-quality, high-carbon steel. Such steel, forged at the right temperature for the correct time, would produce very hard and tough weapons, just like some of the surviving Ulfberht swords.

Some other swords carrying the trademark, however, were made from inferior steel or even iron and thus were not nearly as strong and hard. Apparently, the authentic Ulfberht swords were so good and attractive that a market of pirated copies appeared. An archeometallurgist has found a correlation between the quality of the steel and how the name on the blade is spelled. Most swords with the spelling "ULFBERH+T" are made of top-quality steel.[20] They were very efficient weapons.

Ulfberht produced swords for three centuries, coinciding more or less with the Viking Age, so the name cannot simply refer to an individual smith; it probably refers to a workshop or a family, although, as we have seen, there were also copycats. It is uncertain where "Ulfberht" was active. His swords have been found all around the Baltic Sea, but also in Norway and in Germany. Linguistically, his name belongs, some have argued, to the Rhineland in Germany, but the fact that the metal came from Asia has made other scholars argue that the smithy should be sought somewhere along the Scandinavian trade routes through Eastern Europe. The "Ulfberht" swords were the best swords of the Viking Age, and since early medieval literature talks of the best swords as "Welsh" or

FIG. 5. The Ulfberht swords were the best Viking Age swords, manufactured of very strong high-quality steel that must have been imported from Asia. Such distinguished weapons were eminently worthy to sport exquisitely decorated handles. Photo: Monika Runge, courtesy of Germanisches Museum, Nuremberg.

Frankish, it is tempting to put their manufacture inside the Frankish Empire, for example, in the Rhineland. Suitable trade routes certainly existed along which steel from Asia could reach this area.

A Viking who owned a tough and hard "Ulfberht" sword could consider himself lucky. If he met an enemy with an inferior sword made out of softer or more brittle steel, he might well manage to shatter that sword. "Ulfberht" swords were, however, rare and very expensive, and thus very few Vikings would have been able to acquire them. As the St. Germain author expressed it, the Vikings were "almost unarmed" in comparison to the Frankish army. They had to fight with whatever weapons they had at hand, even if it simply meant fighting with wooden clubs or bringing from home your usual ax for chopping wood or throwing back the spears the enemy had hurled at you.

War and fighting are hazardous. No one can be certain ahead of time that he is going to emerge victorious, and most avoid actual fighting as long as possible. This was true of the Vikings, and yet they have a reputation for cherishing fighting and violence as if for their own sake. This is not a surprising image considering the source material available, the annals and chronicles with their seemingly endless litanies of Viking attacks. This bias is not limited to written sources but also applies to archeological material. Weapons made of high-quality steel or even iron stand a very high chance of surviving until now, to be found by archeologists or others. Some of the preserved "Ulfberht" swords have survived for centuries at the bottom of rivers, to be found when the rivers were dredged, like the one that was taken up from the Elbe close to Hamburg in the 1960s.[21] The implements of many peaceful activities were made of wood, which does not survive as well as weapons of steel in the soil, and certainly not at the bottom of rivers.

Modern imaginations have been thrilled by tales about Norse superheroes in the form of the berserks, a supposed elite group of Viking fighters of remarkable abilities, and about horrendous pagan-tinted tortures like the blood eagle (discussed later in this chapter)—so thrilled, in fact, that the normally well-functioning critical faculties of historians and others have frequently been overwhelmed. Even those who should know better continue to retell these stories long after they have been shown by critical research to be based on little more than misunderstandings combined with the appeal of a good yarn.

Contemporary writers portrayed the Vikings as violent and stereotyped them as "others," and later medieval historians looked back on the Scandinavian raiders as a uniquely destructive phenomenon. The Englishman Henry of Huntingdon, who in the 1150s (almost a century after the last Scandinavian raids on England) wrote a history of his country, considered the Viking raids to have been true catastrophes. They were "much more monstrous and much more cruel" than any other invasions that England had suffered. Vikings wanted only "to plunder, not to own, to destroy everything, not to rule." Henry presented the Vikings as a people interested in violence and destruction for their own sake, despite a preponderance of evidence to the contrary.[22] Vikings from King Guthrum to King Cnut the Great may have been destructive, but they were certainly more interested in ruling than in destroying. In fact, several of them sought royal thrones in England.

In the High Middle Ages, looking back on their ancestors' accomplishments, Scandinavians themselves adopted the image of the Vikings as primarily interested in destruction. They wrote rousing stories about martial prowess and exhilarating adventures resulting in incredible riches taken as booty. Icelandic saga tellers of the thirteenth and later centuries vividly retold the story of the villain of the St. Germain story of 845, Ragnar—"the blasphemer of God and his saints," according to the Frankish monk quoted earlier. In numerous exciting adventure stories, Ragnar Hairy-Breeches (*Loðbrók*), as he came to be known, is portrayed as a heroic fighter, extremely bloodthirsty, and given to extraordinary feats. Nothing about him is normal, not even his death, which becomes a memorable execution. King Ella of Northumbria captured him and put him to death by throwing him into a pit full of poisonous snakes. The snake pit, a refined method of horrific execution, was a literary topos; it was, for example, how Attila the Hun executed King Gunnarr of Burgundy, according to the Old Norse heroic poems *Atlakviða*. In the saga that bears his name, Ragnar's last words in the snake pit were, "How the little pigs would grunt if they knew how the old boar suffers!" This phrase serves to set up the horrendous revenge taken on King Ella by Ragnar's sons (the "little pigs"), themselves Vikings with widespread reputations. In the sagas, they obtain picturesque nicknames that remain hard to explain persuasively: Ivar Boneless, Björn Ironside, Whiteshirt, and Sigurd Snake-in-the-Eye.

In historical fact, the sons of Ragnar defeated Ella in battle at York, England, in 866, and there is nothing in the contemporary sources to suggest anything but that Ella died on the battlefield while fighting to defend his kingdom. That is certainly how the Icelandic poet Sigvat Thordarson presented his death in the celebratory poem, *Knútsdrápa*, that he wrote in the early eleventh century for his patron King Cnut, who counted Ivar Boneless and Ragnar Hairy-Breeches among his ancestors. "And Ivar, he who resided in York, caused the eagle to cut Ella's back."[23] The image is stark and easily misunderstood, but that is in the nature of Viking Age poetry, which typically celebrated martial prowess by circumlocutions referring to how its heroes fed scavenger birds and other animals by killing their enemies. Not only were the enemy humbled and killed, but they also suffered the ultimate humiliation of remaining on the field of battle to become food for carrion-eating beasts rather than enjoying a proper burial.

The eagles and ravens feasting on battle-killed corpses are so much part and parcel of Norse skaldic poetry that they tend to pop up even in the most inappropriate contexts, such as when

FIG. 6. The story of the execution of Ragnar Hairy-Breeches in a snake pit is illustrated on a Gotlandic picture stone from the Viking Age. Photo: Raymond Hejdström, courtesy of Gotlands Museum, Visby.

Earl Ragnvald of Orkney, in wooing Europe's most eligible widow, added carrion-eating eagles to the blandishments of his verses.[24] When the Norse poet Sigvat wrote poetry about his pious pilgrimage to St. Peter's in Rome in the 1030s, he could not resist using images of wild beasts eating his dead enemies. In order to pick up his pilgrim's staff, Sigvat says, he "put down my precious sword . . . , which succeeds in lessening the hunger of the husband of the she-wolf."[25] Sigvat claimed to have sated the he-wolf by providing him a banquet of dead bodies with his sword. Wolfs, ravens, and eagles are most often mentioned in skaldic poetry when poets want to say that someone died on the battlefield, and they do not shy away from graphic images that may seem unpoetic to modern readers. "Ottar fell under the eagle's claws. . . . The eagle trod on him . . . with bloody feet," the tenth-century poet Thjodolf of Hvini told his presumably appreciative audience.[26]

There was nothing extraordinary about Ella's death; hundreds of medieval rulers and chieftains must similarly have fallen on the battlefield, as did Byrhtnoth and the Gokstad chieftain, so that would not be a sufficiently exciting story for later storytellers. Scandinavian high-medieval writers of adventure stories and of histories used skaldic poetry as sources. The art of composing this most intricate of medieval poetry had survived, especially in Iceland, but even Icelanders could have problems understanding the old poems with their strained circumlocutions, allusive style, and free word order. So it was with Sigvat's poem about the death of Ella, which in the original Old Norse is particularly terse, dense, and easily misunderstood. Thus, readers began to understand the stanza as saying not that "Ivar caused the eagle to cut the back of Ella"—that is, Ivar killed Ella, providing carrion for the eagle to eat—but that "Ivar cut the eagle on the back of Ella." Both interpretations are grammatically possible, although only the first makes literary and historical sense. To explain this mysterious statement, the storytellers' imaginations worked overtime. At first, they imagined that Ivar tortured the still-living Ella by carving an image of an eagle on his back. The story reached its full development, however, in the fourteenth century when another storyteller created a truly horrific torture on the basis of his and his predecessors' misunderstanding of this verse: "King [Ella] was taken captive. Ivar and the brothers now recall how their father had been tortured [in the snake pit]. They now had the eagle cut in Ella's back, then all his ribs severed from the backbone with a sword, in such a way that his lungs were pulled out there."[27]

In the imagination of this storyteller, this elaborate execution method, known as "blood eagle," was suitable revenge for Ragnar's painful death in the snake pit. Thus the little pigs avenged the suffering of the old boar, in the literary imagination of storytellers. The legend of the blood eagle has become much beloved in modern times, developing new features (such as salt in the wounds to make it even more painful), inspiring much anatomical speculation (for example, on exactly when the victim dies), and acquiring a religious coating suggesting that this surely was a particularly awful pagan rite. Even long after the skaldic scholar Roberta Frank in 1984 explained how the idea of the blood eagle developed out of misunderstood skaldic poetry, many historians (as well as popular culture) have shown themselves unwilling to let go of this most

cherished demonstration of Viking cruelty. In this, they continue
to be inspired by the medieval spin by Henry of Huntingdon and
others, depicting the Vikings as the most terrible catastrophe in
medieval history. Violence continues to intrigue modern society,
and the Vikings have become emblematic of the most atrocious and
mindless violence.

Similar tales of horrendous violence dominate both medieval
and modern accounts of the feats of the Vikings, and many of them
are similarly hard to take seriously. Prominent in many accounts,
old as well as recent, of Viking fighting are the "berserks." The word
literally means "bear-shirt" in Old Norse. In around 1200, the
Danish historian Saxo Grammaticus described one such berserk:

> At this time a certain Harthben, who came from Hälsing-
> land, imagined it a glorious achievement to kidnap and rape
> princesses, and he used to kill anyone who hindered him in
> his lusts. . . . His towering frame stretched to a height of nine
> cubits. . . . A demonical frenzy suddenly possessed him, he furi-
> ously bit and devoured the rim of his shield; he gulped down
> fiery coals without a qualm and let them pass down into his
> belly; he ran the gauntlet of crackling flames; and finally when
> he had raved through every sort of madness, he turned his sword
> with raging hand against the hearts of six of his henchmen [who
> had conspired against him]. It is doubtful whether this mad-
> ness came from thirst for battle or natural ferocity. Then . . . he
> attacked [King] Halvdan, who crushed him with a hammer of
> wondrous size, so that he lost both victory and life, paying the
> penalty both to Halvdan, whom he had challenged, and to the
> kings whose offspring he had ravished.[28]

The Icelandic sagas from the thirteenth and later centuries similarly feature many berserks, who fought wildly "like wolfs or dogs"
and were as strong as "bears and bulls."[29] Many modern commenta-
tors believe that the berserks existed in fact and speculate about how
they gained their strength, guessing without any basis in historical
sources that they had put themselves into a trance by eating poisonous mushrooms or grain infected by the fungus *Claviceps purpurea*,
or possibly by getting high on self-induced excess adrenaline.[30]

As in the case of the blood eagle, the main historical problem with the berserks is that they are, with one possible exception, mentioned only in sources that were written centuries after any of them would have been alive. The one early reference to the berserks is in a poem dedicated to the ninth-century Norwegian king Harald Fairhair, which simply states that, as the battle of Hafrsfjord began, "bear-shirts [*berserkir*] bellowed . . . wolf-skins howled."[31] Had it not been for the entire later tradition regarding berserks, a modern interpreter expert in the imagery of skaldic poetry would simply translate "bear-shirts" and "wolf-skins" with "[warriors wearing] chain-mail shirts (byrnies)." It is highly probable that this in fact is what the poet intended to convey.

In the Icelandic sagas and in Saxo's work, the berserks are portrayed as people who existed "once upon a time" and more specifically in pagan times, since there is a strong association between berserks and paganism. When a berserk accepted baptism, his berserk powers disappeared, according to the sagas, which thus betray the saga writers' attitude toward the berserk as a part of the distant, pagan past. The stories of berserks carry all the hallmarks of being literary and legendary creations of the imagination of Icelandic saga writers who found the old skaldic verses fascinating but not necessarily easy to understand. They had found the mysteriously named berserks and wolf-skins in the old poem about Hafrsfjord, but they did not understand, or did not want to understand the term as a poetic circumlocution for warriors in armor. Instead, they dreamed up a fantastic kind of elite warrior, which remains titillating to this day, as do many of their other literary creations. The word has entered the English language, and we occasionally read in the news about persons, mostly men, "going berserk."

Just because the blood eagle and the berserks were creations of the vivid imagination of high-medieval writers, combined with their inexact understanding of old poetry, does not mean that the Vikings were not violent. Close attention to the sources, however, reveals that the Vikings' violence was a means toward a goal that was not very different from the goals of other groups in what was, after all, a very violent time, the early Middle Ages. What the Vikings wanted was wealth, which they used for political purposes.

Before fighting in the battle of Maldon, the Vikings tried to negotiate:

Then a Viking messenger stood on the shore
and cried out firmly [to Byrhtnoth]:

—-

"Bold seamen sent me to you,
commanded that I tell you that you must send quickly
rings for protection. And it is better for you
that you pay off this spear-fight with tribute
than that we engage in such a hard fight.
Nor have we any need to kill each other."[32]

Arm rings made of gold and silver were how wealth was stored and carried in the Viking Age. Byrhtnoth carried rings on his arms, if we can believe the poet.[33] So here the Vikings showed up, rattled their weapons, and asked for tribute in exchange for peace. Clearly, it was the wealth of silver and golden arm rings that interested this particular band of Vikings, not violence for its own sake.

In fact, many similar stories show up in other sources. The *Annals of St-Bertin*, for example, record that the Vikings in 852 sailed with 252 ships to Frisia, where they demanded a tribute that was paid, so they continued on to elsewhere without inflicting any damage. Similarly, in 868, they appeared outside Orleans demanding a tribute, which was also paid.[34] In other cases, the tribute was paid only after the Vikings had begun to wreak havoc. Byrhtnoth proudly refused to pay tribute to the Vikings he encountered at Maldon in 991. They killed him and defeated his army. Afterward the English agreed to pay a large tribute of 10,000 pounds of silver. "In that year it was first decided that geld be paid to the Danish men because of the great terror which they wrought along the sea coast," an Anglo-Saxon chronicler commented.[35] It was the first tribute payment in a series of increasingly large danegelds that would be paid out over the next few decades to different bands of Vikings (not all of whom were Danish, despite the name given to the tribute). In 994, 16,000 pounds of silver were handed over. The Swedish Viking Ulf from Orkesta, north of where Stockholm is today, went to England three times to take a share in the danegeld, as he boasted on the runestone that he commissioned: "And Ulf has taken three gelds in England."[36] He had gone there in 1006, 1012, and 1018, following the Viking chieftains Tosti, Thorketill, and Cnut. In fact, the inscription says that it was those chieftains, not the English, who had "paid" Ulf, and that would have been how one Viking warrior among many would have experienced the events. The chieftains negotiated for danegeld from the English, and when they succeeded, they distributed their shares among their followers. In fact, it was essential that the chieftains distributed the booty in this way, for that made the warriors eager to follow them. From the perspective of the warriors, it was the generous chieftain who gave them their just rewards. Such a chieftain was worthy of their loyalty.

The goals and methods of Viking expeditions are similar to those typical of other early medieval warfare. The people of Frankish lands that the Vikings so often attacked looked back to Emperor Charlemagne—Charles the Great—as a founding figure. He ruled the kingdom for almost a half century, from 768 to 814, and during this period he was seldom at peace. Only toward the end of his life did his official historian, the author of the so-called *Royal Frankish Annals*, occasionally note as something exceptional that during a single year the royal army had not campaigned. The army, usually under the personal leadership of Charlemagne, was otherwise usually attacking one or another of the neighbors of the Franks. A result was that Charlemagne's empire at his own death was much larger than the kingdom he had inherited from his father. He had, among other regions, conquered northern and central Italy, large swaths of western and southern Germany, areas in eastern Spain, and even parts of Hungary. Conquest was, however, not the primary goal of these expeditions. They served to acquire booty and tribute payments for the king. In a time when royal taxes were at best marginal, kings needed income to be able to maintain an army and, in general, followers among the important people of his kingdom. The best way to gain wealth was simply to take it as booty in a military campaign, or to force others to pay tribute. Some less powerful neighbors of the Franks, such as the Bretons and the Beneventans (in central Italy) paid tribute regularly to the ruler of the Franks. A Frankish chronicler noted, for example, that in 863 Duke Salomon of the Bretons "paid Charles [the Bald, Charlemagne's grandson] the tribute owed by his land according to ancient custom."[37] Other neighbors, who did not pay tribute, became the objects of military campaigns to gain booty. The Royal Frankish Annalist tells us that Charlemagne in 774 returned from his campaign in Saxony with "much booty." In the same year, he also conquered Pavia, the capital of the old Lombard kingdom in northern Italy, where he took the royal treasury.[38] In 796, he was even more fortunate. The Frankish army had, with surprising ease, defeated the Avars, who lived in Pannonia in Hungary. In conquering their main fortification, the so-called Avar ring, Charlemagne's army discovered undreamed riches, "which had been piled up over many centuries." The army brought the loot back to his residence in Aachen.[39] Some of those treasures had originally been tribute paid by the Byzantine Empire to the Avars to dissuade them from attacking.

These campaigns of Charlemagne were very bloody. Even as biased a source as the *Royal Frankish Annals* does not pretend otherwise. In fact, its authors take pride in the devastation wreaked by the Frankish army on the enemy. That enemy could be many different peoples living around the Frankish kingdom, but the Saxons (in Germany) were particularly hard hit during wars waged by Charlemagne, which lasted for thirty years. In 774, for example, Charlemagne divided his army into three forces, which he sent to different places in Saxony, where they "with fires and pillaging devastated everything, and several Saxons were killed who were attempting to resist."[40] Charlemagne's army went back to Saxony several times—for example, during the winter 784–785, when armies commanded by the king personally or his generals devastated Saxony.[41] During a single day in 782, Charlemagne ordered no fewer than 4,500 Saxons decapitated, according to the *Annals*. He believed that he acted lawfully, punishing oath-breakers; those killed might have disagreed, but there are no Saxon histories that preserve the viewpoint of Charlemagne's victims. The Vikings' execution of 111 prisoners in 845 pales in comparison. In 795, the Saxons killed Charlemagne's ally, King Witzin of the Slavic

Obodrites, which "made him [Charlemagne] hate the treacherous people even more. . . . Once the Saxons had been soundly beaten, their country laid waste, and their hostages received, the king returned to Gaul and celebrated Christmas and Easter at his palace in Aachen."[42] With his large kingdom and well-organized army, Charlemagne was able to inflict much more violence, seize more booty, and demand greater tributes than the Vikings could ever dream of.[43] His wars were not always as violent and bloody as in Saxony; like the Vikings, he sometimes found that his putative enemies were eager to collaborate and pay tribute in order to save their skins.

Yet, the Vikings are the ones on whom the reputation for violence and bloodthirstiness has stuck. Charlemagne, in contrast, is today generally extolled as a founding father of Europe. France and Germany compete about who has the greatest right to claim him as their national founder. The European Union celebrates the great Charles as a symbol of the unification of Europe. One of the largest buildings of the administrative offices of the European Union (EU) in Brussels, for example, is the Charlemagne Building. Europeans still remember that Charlemagne unified great swaths of the continent under his rule, but the EU has chosen to forget that he committed genocide in the process. It is perhaps ironic that Germany is one of the founding and still dominant members of the EU, but the Saxon ancestors of modern Germans were among the longest-suffering of Charlemagne's victims.

Charlemagne's raids among his neighbors brought him much booty as well as tribute. He used this loot to reward his followers. For example, in 796, his army seized the main Avar fortress and sent its considerable treasures to his palace in Aachen. "After receiving it and thanking God, the Giver of all good things, this most wise and generous man, the Lord's steward, sent [a large gift to the pope]. The rest he distributed among his magnates, ecclesiastic as well as lay, and his other vassals." Likewise, after taking the Lombard capital of Pavia in 774, Charlemagne "gave the treasures he found there to his army."[44]

In other words, Charlemagne was sharing his booty with his followers to inspire their loyalty, very much as Viking chieftains like Tosti, Thorketill, and Cnut shared their booty with their followers, men like Ulf from Orkesta. They all fed booty conquered through violence or tribute gained by threatening violence into the gift economy of their societies, obliging their followers to give their loyalty as a countergift. Clearly, the system worked differently in Charlemagne's kingdom from how it worked in the more anarchic society of the Northmen, but it was still the same system. For Charlemagne, and not only him but also his predecessors and successors as Frankish kings and emperors, the influx of silver, gold, and other valuables from outside his kingdom was essential for the survival of that kingdom.

Likewise, Viking chieftains absolutely needed to be successful in winning booty or tribute on their raids. Otherwise, no warrior would follow them, and they would lose whatever position they had managed to attain. Those most successful in raising funds enhanced their position, which would eventually lead to the establishment of kingdoms in Scandinavia. The creation of states was firmly based in violence, and the Vikings were not unique in using it. But since they, unlike Charlemagne, attacked those with a monopoly on writing, it is their deeds, not Charlemagne's, that have gone down in history as infamous, irrational, and bloodthirsty. We will do well to nuance this image.

CHAPTER 3

RÖRIKS AT HOME AND AWAY

Viking Age Emigration

AMONG THE ALMOST FIVE MILLION MEN LIVING IN SWEDEN IN 2014, a single one carried the name Rörik.[1] The name was never very common; among the thousands of men named on Swedish runestones, only five were called Rörik.[2] Among them was a Rörik in Styrstad, a village just west of where the city of Norrköping would be built centuries later. This Rörik appears to have been a well-to-do farmer perhaps with artistic interests. At least, he sponsored a runestone with an unusual design: two thin snakes wriggling alongside and crossing each other, forming ten knots. The runic inscription is placed in the space between the snakes and tells us that HRURIKR (how Rörik spelled his name in runes) raised the stone in memory of his sons Frode and Asbjörn. The sons had died before their father, but we do not know how they died.[3] No other source tells us anything else about the family.

If this Rörik stayed at home on his farm in Styrstad his entire life, there were other Röriks who left Scandinavia. Two of them sailed out in the ninth century, never to return home. They shared their relatively uncommon name but most likely had never heard of each other, or of Rörik in Styrstad. These two Röriks sailed in different directions—one east, the other west—but they nevertheless shared a similar fate, gaining great power in foreign lands. The one going west settled in what is now Holland, where he became a king, even if in name only; he faithfully served Frankish emperors

FIG. 7. Rörik erected this runestone in Styrstad, Sweden, to memorialize his two dead sons, Frode and Asbjörn. The design with two narrow snakes curling around each other and with the runic inscription between them is very unusual. Photo: Håkan Svensson. Reproduced with permission.

and kings. The Rörik going east would beget the Rurikid dynasty, which ruled Russia as grand princes and czars until the sixteenth century.

All three Röriks were successful, each in a different way. One stayed at home on the farm, whereas the other two left to carve out lives for themselves in foreign lands. Like them, many Scandinavians moved elsewhere in Europe and a few to North America. They encountered varied circumstances where they went—from the bitter cold and unpopulated landscape of Greenland to the tribal warfare of Russia and the already occupied lands of the British Isles and the coast of Normandy—but they all desired a better life than Scandinavia was able to offer. Emigration presented multifarious opportunities as well as challenges, and the influx of Scandinavians changed, sometimes fundamentally, the fate of the lands that experienced it. The Scandinavian influence on the English language after masses of Scandinavians settled in eastern

England, for example, is large but so deeply embedded in the language that modern speakers seldom notice it. Scandinavians were on the move in the Viking Age: to Russia and Ireland, to the Low Countries and Newfoundland, and to many other places.

These movements of Scandinavians were typically orchestrated by people who became leaders and chieftains, if they were not that already at home in Scandinavia. Our two emigrating Röriks became chieftains, each having great success in gaining and holding on to power in his new home. This should not make us oblivious to the failure of many similarly ambitious women and men, some no doubt also called Rörik, but as usual in history, we know considerably less about failure than about successes.

The Rörik who sailed west became known in the Latin sources as "Roric" or "Roricus." He belonged to an important Danish family. His uncle Harald had been king in Denmark until he was exiled and instead became a protégé of Emperor Louis the Pious. Roric was a Viking who in the 840s plundered the coastal areas of the kingdom of Emperor Lothar (more or less today's Belgium and the Netherlands). He did this from a base in the kingdom of Lothar's hostile brother, Louis the German, who probably was happy with what Roric accomplished. But Roric had greater ambitions than to be a simple Viking chieftain, or even one who worked for a famous king. He attacked and took the trade town of Dorestad in 850, and he was not going to leave. Lothar realized that he could not drive Roric out without great expense and great danger to his army, so he accepted Roric's occupation, receiving him as his vassal. Everything would be fine as long as Roric paid him the traditional fees and taxes and defended the area against the "incursions of piratical Danes." What better defense than fighting Vikings with Vikings?

When Roric and Lothar made this arrangement, they were in effect resuscitating an older agreement between Roric and Lothar's father, Emperor Louis the Pious, whom the Danish Viking had served as a faithful vassal, only to be expelled after the death of his lord in 840. It was then that Roric sought out Lothar's brother and enemy Louis the German and offered to fight a proxy war against Lothar. But even though Dorestad was in decline as a trade town, it was still a rich and tempting prize, much better than what Louis offered in Germany. Roric settled back into Dorestad, serving both his new lord and that lord's son and successor, Lothar II. Roric's rule stretched beyond the immediate vicinity of Dorestad to include a large portion of Frisia, roughly corresponding to the modern kingdom of the Netherlands. After the heirless death of Lothar II in 869, his kingdom was divided between his uncles Louis the German and Charles the Bald. This included Roric's region, which was similarly divided, although only nominally, for Roric was in effect its ruler, now the vassal of two lords, until he died at some point between 873 and 882.[4]

Practically all Frankish sources that mention Roric—and there are no other sources in which his name occurs—portrays him in a positive light. He appears as a powerful local ruler who could be relied on as a faithful vassal of his various lords. He was so powerful that two Frankish writers who wrote about Roric after his death referred to him as "king." The Irish-born poet Sedulius Scottus wrote in the ninth century about an altar that had been "consecrated in the days of King Roric."[5] In a collection of tales of miracles worked by St. Adalbert, a late tenth-century author recounts that when "King Roric of the barbarians" came to the saint's church, he ordered his followers to dig it out, because it had been covered by storm-blown sand—but the following day, for it was already late. When they came back to begin the work in the morning, they learned that they would not need to dig, for the saint had miraculously removed all the sand overnight.[6]

The Dane Roric may have been a barbarian, but pious Christian writers had no qualms about associating him with Christian miracles and altars. The learned archbishop Hincmar of Reims corresponded with him in the 860s, from which we learn that Roric had become Christian not much earlier. He appears, unexpectedly, to have first been given rule over Frisia while he was still unbaptized. Hincmar wrote to dissuade him from sheltering Count Baldwin of Flanders, who had eloped with Judith, daughter of King Charles the Bald. Hincmar had also heard a rumor that Roric assisted Vikings who had attacked Frankish territory. If true, Roric should undertake whatever penance Bishop Hungarius of Utrecht imposed. Here, Roric appears as a Christian ruler with a bishop and confessor among his subjects (for Utrecht was in his domains), and he controlled his territory well enough to be able, should he wish, to protect even enemies of the powerful West Frankish king.[7]

Roric stayed in Frisia for decades, and other Scandinavians followed him. To conquer and control his quasi kingdom, he must have had a sizable army, presumably made up primarily of fellow Scandinavians. Yet they left no traceable imprint on the region. Unlike in Normandy and the English Danelaw, there are no place-names in Frisia that may be securely derived from Old Norse, and there is little archeological evidence that appears Scandinavian. Roric may not have brought very many Scandinavians to Frisia, or those he did bring may not have stayed for long.

The lack of a Scandinavian heritage in Frisia stands in stark contrast to Russia, where the other Rörik had gone, welcomed by the inhabitants in a way similar to how his namesake had been welcomed in Frisia by Emperor Lothar: guardedly, as the least bad among many bad alternatives. In hindsight, the inhabitants of the region made up a story that they had invited Rörik to rule over them. The story appears only in the twelfth century in preserved sources and is most likely protonationalistic wishful thinking. In the Old Slavonic sources of Russia, Rörik is known as Riurik or Rurik.

A twelfth-century Kievan chronicler recounts that "the Chuds, the Slavs, the Merians, the Ves', and the Krivichians" (peoples of northwestern Russia, south and east of the Gulf of Finland) had in the early ninth century paid tribute to "Varangians," that is, to Scandinavians. In other words, Viking bands had raided among them, forcing the payment of ransoms to stop their raiding, much in the way their cousins did in western Europe. The indigenous peoples had, however, been able to drive the Varangians out, only to start fighting among themselves. They therefore decided to "seek a prince who may rule over us and judge us according to the Law." Thus, they went overseas to the Varangians and asked "the people of the Rus" to "come . . . and reign over us." Three brothers responded and moved across the Baltic Sea. The oldest brother, Rurik, took up residence in Novgorod.[8] His descendants, the Rurikids, would continue to rule Russia until the sixteenth century.

The principality that Rurik created would grow and soon become important enough to make trade treaties with the Byzantine Empire. In the delegation that went to Constantinople to negotiate a treaty in 907, several carry Scandinavian-sounding names, such as Karl, Velmud, and Rulav. The rulers of the principality likewise preserved Scandinavian names in their families for a couple of generations: Olga (whose name derives from Old Norse *Hælga*), Oleg (*Hælgi*), and Igor (*Ingvarr*). A similar story is told by the archeological evidence. The typically Scandinavian women's dress fastened with two brooches is found in several graves from the area ruled by Rurik and his companions, which does not necessarily mean that the women buried in those graves were Scandinavian, but only that they experienced cultural influence from Scandinavia and chose to wear Scandinavian-style dress.[9]

The Scandinavians who settled in Russia under Rurik's leadership made an impact on the region, but it was fleeting, and the Scandinavian flavor disappeared after a few generations. Only the leading aristocracy maintained their ties back home, for instance with the eleventh-century Grand Prince Iaroslav marrying Ingegerd, the daughter of the Swedish king Olof Eriksson. What otherwise remained was the label "Rus," which may derive from the Finnish word for Sweden, *Ruotsi*, and is associated with the Scandinavians in the region.

What the stories of Roric and Rurik show are two entrepreneurs in lordship who sought power, achieving it in lands outside Scandinavia. The Frisian Roric at one point tried to take power at home in Denmark, but he failed, much as his uncle Harald had failed in the 810s and 820s. They were Scandinavian warlords who did not succeed in the power games of Scandinavia, or who simply saw greener pastures farther away. From the perspective of their subjugated peoples, the two Röriks provided stability and security in a very unstable and violent time. As the *Russian Primary Chronicle* said about the situation in Russia immediately preceding Rurik's assumption of power: "There was no law among them, but tribe rose against tribe."[10] Any chieftain who was able to protect his people and maintain order was welcome, whatever his origin.

Every Scandinavian chieftain dreamed of accomplishing what the two Röriks had achieved: to create a secure position of power for himself. The immediate goal for most of them was surely to do so at home in Scandinavia (as Roric attempted in Denmark), but many succeeded only away from home. Thus, the North Atlantic islands, from Greenland and Vinland to Iceland, the Shetlands, the Orkneys, Ireland, and Britain became the homes of chieftains born in, or descending from Scandinavia, just as Scandinavians held power in Russia, Frisia, Normandy, and other places on the European continent. Various men with Scandinavian names considered themselves kings or lords or simply chieftains in Novgorod, Dorestad, Rouen, Dublin, the Isle of Man, York, the Shetlands, the Hebrides, the Orkneys, the Faroes, Iceland, and Greenland at different points during the Viking Age.

We should not forget that this was an emigration of power-hungry chieftains, not primarily of people. The chieftains would, to be sure, all be accompanied by their warrior bands, which could vary considerably in size, but this is basically not an early instance of mass emigration like that from nineteenth-century Scandinavia, in which a sizable portion of the population moved to North America. Also, Viking Age emigration from Scandinavia was not driven primarily by population pressures at home, as is often imagined. Populations always tend to grow, but such growth is typically balanced by famine, war, and disease, as Thomas Malthus (1766–1834) postulated. People may always feel pressured by the lack of opportunity at home; what made the Viking Age different was not exceptionally great pressures at home but the appearance of real opportunities elsewhere. The topos of Scandinavia as a great producer of surplus population, a source of barbarian peoples, was established long before the Viking Age and derives from ancient climate theory, which Hippocrates and Aristotle developed and which medieval intellectuals knew well. For example, the learned Paul the Deacon (d. 799) wrote that the cold regions of the north were "so much the more healthful to the bodies of men and fitted for the propagation of nations." He continued, "From this it happens that such great multitudes of peoples spring up in the north."[11] When the historian Jordanes, writing in Constantinople in the mid-sixth century, tried to explain the origin of the Goths who invaded the Roman Empire, he looked to the same theory and concluded that the Goths must have come from Scandinavia, which he considered a "hive of races or a womb of nations."[12] When latter-day scholars speak of the overpopulation of Viking Age Scandinavia, they are continuing the tradition from Paul and Jordanes and simply repeating an ancient cliché that has no basis in fact.

Warlords, not any extraordinary population pressures at home, propelled the Viking Age movement of people from Scandinavia, as the story of the Viking chieftain Halvdan illustrates. After his army had conquered Northumbria (in northeastern England) in 876, "Halvdan divided up the land" among his followers, "and they plowed and provided for themselves."[13] In other words, Halvdan no longer needed to provide for them. Exactly what is meant by "the land" that he divided up has been much debated without reaching any conclusions—whether one should see Northumbria as entirely depopulated after years of Viking raiding, or Halvdan simply disposed of land that had been abandoned in pockets among otherwise inhabited areas. He may also have expelled or killed the existing population.[14] Halvdan did, at any rate, command a large army of Vikings, so he was certainly able to take land violently, should he wish.

Nowhere did Scandinavian immigrants have a greater impact on an existing population than in the British Isles. Halvdan was only one among many Norse Viking leaders who succeeded in carving out positions of power for themselves there. Another of the leaders of the "Great Heathen Army," Guthrum, did the same thing in East Anglia, where he even adopted an Anglo-Saxon name, Ethelstan, which had been given him by no less a luminary than King Alfred the Great of Wessex when the former Viking chieftain was baptized in 878 with the famous king as his godfather.[15]

It is typical that a Viking leader like Guthrum/Ethelstan appeared eager to assimilate the culture of the land where he settled. Viking chieftains who became rulers in Europe quickly adopted the trappings of rulership prevalent there. This included reliance on the Church for support and the use of written documents in government. Like most of his colleagues among the Viking rulers of the British Isles, Guthrum also performed an important royal function that was at the time more or less unknown in Scandinavia: he issued coins that reproduced the conventions and imagery of English coinage, including inscriptions in Latin. Only exceptionally did a Viking ruler issue a coin with a Norse word inscribed, as did King Olav Guthfrithsson of York, who in ca. 940 called himself *cununc*, "king" in Norse, rather than *rex*, in Latin.[16]

Like their leaders, ordinary Viking settlers adopted many of the habits of the indigenous inhabitants where they settled. This appears clearly in the burial customs in those parts of England where we know that large numbers of Scandinavians settled: the graves of Scandinavians are, with a few exceptions, impossible to distinguish from those of the English.[17]

Some Viking leaders settled in Ireland, Scotland, and the islands north and west of Britain: the Orkneys, the Shetlands, the Hebrides, and the Isle of Man. Their history, and the history of the kingdoms, principalities, and lordships that they created or took over are incompletely known from the sources, but it is obvious that they seldom had a chance to rest on their laurels. Other Scandinavians as well as inhabitants of the British Isles often attacked to challenge their rule. Halvdan, for example, was killed in 877, apparently after being expelled from his newly conquered Northumbrian kingdom. Guthrum and his East Anglian kingdom, likewise, soon disappear from the sources. The area that the two conquered, however, remained under Scandinavian control, at least off and on, for the next century or so. It would become known as the Danelaw, the area where "Danish" (i.e., Scandinavian) law applied.[18]

In the history of Norse occupation of areas in the British Isles, a remarkable family stands out: the descendants of one of Halvdan's successors as Norse king of York and Northumbria, King Guthred.[19] Like Guthrum, Guthred became a Christian (or he may already have been one before moving to Northumbria). Later traditions claim that St. Cuthbert, the patron saint of the kingdom, wanted Guthred as king of Northumbria; the saint had revealed this in a dream to the abbot of the monastery that carried his name. Guthred ruled Northumbria for at least ten years until his death in 895, when he was buried in York Minster. After his death, rule there became contested and exactly what happened around 900 to the kingdom of Northumbria and to Guthred's family remains unclear.

Guthred's sons Ragnall and Sitric had probably been children when their father died; they showed up in 917, each with a Viking fleet, in Ireland, where they routed an Irish army. Sitric took control of an old Viking settlement on the Liffey River and set his men to construct a fortress with carefully laid-out streets on a ridge above a small pool known as *dub lind* (the black pool). This is the beginning of the city of Dublin, which, into the nineteenth century, in its center maintained traces of the city plan laid out by Sitric. Ragnall went elsewhere, first plundering around Waterford in Ireland, and then returning to Britain, where he eventually became king of Northumbria, with his residence in York. When Ragnall died in the early 920s, Sitric succeeded him in York, leaving a third brother, Guthfrith, in charge in Dublin.

Sitric and his brothers were no longer pirate chieftains; they had become powerful kings, and other kings in the British Isles recognized them as such. In the mid-920s, the Anglo-Saxon king Ethelstan of Mercia acknowledged Sitric's royal status by giving him his sister in marriage. We are not certain what her name was—the historian William of Malmesbury stated in the twelfth century that he was unable to find out—but she probably became the mother of Sitric's famous son Olav Cuaran.

Olav was certainly a small child when his father died about a year after his marriage. He turns up in history as a teenager in 941, when he became the ruler of Northumbria together with his cousin Ragnall Guthfrithsson. They were driven from their kingdom in 944, and Olav then went to Ireland to take over his father's city of Dublin. He was eventually defeated there also, so he went back to York, where he managed to make himself king for a few years around the middle of the century. Scots and Anglo-Saxon allied against him and he fled back to Ireland in 952, being succeeded in York by the last Norse king of Northumbria, the Norwegian Erik Bloodaxe, who in turn was ousted in 954.

Back in Ireland, Olav regained Dublin, where he remained in charge for almost three decades. During this period, he married, in succession, two Irish princesses, and Dublin grew into a substantial commercial center, the first city in Ireland. As king of Dublin, Olav patronized both Norse and Irish poets, such as Thorgils Orraskald

and Cináed ua hArtacáin, suggesting (but not necessarily proving) that he was bilingual. Olav's poets saw to it that his reputation
did not perish; indeed, he was portrayed as a noble savage called
"Havelok the Dane" in French and English poetry from the twelfth
century and later. After being defeated in the great battle of Tara
in 980, Olav, who earlier in his life had not hesitated to plunder
churches, retired to St. Columba's monastery on Iona in the Inner
Hebrides, where he died the following year.

Olav's sons and descendants continued to be major political
players around the Irish Sea for more than a century, especially his
charmingly named son Sitric Silkenbeard (d. 1042), who is famous
from Icelandic sagas. Sitric's mother was an Irish princess, his
father's mother an Anglo-Saxon princess, and his great-grandfather
a king of Northumbria, yet he was still considered a "foreigner" in
the twelfth-century Irish history *Cogad Gáedel re Gailab* (The War of
the Irish against the Foreigners). The work describes the battle of
Clontarf just north of Dublin in 1014, when Sitric's forces fought
against those of his father-in-law, who was also his step-father, the
Irish high king Brian Boru. This provides rich opportunities to
describe "the foreigners" in highly pejorative terms: "Now on the
one side of that battle were the shouting, hateful . . . [altogether
twenty-seven negative adjectives are lined up] . . . poisonous, mur-
derous, hostile Danars; bold, hard-hearted Danmarkians, surly,
piratical foreigners, blue-green, pagan; without reverence, without
veneration, without honour, without mercy, for God or for man."[20]
Sitric was not all that pagan; after all, he went on a pilgrimage to
Rome in 1028, when he appears to have petitioned the pope to
make Dublin the see of an archbishop.

In fact, Irish fighters, especially men under Sitric's uncle King
Máel Mórda of Leinster, fought on Sitric's side at Clontarf. His
army also contained units sent by Norse rulers in the British Isles,
such as Earl Sigurd of the Orkneys and Olav, son of King Lagmann
of the Isles (Hebrides and Man). Rulers with a common heritage
from Scandinavia may have felt that their shared culture and language obliged them to remain loyal to one another, but Sigurd and
Olav were more likely to be grabbing opportunities to enrich themselves and enhance their reputations. Brian Boru had, as we would

expect, other Scandinavians on his side in the battle. Warfare in Ireland was not simply inherited archhostility between "Vikings" and the Irish, however much the author of *Cogad* and other writers liked to imagine this to be the case; the warriors on the battlefield of Clontarf were there to promote their self-interest.

The *Cogad* leaves no doubt about the outcome of the battle: Brian Boru's "Irish" side won, even though the king himself was killed. A near-contemporary Norse skaldic poem known as *Darraðarljóð* (The Banner Song), on the other hand, claims the victory for Sitric. What is certain is that the Irish were unable to expel Sitric from Dublin until he was finally driven out in 1036, after almost a half century of rule. He survived until 1042 in a location that is no longer possible to determine.

Sitric's expulsion does not mark the end of Scandinavian rule over Dublin, which continued (by, among others, his nephew Ivar) until the invasion of Ireland by the Norman rulers of England in the twelfth century. Members of his brother Harald's family were for several generations kings of the Isles, that is of the Isle of Man and the Hebrides, and Sitric's granddaughter Ragnhild became the mother of the Welsh king Gruffudd ap Cynan (d. 1137) and thus the ancestor of several later Welsh rulers.

The last twenty years of Sitric's rule over Dublin coincided almost exactly with that of another Scandinavian ruler in the British Isles, the Danish king Cnut, who conquered England in 1016 and ruled there until his death in 1035. Historians have speculated about contacts or an alliance between Cnut and Sitric, and perhaps even a relationship between Cnut's death and Sitric's expulsion from Dublin the following year, but the evidence does not support such guesses.[21] Cnut's English kingship may be seen as the culmination of more than a century of Scandinavian power grabs in the British Isles. Where Guthrum and Guthred in the ninth century had been content to rule over county-sized areas, Cnut in the early eleventh century conquered England wholesale and, when he also inherited Denmark from his brother, he became one of the most powerful rulers of northern Europe. He thus followed in the footsteps of his father Svein Forkbeard, who also conquered England but was unable to enjoy his new kingdom for long, since he died only a few weeks after the English had proclaimed him king at Christmas 1013.

Scandinavian immigrants had a huge impact, still discernible today, on society and culture in the British Isles. Modern genetics researchers often look for the genes of Scandinavian ancestors in the current populations of these islands, and often (but not always) find them.[22] A survey of the genetic materials of the inhabitants of the islands around Britain has shown, for example, that 44 percent of the ancestry of Shetlanders is Scandinavian. The corresponding figure for the Orkneys is about 30 percent, and for the Western Isles only 15 percent.[23]

In accordance with modern stereotypes, we often imagine the Scandinavians who settled in Britain and Ireland as sturdy and robust men who married indigenous women, but the evidence, both historical and genetic, suggests that Vikings often brought their own families. In the 890s, a large Viking army raided in England under the leadership of a chieftain called Hæsten. They built a fortification in Benfleet, Essex, where they put "money and women and also children." The English took this fortification in 893 and captured, among others, Hæsten's wife and children.[24] This historical testimony is corroborated by archeological evidence suggesting that a larger proportion of Scandinavians moving to the British Isles were women than was previously thought.[25] Likewise genetic evidence has revealed that the Scandinavian ancestry of people on the Shetlands and the Orkneys derive as much from women as from men. The results for the Western Isles suggest, in contrast, a disproportionally large genetic contribution from Scandinavian males. Exactly how to explain these results is still hard to say.

The Norse language of the Scandinavian immigrants greatly influenced the languages spoken in the British Isles.[26] The impact is less noticeable in Irish, although several Norse words were borrowed into the language. One example is the Norse word for skin and hide, *skinn*, which became Middle Irish *scing*, meaning "garment, clothes, cloak." The word of course also survives in English as *skin*. The Old Norse word *rannsaka* (search a house) was taken into both Irish, as *rannsughadh* (search, rummage) and into English, as *ransack*. The influence on modern English is so profound that modern speakers seldom notice that they use a plethora of Norse words. The words that English borrowed from French and Latin are, in contrast, often obvious; we know that *mutton* and *prescribe* come from foreign languages, but it might not occur to us that *window* and *flawed* also are loanwords. It is, in fact, possible to construct entire narratives in which every word (except conjunctions, the verb *to be*, articles such as *the* and *a*, and prepositions such as *of* and *at*) is arguably derived from Old Norse. Here is an example:

> The odd Norse loans seem an awesome window onto a gang of ungainly, rugged, angry fellows, bands of low rotten crooks winging it at the stern's wake, sly, flawed "guests" who, craving geld, flung off their byrnies, thrusting and clipping calves and scalps with clubs. But for their hundreds of kids, the same thefts, ransacking, and harsh slaughter, the wronging of husbands, the bagging and sale of thralls, the same hitting on skirts and scoring with fillies, the lifting of whoredom aloft, the scaring up and raking in of fitting gifts, seemed flat and cloying, and got to be a drag. They shifted gears, balked at gusts, billows, rafts, and drowning, and took to dwelling under gables, rooted in their booths and seats on fells beneath the sky. Dozing happily on dirty eiderdowns, legs akimbo, they hugged their ragged, nagging slatterns, bound to birth and raise a gaggle of wall-eyed freckled goslings—ugly, scabby, wheezing, bawling, wailing tykes in kilts. Though our thrifty swains throve in their bleak hustings, wanting not for eggs or steak, bread or cake, they gasped and carped at both by-laws and in-laws and—egged on by the frothy blended dregs of the keg—got tight, crawling, staggering, swaying, loose-gaited athwart muck and mire and scree.[27]

The influence of the Norse language remains strong, but often overlooked, also in the family names of people from the British Isles. The Gaelic surname prefix *mac* ("son") is frequently combined with a Norse name, as in McLeod (from *Ljotr*), Macauley and MacAuliffe (*Óláfr*), MacSweeney (*Sveinn*). This does not mean that these families necessarily descend from Norwegians, Danes, or Swedes, for people without any Norse ancestry began to use Norse names, apparently fashionable in some Viking Age circles.

The many British place-names containing Norse words and personal names are important evidence for the extent of Scandinavian settlements. Swansea, for example, derives from the name *Sveinn* and the Scandinavian word for "island," *ey*. Kirkby and Kirby (there are forty-seven examples in the British Isles!) derive from the words *kirkja*, "church," and *by*, "farmstead, village." Kettlethorpe comes from the name *Kettil* and *thorp*, "outlying farm." Some place-names are compounded with female names, like Raventhorpe, which derives from *Ragnhild*. A scholar who has studied the place-names of Yorkshire and Lincolnshire (both in the Danelaw) found fifty-seven place-names that derived from twenty-eight different female names. Perhaps this is further evidence that Scandinavian women came to England with Viking armies, but the women remembered in the place-names could also be second- or third-generation immigrants.[28]

The Scandinavian settlers in the British Isles also had some influence on the institutions of the kingdoms there, although the most noticeable influence flows in the opposite direction. When Cnut was king of both England and Denmark, the latter country adopted many administrative structures and forms from the more advanced English kingdom. Scandinavian-derived laws were, however, valid in the Danelaw (as the name suggests) even after the demise of its Norse rulers. Perhaps the most important Scandinavian influence on English institutions was the creation of a tax collection system. When King Ethelred in 1012 employed Viking troops led by the chieftain Thorkell, he paid them out of the revenues of a new tax called *danegeld*, *heregeld*, or later simply *geld*, which was collected annually from every landowner. Subsequent English kings continued to collect this tax long after Thorkell and his army had left. It was abolished only in 1162, under Henry II.

In the British Isles, the invading and immigrating Vikings had a continuing impact. It stands to reason that this was because they took the place of people who lived there before, who may have been killed or hauled off into slavery elsewhere in Europe, or who simply moved. After all, a "great army" of Vikings had brought down three Anglo-Saxon kingdoms in the late ninth century, wreaking considerable havoc in the process. In the cases of Orkney and

Shetland, scholars have wondered if the original inhabitants disappeared entirely and were replaced by Scandinavians, whose dialect of Norse known as Norn was still spoken there into the nineteenth century.[29] Scandinavian immigration into the British Isles came about through a process of accommodation and encounter, peaceful as well as violent, with an existing population.

Some Scandinavian emigrants, in contrast, settled scarcely populated or unpopulated lands, such as Greenland. This large island is known for the huge glaciers that cover most of it, but we should not forget that strips of land along the coasts, especially on the western side, are free of ice. The climate is too cold to sustain forest growth or more than marginal cultivation of grain, but the green grass that grows on these strips has given the island its name and can sustain grazing domestic animals. The area is, furthermore, full of game such as caribou, foxes, and bear. The waters outside Greenland team with fish and other valuable animals such as walrus, seals, and whales. Therefore, people were not only able to survive there but also make a good living exporting the arctic riches of the region—for example, walrus ivory and ship ropes made of whale hide—to Europe.

Scandinavians settled Greenland toward the end of the tenth century. The much later *Saga of the Greenlanders* and *Saga of Erik the Red* depict the colonization of Greenland as the initiative of a single man, Erik the Red. He is a portrayed as a ne'er-do-well and troublemaker who had to leave Iceland for committing murder. He persuaded other Icelanders to move with him to Greenland, where he became an uncontested chieftain. Thus, Erik's story fits the template of the two Röriks: having little possibility of gaining power at home, he opportunistically grabbed the chance for a fresh start in life away from home. The sagas probably exaggerate for literary effect the contrast between Erik's sad existence in Iceland and his glorious chieftaincy in Greenland, but it is hard to escape the impression that Erik was yet another enterprising man who achieved his ambitions by emigrating.

In Greenland, Scandinavians settled in two areas, known as the Western and the Eastern Settlements.[30] The Western Settlement was some 650 kilometers to the northwest of the Eastern Settlement,

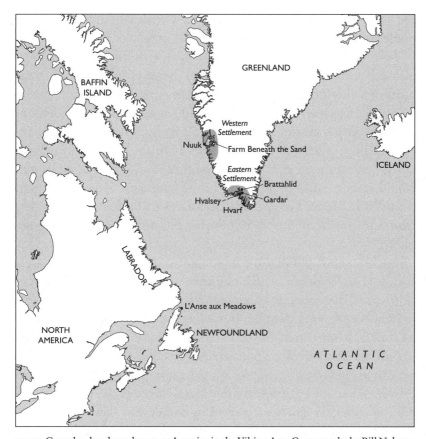

MAP 3. Greenland and northeastern America in the Viking Age. Cartography by Bill Nelson.

where Erik picked a splendid site for his farm. He called it Bratta-hlid and it was situated on a fjord known as Eriksfjord—a location that today is known as Qagssiarssuk on the fjord Tunugdliarfik. Here he built his hall and various other buildings. According to the sagas, his wife Thjodhild, who converted to Christianity before her husband, built a church, which archeologists believe they have found a few hundred meters from Brattahlid. The church was very small, only 2 by 3.5 meters, with a wood-clad interior surrounded by thick turf walls. Wooden benches along the walls provided seats. Around the church, a cemetery has been excavated with 144 graves (24 children, 65 men, and 39 women) dating from the end of the tenth century to the twelfth. It is reasonable to assume that Erik the Red, Thjodhild, and their son Leif Eriksson are among the bodies found in this cemetery.

Installed in his hall on the Eriksfjord, Erik the Red could feel pleased with himself. From dubious beginnings, he had made himself a chieftain. The Eastern Settlement, which looked to him as its political leader, by the 1350s had some 190 farms and about a dozen parish churches. In 1126, Greenland was even given its own bishop, who resided in Gardar (Igaliko), not far from Brattahlid but on the next fjord, Einarsfjord. The Western Settlement would number ninety farms and four churches. How many people lived in Norse Greenland? Estimates diverge widely, ranging from some 1,500 to 6,000, but the lower number is probably more likely.[31]

Such a small population in such a marginal climate is barely sustainable. Epidemics and violence constantly threatened the very survival of the entire settlement. Greenlanders were no strangers to violence. Among the men buried at the little church at Brattahlid, one had been stabbed with a knife that was still stuck between his ribs when archeologists excavated his body. The cemetery also contains a mass grave containing the disarticulated bones of thirteen men and a boy of about nine years. Three of the men had cranial injuries that had been caused by something sharp, such as an ax or a sword. The most likely interpretation is that the fourteen corpses come from some expedition or raid that had gone wrong, illustrating the violent nature of Norse society with its competing chieftains. The skeletons had been transported back to Brattahlid and the sacred ground of the cemetery. Either the bodies had been unburied for so long that they had become skeletons, or they had been boiled so that the flesh could be separated from the bones, and the bones transported home. This custom is documented by medieval histories, such as the story in the *Greenlandic Annals* of the Greenlander Einar Sokkason's expedition to what appear to have been distant hunting grounds. There, Einar and his men encountered the remnants of a shipwreck, including several corpses. He ordered his men to "put the bodies in boiling water . . . , so that the flesh can be separated from the bones, which then will be easier to bring to church."[32]

FIG. 8. When the third bishop of Gardar, Greenland, Jon Arnason, died in 1209, he was buried with his episcopal ring and his crozier, made of finely carved walrus ivory, one of the most desirable export articles of the arctic North. Photo courtesy of Nationalmuseet, Copenhagen.

The Norse population of Greenland disappeared later in the Middle Ages. They were still there in the early fifteenth century, but repeated expeditions sent by King Christian IV of Denmark-Norway at the beginning of the seventeenth century failed to find any Scandinavians in Greenland. Exactly what happened to the

Greenland Norse is a mystery, with guesses running the gamut from defeat in armed conflicts with the Inuit to Norse failure to adopt a diet more suitable to a deteriorating climate. Another proposal is that the Norse took English employment as fishers and moved to northeastern North America.[33] The flourishing of Norse civilization in Greenland followed by decline and abandonment is strikingly illustrated by archeological excavation at an unusually well preserved site, where the ruins of a farm were covered by sand and then deep-frozen in permafrost for some five centuries. The farm, now known as "The Farm beneath the Sand," is located on the outskirts of the Western Settlement, close to a river on a plateau some distance from the sea.[34]

The Farm beneath the Sand, the Norse name of which is unknown, was settled in the first decades of the eleventh century. We know the names of two men and one woman who lived there— Thor, Bardur, and Bjork—because their names appear in runic ownership marks on wooden artifacts. The central building on the farm was a small, three-aisled hall, measuring twelve meters by five meters on the inside. Its thick walls (1.2–1.9 meters) were made of turf, the most common building material in medieval Greenland. The turf isolated against the cold, which would have been needed, since temperatures at this site can drop to as low as –50°C in the winter. Inside, there were benches along the walls and wooden posts holding up the turf roof. This small hall was a distant reflection of the great chieftain's halls known from Lejre, Slöinge, and Gamla Uppsala on the Scandinavian mainland. Whatever ambitions these Greenlanders may have had, they soon abandoned them. The hall provided living space for people only for a short period, after which it was adapted to serve as a shed for animals, mainly sheep. Sheep's wool formed the basis for a cottage industry at the Farm beneath the Sand, where it was spun and then woven. One of the rooms at the farm contained the remains of an upright loom, which is the best preserved Viking Age loom anywhere. The room contained no less than eighty weights used to keep the threads of the warp taut. Archeologists also found tools for spinning, such as many spindles and spindle whorls. This large room was used for preparing textiles during the entire lifetime of the farm. Finished cloth and also a small stash of raw wool were found. The woven cloth was of high quality and would certainly have helped to keep the inhabitants of the farm warm, although it is possible that Greenland also exported wool cloth to Europe. An interesting oddity is that an analysis of the woven cloth from the Farm beneath the Sand reveals that it contains not only the expected fiber from sheep, goat, and oxen, but also hair from wild animals such as caribou, arctic fox, polar bear, brown bear, and bison. Brown bear and bison do not live in Greenland, so this hair must have come either all the way from Europe or, more likely, from North America. Either the Norse of Greenland went to North America to hunt bear and bison, or they traded with the Inuit for the fur of such animals.

The Farm beneath the Sand was abandoned at some point around 1400. The abandonment seems to have proceeded calmly and in a planned fashion, for very little of value was left behind. We do not know where the people of the farm went, but they must have gone by boat, for otherwise it is hard to explain why they left some of their animals behind. The animals stayed close to and inside the structures for shelter, as demonstrated by the large quantities of manure found inside some of the buildings. Rain, snow, and wind would have slowly destroyed the buildings as would wear and tear caused by the animals. One of the last dwellers at the site was a goat who had the misfortune of being killed by a collapsing wall; his skin, fur, and skeleton have been well preserved through the permafrost that soon froze his corpse. If there had still been people in the area, it would be hard to imagine that they would not have eaten the meat of the goat.[35]

The fate of the Farm beneath the Sand as revealed by archeologists strikingly confirms what one of the last medieval Europeans to visit the Western Settlement said about his experiences. While the priest Ivar Bardarson resided in the Eastern Settlement as administrator of the bishopric of Gardar from the 1340s to the 1360s, on behalf of a bishop who preferred to stay in Norway, one summer in the mid-1350s nothing was heard from the Western Settlement. The following summer, he set out to investigate what might have happened. In the Western Settlement he found only abandoned farms and half-wild farm animals, but no people.[36] It is odd that Ivar claims not to have found any people in the Western Settlement already in the 1350s, whereas the archeological date for the abandonment of the Farm beneath the Sand is around 1400. Either the scientific (but imprecise) date is incorrect or Ivar did not look carefully everywhere in the Western Settlement.

The Eastern Settlement also disappeared eventually. Excavated clothes from a well-preserved cemetery in the Eastern Settlement demonstrate that the Greenlanders, far from living in an isolated outpost, actually kept up with fashion in the Scandinavian mainland. This still applies in the middle of the fifteenth century, but no later. The Norse population disappeared at some point after that date. The last we hear of them in written sources is when a young couple, Sigrid Björnsdottir and Thorstein Olafsson, got married in the church at Hvalseye, Greenland, in the fall of 1408. It may be suggestive that Sigrid and Thorstein then moved to Iceland. Archeological investigations in both Greenlandic settlements have not revealed any traces of a sudden, catastrophic end to the Norse society there. The end seems to have been orderly and planned. Perhaps the Norse of Greenland opted to move elsewhere, especially when worsening climatic conditions from the thirteenth century made their already marginal existence less sustainable, forcing them, for example, to find new sailing routes between Greenland and Iceland so they could avoid the expanding ice masses.

In the place of the Norse, the Inuit moved in. When their legends and tales were written down in the middle of the nineteenth century, they appear still to remember their encounters with the Norse:

> In former times, when the coast was less peopled than now, a boat's crew . . . near Kangiusak . . . came upon a large house; but on getting closer to it, they did not know what to make of the people, seeing that they were not Inuit. In this manner, they had quite unexpectedly come upon the first Norse settlers. These likewise for the first time saw the natives of the country.[37]

Life in a cold and distant place like Greenland must have provided many kinds of challenges as well as opportunities. Among the challenges was the lack of trees on the island. In the Scandinavian homeland, the inhabitants would be used not only to building their ships and homes of wood, but also to heating their houses with fire-wood and to manufacturing all kinds of tools, furniture, and other implements from wood. The later sagas claim that Iceland had been wooded when first settled, but that the settlers cut down the trees within a generation or so of the first settlement. Sheep and other grazing animals prevented the woods from growing back. When Greenlanders needed wood, their closest known source was, thus, Norway, many days sailing away.

To make up for the lack of indigenous wood in Greenland, the inhabitants were inventive in using other materials. We have already seen that they built their houses of turf and stone, except for roof posts and other parts of the supporting structure that needed to be made of wood. Some Icelanders similarly lived in turf houses into the twentieth century.[38] Greenlanders burned some firewood, as is clear from charcoal found in their hearths, but they must otherwise have burned animal manure. Instead of wooden chairs, the inhab-itants of the Farm beneath the Sand sat on whale vertebrae. Their inventiveness is clear from many archeological finds. Instead of the standard wooden spades, Greenlanders fashioned spade blades from whalebone. The door to a dwelling room at the farm consisted of three wooden planks held together with two wooden cross-pieces. The wood is worm-eaten and was thus most likely Siberian driftwood that Greenlanders had collected on the beaches of their island; shipworms eat any wood that is in the ocean for any length of time. When the door needed repairs, they lashed the planks with whale baleen and used a piece of caribou antler to strengthen the door, rather than employing expensive wood. The door contains no piece of rare, imported wood.

Greenlandic archeological sites have also, however, produced wooden things without wormholes—for example, a plate and a bowl from the Farm beneath the Sand. Those things, or the wood they were made from must, thus, have been imported. It was prob-ably to seek new sources of wood, among other things, that Green-landers began to sail to the west and south, toward the North American continent, shortly after Greenland was settled. They became the first Europeans known to have visited North America, some five centuries before Christopher Columbus. The Labrador peninsula would have provided plenty of wood much closer at hand than Norway, and it is possible that much of the nondriftwood found in Greenland comes from there.

The *Saga of the Greenlanders* and the *Saga of Erik the Red* tell rousing tales about the discovery of Vinland, a wonderfully fertile land where wheat and grapes abound and the rivers team with fattened salmon. The land was first explored and, in one version of the story, also first discovered at some point close to the year 1000 by Erik the Red's son Leif Eriksson. An attempt was made to settle in Vinland but given up due to hostile encounters with the original inhabitants, whom the Norse called *skrælingar*. The word is clearly pejorative, but its exact meaning is much debated.

The sagas were written down hundreds of years after the discovery of Vinland, and their stories have clearly undergone literary shaping, but there is no doubt that the basic fact of Greenlanders sailing to North America is correct. The archeological discovery of a Scandinavian farm at Anse-aux-Meadows, close to the northern tip of Newfoundland, puts the Norse discovery of America beyond doubt. This does not mean, however, that every detail in the sagas is reliable. We might, for example, be suspicious of the claims about self-sown wheat and grapes. To anyone telling the story of the expeditions it may have seemed natural to conclude from Vinland's name that grapevines grew there, so this claim may be based more on folk etymology than on stories transmitted orally through the centuries before being written down. We should also be suspicious of sundry other evidence for Scandinavian colonization of America—runestones and the like—much of which was fabricated in modern times.

We should see the Vinland trips, which clearly continued after the original expeditions made famous through the Vinland sagas, as an expression of the opportunism of the Scandinavians living in Greenland. They needed wood, so they got it from a place as close as possible to their homes, rather than from Norway. According to the sagas, the route to Vinland passed by Markland, a name that means "Forest Land," suggesting what the Greenlanders valued about the area. This is probably the heavily forested Labrador

FIG. 9. Archeologists have excavated a Norse settlement from about 1000 at Anse-aux-Meadows, close to the northern tip of Newfoundland, Canada, proving that Scandinavians reached North America hundreds of years before the "Age of Discovery." An open-air museum contains a replica of the turf house that Viking Age settlers built there, reminiscent of the buildings common in Norse Greenland as well as in Iceland until relatively recently. Photo: D. Wilson. © Parks Canada. H.01.11.01.04(84), 31/12/2003. All rights reserved.

peninsula. Some Greenlanders looked for new places to settle and build farms, but the population of Greenland was so small that it could not sustain any large-scale colonization of Vinland. It is likely, or at least possible, that farms were built in other American places beyond Anse-aux-Meadows but most traces were lost when Europeans began cultivating the American soil in earnest during the early modern period, since they were likely to choose the same locations for their farms as the Norse had centuries earlier.

During the Viking Age, Scandinavians settled almost everywhere between Newfoundland and Novgorod, between Dublin and Dorestad. They encountered very different circumstances in the various places they went, and they had very different objectives. Rurik looked for trading opportunities when he moved into a region with people but no strong states. Roric conquered a great

trade emporium, Dorestad, and occupied the outskirts of a powerful empire, reaching an understanding with emperors and kings.
The settlers of Greenland and Iceland colonized previously unin-
habited lands, where they, like Rörik in Styrstad, pursued agriculture and animal husbandry. Other Viking chieftains, such as
Guthrum and Halvdan in England and Sitric Silkenbeard in Ireland, had set their sights on existing states, which they sought to
topple. They arrived with large armies that could match the defensive forces. When they were victorious, they could move in with at
least some of their warriors on previously inhabited territory. All
these Scandinavians had, however, one thing in common: they left
Scandinavia to pursue what they saw as opportunities elsewhere.
This applies especially to chieftains, who sought power. They all
appear eager to adopt European culture and civilization, to become
Europeans, as did Guthrum when he accepted Christianity and the
Anglo-Saxon name Ethelstan. Wherever they went, Viking Age
Scandinavians brought with them their language, their traditions,
and their genes. These features are to this day more or less traceable
in different places in Europe. While almost no Norse loanwords
were taken into the Slavic languages of eastern Europe, English
has many, Irish some, and French a few. Norse customs were long
reflected in traditions of the English Danelaw, but the dukes and
other inhabitants in Normandy quickly became more French than
Scandinavian, and the Scandinavian occupation of Frisia is almost
forgotten. The Viking Age settlement that retains most of its Scandinavian heritage is Iceland, where the language has changed so
little since the country was first inhabited that modern Icelanders
have little difficulty understanding Old Norse texts.

CHAPTER 4

SHIPS, BOATS, AND FERRIES TO THE AFTERWORLD

EMPEROR CHARLEMAGNE WAS ALREADY AN OLD MAN WHEN, IN 810, he "received the news that a fleet of 200 ships from Denmark had landed in Frisia" on the northern coast of his empire. The Vikings ravaged the region, fighting three battles against the Frisians and finally forcing the inhabitants to save their lives by paying a large ransom. The emperor was furious and ordered his army to assemble to march north and defeat them. Charlemagne himself rode toward the plundering Northmen, bringing with him his beloved pet elephant, Abul-Abbas, a gift from Caliph Harun ar-Rashid in Baghdad. The elephant suddenly died after crossing the Rhine River, a bad omen. The bereaved emperor continued north, only to be met with the news that "the fleet that ravaged Frisia had returned home." The fearsome Frankish army had marched out in vain; it never engaged the Scandinavians in battle.[1]

The incident demonstrates how the Vikings used the speed of their ships to good effect, to show up in force suddenly and without warning and to disappear just as quickly without risking a fight with the well-armed and powerful but slow regular army of the Frankish Empire. Contemporary chroniclers often emphasized the surprise element in Viking attacks, describing the Northmen as "rushing in," "falling upon," or "bursting in" with their ships.

Sea trials with reconstructed Viking ships confirm the impression that they were very seaworthy and fast. *Helge Ask*, a modern copy of the Viking Age ship *Skuldelev* 5, for example, has sailed at speeds of more than fifteen knots and it can be rowed at almost six knots. Other reconstructed Viking ships have managed to ride out gale-force winds in the North Atlantic.[2] The shipwrights of Viking Age Scandinavia designed great ships that continue to impress.

Contemporaries often noted that the Vikings arrived on ships. "Three hundred and fifty ships came into the mouth of the Thames" in 851, noted the Anglo-Saxon Chronicler; Archbishop Hincmar of Reims observed in 859 that "Danish pirates made a long sea-voyage, sailed through the straits between Spain and Africa and then up the Rhone," where they "ravaged cities and monasteries."[3] The Vikings were nothing if not sailors. The Anglo-Saxon poet who composed *The Battle of Maldon* pointed to this fact in about 1000 when he gave a Viking spokesman a speech referring to his band of warriors as "brave seamen," who would "go [back] to their ships and take to the sea" if only the English would pay them off with a suitable tribute.[4]

If early medieval Scandinavians had not become exquisite shipwrights, there would have been no Vikings and no Viking Age. They learned to build fast and flexible ships, oceangoing but also suitable for shallow river waters, that could transport large numbers of warriors. As a consequence, those parts of Europe that could be reached by the sea or navigable rivers bore the brunt of the Vikings' fury. The Scandinavians themselves were acutely aware of the importance of their ships, which they celebrated in their mythology, poetry, runic inscriptions, and funerary customs. A widespread belief circulated, for example, that the Afterworld was most appropriately reached by ship, so many a Scandinavian—Viking warrior as well as peaceful peasant—was buried in some kind of boat or at least accompanied by a symbolic ship.

For centuries before the beginning of the Viking Age, Scandinavians had built sleek and fast ships. These were propelled by rowers, not by sails, but they were still formidable warships. A well-preserved example from about 320 CE was found in Nydam in the nineteenth century; it is a large ship, 23.5 meters long by 3.5 meters wide, and it was capable of high speeds when manned by the full complement of twenty-eight rowers/warriors. The threat from such ships explains why settlements on the Baltic Sea island Gotland in pre-Viking times pulled back from the coasts. Although its distance from the nearest land—some one hundred kilometers—would previously have protected the island from surprise attacks, the development of warships like the one at Nydam forced the inhabitants to take the defensive measure of moving away from the shore.[5]

Even though large rowing ships easily reached Gotland and other islands closer to the mainland, they would not have been particularly suitable for going on Viking raids in western Europe or for traveling to Iceland, the Faroe Islands, or the British Isles. They were simply not built for the demands of ocean travel. Long-distance travel had to wait for Scandinavian shipwrights to construct ships with masts—sailing ships. One of the great mysteries of Scandinavian shipbuilding is why it took so long before the Norse began to use sails. The Romans had brought sailing ships to the North Sea and some non-Roman people in Germany and the British Isles adopted their sailing technology, while Scandinavians did not, at least until the late eighth century. Only around the year 800 do the picture stones on Gotland start to depict ships under sail rather than rowing boats. The oldest Scandinavian sailing ship to have been found by archeologists is the Oseberg ship, which was built in Norway in about 815–820. Its pine wood mast had been rather awkwardly attached to the ship, suggesting that the shipwright was not very familiar with the new design. Also, the Oseberg ship is low, only 1.6 meters from the keel to the upper edge of the sides. It has a moderate draft (depth under water) of only 80 centimeters, useful for maneuvering in shallow waters, but its freeboard (the distance between the water and the upper edge of the boat's side) is similarly modest, which means that the ship is not very safe in windy weather. Experimental journeys with reconstructions of the Oseberg ship have shown it to be very fast, but quite unsafe in gusty winds and at speeds faster than ten knots.

By around 900, Scandinavian shipwrights began to develop two different types of ships: long and sleek warships, on the one hand, and broad and comparatively short cargo ships, on the other.

FIG. 10. One of the best-preserved Viking ships was excavated from a grave mound in Gokstad, Norway, and is now on display in Oslo. A large, robust man, who clearly had been killed
in battle, was buried in the ship together with rich grave goods, including horses and dogs.
Photo: © Kulturhistorisk museum, Universitetet i Oslo.

Scandinavian ships could reach impressive loading capacity, such
as a twenty-five-meter longship from around 1025 found in the harbor of Hedeby, which is estimated to have been capable to carry a
load of 60 metric tons. A more typical cargo ship might be exem-
plified by the so-called *Skuldelev* 1 ship found close to Roskilde in
Denmark, a robust oceangoing ship of great seaworthiness. It was
built in around 1030, and could load about 24 tons on a length of a
little more than 16 meters. Several full-scale reconstructions of this
ship have shown that it can be sailed handily with a crew of five to
seven. It would have been provided with a few oars to help maneuver the ship in harbors and other tight places, but they would not
have been used for propelling the ship; that would have been done
only by sail.

Scandinavian shipwrights also built long and sleek ships that
were used as warships. Such longships were provided with sails, but
they also had places for sometimes dozens of rowers. A ship from
985 found in the harbor of Hedeby measures almost 31 meters by

only 2.6 meters. It could be propelled by sixty rowers using thirty pairs of oars. An even longer ship from after 1025 was recently found in fragments; amazingly, the find was made when the ground next to the harbor in Roskilde was excavated for the purpose of expanding the Viking Ship Museum. It had a keel composed of three separate wooden pieces, together 32 meters, and thus the ship should have been about 36 meters long. The high-medieval sagas often include what used to be thought of as exaggerated claims for the size of the greatest longships. The thirteenth-century historical narrative *Heimskringla*, for example, claimed that Olav Tryggvason's great ship *Long Serpent* (from just before 1000) had space for sixty-eight rowers.[6] The recent discoveries of the Roskilde and Hedeby longships, however, corroborate such claims.

The great chieftains of the Viking Age competed with one another about who had the longest and most magnificently decorated warships, but there were also longships of more modest proportions that would have served perfectly well for Viking raids. The ship known as *Skuldelev 5* was a little more than eighteen meters long and had space for thirteen pairs of oars. Its size is probably more typical of normal Viking ships.

The secret behind the excellence of Viking Age ships lies in how they were constructed. Centuries earlier, Scandinavian ships were constructed through the so-called clinker or lap-strake technique: the primary component of such a ship was the shell made from planks that had been placed side by side with a slight overlap, through which small clinching nails ("clinkers") hold the planks together. This makes the sides of the hull appear with small "steps" between the planks. The technique produces a strong and flexible hull, which was stiffened by inserting frames and ribs to fix the shape firmly. An Old English poet describing the battle of Brunanburh (937) between Anglo-Saxons and Vikings appears to allude to the typical Scandinavian ship construction when he refers to the ships of the invaders as *nægledcnearr*, "nailed knarr," or perhaps "clinkered knarr." The word "knarr" is a loanword from Old Norse *knörr*, which refers to a type of ship, most likely a broad and sturdy ship.[7]

In the Viking Age, the planks were not sawed but rather split from logs using wedges and axes. This meant that the planks

FIG. 11. A fourteenth-century manuscript known as *Skarðsbók* illustrates the laws of Iceland with delightful miniatures. This initial S in the section dealing with seafarers depicts two shipbuilders constructing a ship. Photo courtesy of © Stofnun Árna Magnússonar í íslenskum fræðum, Reykjavik. From AM 350 fol., fo. 61v.

followed the natural grain of the wood, making them more flexible and easier to bend than sawed planks. The best wood for boatbuilding was oak, strong and flexible, where it was available in southern Scandinavia. The Hedeby and Roskilde grand longships as well as the prestigious ships from the Oseberg and Gokstad graves are all made entirely of oak, except for their masts. In skaldic poetry the Norse word for "oak" is often used figuratively to signify "ship," as in Sigvat Thordarson's poem celebrating King Olav Haraldsson's victory over the local magnate Erling Skjalgsson. The lethal war between these two great men began when the latter "caused the oak [= ship] to be launched."[8] Pine was also used to build ships, perhaps especially in northern Scandinavia, where no oaks grew. The remains of Viking Age ships also include a few pieces of other kinds of woods, such as maple and birch.

With warships like those mentioned, bands of Vikings were well prepared to attack and raid in Europe. With a sail and so many pairs of oars available, they were able to show up suddenly and without warning on a seashore, or even on the banks of larger rivers. The ships' relatively shallow draught allowed them to travel on rivers and to be pulled up on land. When the raiding was done, or when Vikings encountered unexpected resistance, they could quickly row out to safety beyond the reach of arrows and spears. With the larger ships they did not need to hug the shore when they sailed; they could cross huge expanses of open water: the Baltic Sea, the North Sea, the Bay of Biscay.

Vikings ships' square sails were their greatest liability. Such sails worked marvelously well as long as the wind blew in the direction they wanted to go. But when headwinds persisted, ships rigged with square sails were very poor at beating to windward, certainly when compared to modern sailboats with their triangular Bermuda rigs. In addition, oars were not of much use with a headwind of any strength. Experiments with reconstructed Viking ships performed by the Roskilde Museum show that, when zigzagging against the wind, square sails were not quite as bad as previously thought. A reconstruction of *Skuldelev* 1 was able to tack against the wind in a very rough sea, covering thirty nautical miles in twenty-four hours. That amounts to an average speed of only 1.3 knots, but at least no distance was lost while the headwind lasted.[9]

Vikings enjoyed rushing forward in their large and impressive warships, sails bulging and planks creaking. Any chieftain who wanted to be thought of as a great leader was expected to have a really good and prestigious ship. The court poets, therefore, heaped praise on their lords' ships. The skald Thjodolf Arnorsson extolled the longship of King Magnus Olavsson of Norway. It had place for sixty rowers and was called *Bison*. Thus it was the same size as the ship excavated in Hedeby. Its name is typical of Viking Age boat names, which often refer to animals, and the strong and sturdy bison, which is in the habit of dashing unrestrainably ahead, must have been particularly attractive. Thjodolf praised *Bison* and the king:

Mighty ruler, you launched a ship, and [made] the thirty-benched ship glide at full stretch over the sea at that time; the driven sailyard shuddered. The raging wind did not spare the swayed mast above you, lord; splendid retainers took down the decorated cloth of the mast-top [= sail] in Sigtuna.

——-

You used long ships boldly, battle-strong lord, as men steered seventy vessels eastwards. Strakes [= hull planking] roared south; high-hoisted sails conversed with the forestay; the tall-masted oak [= ship] sliced the sound; Bison plunged its curved rail.[10]

Obviously, King Magnus was proud of his magnificent longship with swaying mast, decorated sail, thirty rowing benches, and splendid warriors to man the oars. He had every reason to be delighted. A truly royal longship like *Bison* represented a major investment of resources that paid off handsomely in military strength and power.

The Viking Ship Museum in Roskilde has for many years experimented with building reconstructions of historical Viking ships from the museum's collection. In 2000–2004, the turn had come to reconstruct the largest ship in the museum, the longship *Skuldelev 2*, which was originally built in about 1042 somewhere close to Dublin in Ireland, but using a Scandinavian design. A Norse chieftain who had settled in Ireland most likely commissioned it. Only about 25 percent of the original ship survives, in eighteen hundred pieces, after nine hundred years at the bottom of the Roskilde Fjord, but these fragments included enough key features that scholars can figure out the dimensions and construction of the ship. It was a giant, thirty meters long and capable of seating some sixty rowers.

To reconstruct such a huge ship required altogether 27,000 man-hours, working with 150 cubic meters of oak. If one assumes that a master builder and ten shipbuilders worked on the original *Skuldelev 2*, it would have taken seven months to build the ship, assuming that they had access to plenty of low-skilled workers to fell and transport the necessary wood. That calculation includes only the woodworking. An additional 13,000 hours would have been required to forge the nails and other iron details, to burn the tar (from 18 cubic meters of pine wood), to make the ship ropes, and to weave and sew the sail (from linen or wool). In sum, a great many men and women worked some 40,000 hours to build this ship and equip it with all its fittings. We may be sure that women would have been involved with some of the tasks; if we take the stereotypes in medieval literature seriously, that would certainly include weaving the sail. The skald Ottar the Black, for example, mentioned "the sail spun by women" when he praised his king's ship in the early eleventh century. The person who had the original *Skuldelev* 2 longship built clearly expended huge resources, in terms of both human workforce and raw materials.[11]

Scholars reckon that the sail of the *Skuldelev* 2 longship would have been about 120 square meters, whereas the sail of the ocean-going cargo ship *Skuldelev* 1, built about 1030, would have been approximately 90 square meters. During the Viking Age, sails were made from either linen or wool. In 1999, the Roskilde Museum produced a large woolen sail for its reconstruction (called *Ottar*) of the cargo ship *Skuldelev* 1. For this, the wool from 200 Norwegian heritage sheep was spun very taut and then woven tightly to produce an appropriately windproof textile. The sail was then smeared with ochre, horse mane fat, and beef suet to make it even more windproof and durable. For the rigging, the museum has experimented with horsehair rope, hemp rope, and linden bast rope. In the Viking Age, shipwrights also rigged their ships with twined walrus skin, which made very strong and durable rope. When the north Norwegian chieftain and merchant Ottar visited King Alfred of Wessex in the late ninth century, he told him about the walrus, which he said was a kind of whale, "smaller than other whales; it is no longer than seven ells long." Ottar hunted walrus for the sake of the very fine ivory in their tusks and, he added, "their hide is very good for ship-ropes."[12]

Viking ships did not have very long lifespans. If they saw much action, they soon needed repairs and were eventually scrapped. The five ships that form the core of the collection at the Roskilde Viking Ship Museum were old and worn out when they were purposely sunk in about 1070 to block the narrow entrance to the Roskilde Fjord. They were then only some thirty to forty years old. Several of the ships had already been repaired. The great longship *Skuldelev* 2, for example, had been repaired in Ireland, where it had been built. Written sources sometimes tell us that the Vikings used lulls in the fighting to repair their ships. In 862, for example, a band of Vikings had after partially unsuccessful raids around the river Seine retreated to Jumièges in Normandy "to repair their ships." Four years later, some of the same Vikings stayed at a place, apparently also in Normandy, that was "suitable for making repairs to their ships and for building new ones."[13]

Ships could be built or repaired anywhere, not just in permanent shipyards. We must imagine that the proximity of mature oak or pine trees determined where Viking shipwrights decided to build their ships. The old Norwegian law book *Gulatingslov* allowed ships to be built wherever the right wood was available.[14] Archeologists have, nevertheless, found remnants of permanent shipyards all around the areas where Viking Age Scandinavians ventured. In the trading community at Paviken on the island of Gotland in the Baltic, for example, a small shipyard specialized in repairing ships. The ground has yielded expert tools for removing the clinching nails used to hold together the clinker-built hulls of Scandinavian ships as well as large quantities of such nails.[15] Archeologists have found several workshops where ships could be repaired and surely also built in the large settlement Gnëzdovo, ten kilometers west of the present center of Smolensk.[16] This town needed shipyards, since it was of special importance as a transportation hub during the Viking Age, situated close to the crossroads of eastern Europe.

Any Scandinavians reaching Gnëzdovo would have traveled on a vast network of riverways stretching across eastern Europe, after first crossing the Baltic Sea. They would have used several different ships on such a trip, suitable for the varying conditions in which they traveled: sturdy seaworthy ships on the Baltic and smaller, lighter boats on the rivers, particularly in the shallow waters of their upper reaches. When approaching the river's sources, they could portage small vessels over to river systems on which they might reach their destination.

Some of the riverboats used on the Russian rivers were probably dugout canoes, that is, logs that have been hollowed out to a thin skin that could be stretched to form a hull. An informed Byzantine observer in the tenth century said that each spring the Rus constructed *monoxyla*. This obscure Greek word, which clearly refers

FIG. 12. To get from one river to another, Scandinavians in the Viking Age portaged their boats overland. Photo courtesy of the Beinecke Rare Book and Manuscript Library, Yale University. From Olaus Magnus, *Historia de gentibus septentrionalibus* (Rome, 1555), 369, but the same woodblock was previously used for an illustration in the same author's *Carta marina* from 1539.

to some kind of boat, is compounded of the words for "one" and "wood"; a likely translation is "dugout canoes."

The observer, who is none other than the highly literate Byzantine emperor Constantine VII Porphyrogennetos (913–959), recounts how the Rus, starting from Smolensk, would travel down the Dnieper River. He describes in detail how they managed to pass the dangerous Dnieper cataracts or rapids, through which the river drops some thirty-five meters over a stretch of seventy kilometers. These rapids are no longer visible, since a Soviet-era hydroelectric dam covers them with water. To avoid the greatest of them, Constantine says, the Rus would "partly drag their boats and partly carry them on their shoulders" overland around the rapids, which meant that they had to watch out for the steppe nomads known as the Pechenegs, who might take the opportunity to attack and plunder the travelers while they were vulnerable. Constantine names the rapids, giving most of them two names, one in Slavonic and one in "Russian." Many linguists consider the "Russian" names to be derived from the Norse language.

Constantine names the largest Dnieper rapid "Aifor" in Russian. The same name appears on a runestone from Gotland in Sweden, raised in memory of a man called Ravn by his brothers. "They came far in Eifor," the inscription says. Perhaps Ravn together with his fellow travelers, possibly his brothers, had tried to ride the rapid in their boat, but failed. Even in the nineteenth century, Cossack river pilots still took pride in being able to steer a boat through all the rapids. Ravn may have been one of their equally proud, but less fortunate, predecessors.

A beautiful runestone now built into the wall of a church in central Sweden commemorates a man called Banki (or Baggi). His bereaved parents, Thjalvi and Holmlaug, had commissioned the inscription and they remembered two facts of Banki's life that made them very proud: he owned a ship, and he had steered that vessel to the east as a companion of the Viking chieftain Ingvar. The inscription provides more clues to how Viking raids and Scandinavian society were organized.[17] Ingvar set out from Sweden in the early eleventh century with a large following to raid the shores of the Caspian Sea on the border of Asia and Europe, an unusual destination. The band succeeded in getting there, but their plan to raid failed spectacularly, since they met strong resistance and most of them perished. Twenty-six runestones spread over central Sweden still memorialize warriors who "died in the east, with Ingvar." That number also includes the famous runestone that remembers Ingvar's brother Harald with a sparse verse distilling not only a mother's pain at the loss of a warrior son, but also her pride:

> They traveled valiantly far for gold
> and in the east gave [food] to the eagle.
> [They] died in the south in Serkland [= land of the Saracens][18]

Like Harald, Banki had responded to Ingvar's call for warriors to go with him for what they hoped would be lucrative raiding. Surely, Ingvar had been careful to build up a loyal following over the years before setting out on his proud venture, and we may guess that Banki had exchanged gifts with Ingvar and that he had visited Ingvar's hall to drink mead and other drinks many times. To afford and to man a ship, Banki must himself have been a chieftain, who chose to sail with Ingvar although he could have chosen to do something else, such as raiding on his own or following another Viking chieftain in some other direction. Large Viking fleets were made up of many smaller contingents whose leaders had decided to join together for the occasion. This explains how large forces could appear so suddenly, only to disappear again just as quickly. Such fluid and transient configurations were typical of the early Viking Age.

Banki owned his own ship, something his proud parents did not fail to point out. He had also steered his ship himself, manning the large steering oar or rudder hanging alongside the starboard (right) side of the back of the ship. He thus took upon himself the great responsibility of directing his valuable ship safely, avoiding skerries and shoals. That said, his ship would have had a crew of warriors, who were his friends and clients, no doubt recipients of his gifts and participants in the feasts that he had organized in his hall.

The warriors rowed the ship when necessary, for example on the rivers of Russia that they needed to traverse in order to get to the Caspian Sea where Ingvar had planned to raid and plunder. When rowing they may have sat on cross-beams (thwarts), but more often on chests in which they could store their belongings, perhaps including their booty from raids. At some point in the Viking Age, a sailor was robbed of his chest in Hedeby. The perpetrators broke the lock and emptied the chest of its valuables. They then put a large stone into it and sank it in the harbor, thus preserving it, but not its contents, for posterity. This chest, measuring 52 by 23 centimeters, is a typical sea chest, with its base broader than its top, preventing it from tilting over in rough seas. It is made of oak and 27 centimeters tall with a slightly vaulted cover, making it a suitable seat for rowing.

Each rower handled a single oar, while his benchmate, whether on his own chest or a thwart, handled an oar on the other side of the boat. Oars were typically made of alder and pine wood, and they wore out quickly, which explains why new oars were made for the Oseberg ship, itself already several decades old when it was buried. Its original oars must have been destroyed long before. If rowers had their customary seats at specific oarports (holes in the top plank) or tholes (pairs of wooden pins in the gunwhale between which the oar is placed), it is easy to understand that friendships and, perhaps, sometimes enmity developed between benchmates. The poet Sigvat Thordarson addressed his partner in rowing, Teitr, in a stanza that alludes to their shared experience as Olav Haraldsson's warriors:

> Teitr, I saw chill mail-shirts fall over the shoulders of us both in the glorious war-band of the mighty ruler . . . bench-mate, I knew us both to be thus prepared against the [enemy] army.[19]

When the ship was under sail on the open sea, the full complement of warriors was normally not needed to maneuver it, so those off duty would entertain themselves as best they could by telling stories and playing games. Archeologists often find gaming pieces and boards in the graves of Viking Age warriors.

Scandinavian seafarers clearly were able to find their way in many different kinds of watery contexts between Newfoundland in North America and the Caspian Sea. This was because they simply knew their way, not because they had access to any advanced navigational tools. They passed down information about sea routes from generation to generation. This was easy on rivers, along the coasts, and in small bodies of water such as the Baltic. The northern shores of the Baltic Sea are protected by thousands of islands and islets in archipelagos that stretch almost uninterrupted from eastern Scania to the tip of the Gulf of Finland close to St. Petersburg. There are sufficient landmarks by which to remember any route, and land is never far away should any sudden storm arise, as is wont to happen in the Baltic. Even ships that avoid the route through the archipelagos are never very far from land, since the Baltic is nowhere broader than 330 kilometers across.

Other Scandinavian coasts, such as most of the long coast of Norway, also offer protected navigation routes within archipelagoes. In the late ninth century, the chieftain and merchant Ottar regularly made the trip from where he lived in the far North to a trading place that he called Sciringes healh in the Oslo Fjord. "He would sail by the coast the whole way" and this would take a month, "assuming he made camp at night," he told King Alfred in Wessex. Ottar would have known the landmarks on the way, and he probably had favorite places where he would stop for the night.

Vikings would similarly have been able to learn the routes along the coasts of continental Europe as well as the British Isles so that they could find their way to rich raiding opportunities. Yet, Viking Age Scandinavians clearly were also adept at crossing the open ocean and finding their way not only across the North Sea to the British Isles, but also across the Atlantic to Iceland and Greenland. Today, it is so difficult to imagine this being done without maps, compass, or a satellite navigating system that there has been much unfounded speculation about advanced navigating tools that the Vikings are supposed to have used. But we simply have to accept that Scandinavians, like other seafaring peoples before the modern era, were well able to find their way across the ocean simply by observing nature around them. We get some hints about how it was done through sailing instructions written down in Iceland in the early fourteenth century, which surely reflect the navigation practices of the Viking Age. To sail straight from Norway to Greenland, across the huge expanse of the North Atlantic, a sailor needs to observe the surroundings carefully:

> From Hernar [on the western coast of Norway] one should keep sailing west to reach Hvarf [close to the southern tip of] Greenland and then you are sailing north of Shetland, so that it can only be seen if visibility is very good; but south of the Faroes, so that the sea appears half-way up their mountain slopes; but so far south of Iceland that one only becomes aware of birds and whales from it.[20]

Travelers to Greenland would have been able to keep a course due west by observing the sky and sea currents. The instructions talk about visually observing the Faroes and, in good weather, Shetland, while other clues would let the sailors know that they were at the right distance from Iceland. Each kind of seabird flies only a certain distance from land, and whales like to stay in certain areas of the sea where they are able to find rich food supplies. By knowing the species of birds and whales and their idiosyncrasies, Viking Age sailors knew where they were, even when they could not see land. Additionally, cloud formations and even smell could tell experienced sailors where there was land beyond the horizon.

Despite their navigational expertise, ship's crews sometimes got lost. Navigational mishaps might take sailors to where they did not intend to go. In fact, the high-medieval sagas from Iceland frequently tell of such adventures, claiming for example that Greenland, "Vinland" (certainly some part of North America, perhaps Newfoundland), Svalbard (probably Spitzbergen), and even Iceland itself were discovered after seafarers had been blown off their intended course in storms. Even if these stories are based in a literary cliché, they surely reflect the reality of sailing on the ocean. But storms could do worse things than blow ships to new and unexpected lands; sometimes they simply wrecked ships or entire fleets, drowning the crews. European chroniclers occasionally recount with some satisfaction that Viking fleets met this fate. In 838, for example, "Danish pirates sailed out from their homeland but a sudden severe storm arose at sea and they were drowned with scarcely any survivors."[21] Or in 876: "The raiding ship-army sailed around west, and then they met a great storm at sea, and 120 ships were lost there at Swanage."[22]

A runestone in Sweden memorializes the man Geirbjörn, who had been killed in a fight: "Norwegians killed him on Asbjörn's ship." It is tempting to think that Asbjörn was a Viking chieftain and that Geirbjörn died during a sea battle, but perhaps the ship was a merchant vessel and Geirbjörn was killed during a quarrel among merchants, or when a cargo ship was attacked by raiders.[23]

Be that as it may, Vikings certainly knew how to fight at sea, although they did not at first have to do it much when they attacked their victims on raids in Europe, for the kings there did not have navies that could meet the Vikings on equal terms. The Europeans eventually learned to challenge the Vikings in their own element, on the water, as when, in 882, "King Alfred went out with ships and fought against four ship-loads of Danish men and took two of the ships, and killed the men; and two surrendered to him, and the men were badly knocked about and wounded before they surrendered."[24] Still, European navies never became very effective in defending against the Vikings, and the kings preferred to "fight fire with fire," that is, to rely on Viking mercenaries to defend territory against other Vikings.

In Scandinavia itself, ambitious chieftains and kings often fought one another in great sea battles. The skalds liked to describe such heroic occasions in some detail, so we are happily able to learn much about how Vikings fought on ships. Later saga literature, such as the *Heimskringla*, tells with great verve exciting stories about sea battles, but they represent simply later authors imaginatively weaving narratives that have very little value as historical sources.

Before the actual sea battle began, the chieftain exhorted his warriors to fight bravely. Before he battled the Danish king in 1062, King Harald Hardruler of Norway, for example, "told the troops of warriors to shoot and strike," and "the famous ruler said each of us must fall crosswise on top of one another rather than yield."[25] Then the ship would be rowed to an enemy ship, preferably the leader's: it would "lie alongside the ship."[26] When the warriors "join[ed] together the stems of the longships," they created a platform on which they could fight.

Then the battle started. As one poet expressed it, with typical northern understatement, "it was not as if a maiden was bringing a man leek or ale": in other words, it was a horrid experience.[27] "The bold lord cut down warriors; he walked enraged across the warship."[28] "We [warriors] went enraged onto the ships under the banners," the warrior poet Sigvat recounted after fighting under Olav Haraldsson in the battle of Nesjar in 1016.[29] Different poets celebrating different battles fill in the details. Warriors and, especially, their leaders were supposed to be "angry" during the fight— the word shows up repeatedly in the poetry. Their enemies suffered their anger; there was blood everywhere: "Dark blood splashed on the pliant row of nails [= ship], gore spurted on the shield-rail, the deck-plank was sprinkled with blood."[30] "The army fell on the deck" so that "the slain lay tightly packed on the boards," unless they "went wounded overboard."[31] In the end, "the prince won the victory" and could take over the ships of those he had defeated.[32] If they were still in a repairable state, ships were extremely valuable war booty, not surprising considering the amount of work that went into constructing the great longships.

Afterward, the bodies of the dead washed up on the beaches. With their characteristic fascination with gore, skalds like Arnorr jarlaskald did not hesitate to describe the grisly scene, where carrion eaters like eagles and wolves had been given a feast:

> Sandy corpses of [the loser] Sveinn's men are cast from the south onto the beaches; far and wide people see where bodies float off Jutland. The wolf drags a heap of slain from the water; Olav's son [= King Magnus Olavsson of Norway] made fasting forbidden for the eagle; the wolf tears a corpse in the bays.[33]

Sea battles often had momentous effects, with the lives and reputations, not only of warriors, but also of entire kingdoms, hanging in the balance. Many a Scandinavian king and chieftain met his end in battle, like the Norwegian king Olav Tryggvason, who fell in the battle of Svölðr in 1000, fighting a coalition of the Danish and Swedish kings as well as a Norwegian chieftain. His namesake Olav Haraldsson won Norwegian kingship at the battle of Nesjar in 1016. Olav's half-brother Harald Hardruler tried to conquer Denmark from his rival, King Svein Estridsson, in the battle of Nissan River in 1062, but although the Norwegians were victorious in the battle, Harald did not gain Denmark. The battle was inconclusive since King Svein and some of his warriors managed to escape Harald's clutches by ignominiously rowing ashore in a small boat. Great sea battles were often the decisive events when Scandinavian rulers fought wars with one another, and the skalds of the victorious ruler would make sure that his lord's exploits became famous. In the historical sagas of high-medieval Iceland, battle narratives often allow for the most impressive and rousing prose. The *Saga of Olav Tryggvason* from the early thirteenth century ends, for example, with a climactic retelling of the battle of Svölðr. The story has fascinated generations of Scandinavian schoolchildren, and it continues to impress modern readers.

Ships loomed large not only in the life but also in the imagination of the Viking Age. We have already seen what a prominent place ships had in Viking court poetry flattering kings and chieftains, but ships also show up in the art of the time—for example, on picture stones and runestones. They are particularly prominent on the great inscribed stones of Gotland, where they often dominate the composition. The large picture stone Stora Hammars I is divided into six panels, and ships appear in two of them. The fourth panel depicts a ship without a sail, but with round shields along the gunwale. Four men with raised swords in the ship appears to attack a group of four persons on land, one of whom looks like a woman. This has been interpreted as a mythological scene. The viewer's gaze is, however, most attracted by the large bottom panel that is almost entirely filled by a great ship sailing on elegantly out-lined waves. The square sail is fully raised on a mast amidships and people fill the ship. The composition is characteristic of the Viking Age picture stones on Gotland, which often devote almost half of their surface to a large image of a ship. These monuments are to be understood as memorial stones, or stones marking the graves of distinguished men and women, and it is therefore reasonable to assume that their depictions represent the ships that would take the dead person to the Afterworld.

Many runestones also have images of ships, but only one also mentions the ship in its text. This is a Swedish runestone at Spånga, now on the outskirts of Stockholm, that outlines a ship that instead of a mast has a richly decorated cross. Two brothers, Gudbjörn and Oddi, raised this stone in memory of their father, Gudmar. They appended a brief verse: "He stood valiantly in the stem of the ship; he who died lies buried in the west." The poem emphasizes that Gudmar was not just an ordinary warrior; he stood in the stem, a distinguished position, whether it means that he occupied the prime fighting position at the forestem or that he captained and steered the ship from its rear stem, perhaps also owning it. The context seems to suggest that Gudmar was a warrior who had been killed on a Viking raid in western Europe or in a sea battle in Scan-dinavia. The runestone emphasizes that he received a proper burial even though he died away from home.[34]

We like to imagine that the ship depicted on the Spånga stone was Gudmar's own ship, the one he steered or manned in the prow during this lifetime, but another interpretation stands out as per-haps even more likely: his sons may have chosen to portray the ship that they thought would transport their fallen father into the realm of the dead. If great ships were appropriate vehicles for great men and women in their lifetimes, should they not travel in similar style after death? The cross on the stone suggests that Gudmar, or at least his sons, were Christians; although the idea of a ship ferrying the dead to the Afterlife is not really consistent with Christian ideas, we have to be prepared to accept some apparent inconsistencies in what was, after all, a time of rapid religious change.

Allusions to ships sometimes appear in unexpected circumstances. Anyone who moves around the Scandinavian countryside is likely to encounter mysterious arrangements of large stones, often aligned to form the outline of a ship. Such structures are known as ship settings, and they are very common although usually hard to discern if they are overgrown or ruined. Many ship settings were built on top of graves. Scandinavians created these figurative ships through much of prehistory, beginning in the Neolithic Era, but a substantial portion are from the Viking Age. These ancient monuments tell us that Viking Age people associated death with sea travel. The idea seems to be that the dead person sailed to the Afterworld in a ship and that a symbolic stone ship was quite sufficient.

Such ideas must have been widespread, for numerous ship settings are known from all over Scandinavia. They are concentrated in Sweden from its southern tip in Scania up to Uppland just north of Stockholm, with an especially large number found on the island of Gotland. They have never been completely catalogued. In 1986, a scholar listed close to two thousand examples spread all over Scandinavia, but the list is very incomplete, since he based it mostly on information available in print.[35] We get a sense of how much might be missing from a detailed study of a single Swedish region (Södermanland), published in 2003, which showed that very many ship settings had never been mentioned in print.[36] Whereas the 1986 catalogue lists only twenty-six locations in the region, the 2003 study identified ship settings in no fewer than 186 locations, including 228 individual ship settings. Overall, there must be thousands of ship settings in Scandinavia, demonstrating yet again the importance of ships in the imaginary world of the Norse.

The idea that the dead sailed to the Afterlife in a ship appears when the Old English poet of *Beowulf* imagines how a chieftain would have been buried in ancient Scandinavia when he narrates the Danes' mythical ancestor Scyld's funeral, which quite literally includes his sailing away in a ship. This description, surviving in a manuscript from about 1000, might perhaps seem more valuable for its literary merits than for any historical accuracy, but it appears to capture at least some aspects of Viking Age ship burials, including the rich grave goods and the idea that funeral ships were intended for transport to the Afterlife:

> Scyld passed away at his appointed hour,
> the mighty lord went into the Lord's keeping;
> they bore him down to the brimming sea,
> his dear comrades, as he himself had commanded
>
> —
>
> In the harbor stood a ring-prowed ship
> icy, outbound, a nobleman's vessel;
> there they laid down their dear lord,
> dispenser of rings, in the bosom of the ship,
> glorious, by the mast. There were many treasures
> loaded there, adornments from distant lands;
> I have never heard of a more lovely ship
> bedecked with battle-weapons and war-gear,
> blades and byrnies. In its bosom lay
> many treasures, which were to travel
> far with him into the keeping of the flood.
>
> —
>
> Then they set a golden ensign
> high over his head, and let the waves have him,
> gave him to the Deep with grieving spirits,
> mournful in mind.[37]

There are no parallels elsewhere in literature to the very impractical idea that a corpse would be buried by being put on a ship set adrift in the ocean. This journey is perhaps better read as a figurative one, like that imagined for the Oseberg burial (see below), than an actual one. The destination of the trip remains unclear in the poem. In fact, the poet points out that "men do not know . . . who received that cargo," although that may reflect a Christian writer's discomfort with an idea of the Afterlife that is not reconcilable with Christendom.[38]

The idea of traveling by ship to the Afterworld inspired literary compositions and dozens of images of ships, but also the actual burial practices of the Viking Age. Hundreds of people buried in ships have been identified throughout Scandinavia.[39] The vessels involved ranged from quite small rowboats to full-fledged Viking longships like the beautifully decorated one found remarkably well preserved in a clay mound in Oseberg, Norway. Sometimes the funerary ship was burned in a great conflagration that also cremated the bodies of the dead. Among the smaller ships used for an actual burial is one six meters long by one meter across that was buried in a mound in Vatnsdalur on the shore of the starkly beautiful narrow sea bay Patreksfjörður in northwestern Iceland. A woman was buried here, probably in the tenth century, in a clinker-built hull constructed with twelve strakes, most probably of larch wood. Two pieces of whalebone attached to the gunwale served as cleats, to prevent an anchorline or a towline from cutting into the wood. Almost nothing of the wood is preserved, making determination of the species difficult, but the clinching nails still outlined the shape of the boat when the grave was excavated in 1964. The woman buried in the boat was accompanied by her dog and relatively rich grave goods, including two arm rings of bronze, a necklace with glass beads and two pieces of amber, a small, round silver disk probably made from an Arabic silver coin, and a simple Thor's hammer amulet of silver. The woman buried here would have arrived well attired in the Afterworld, traveling in her ship.[40]

Two other Scandinavian women, splendidly dressed in decorated woven clothes and with uniquely rich grave goods, were buried in the great Oseberg ship in 834 or shortly thereafter. This ship, made out of oak and exquisitely carved in the animal style typical of the time, was twenty-two meters long and five meters broad. Notable among the grave goods is a wooden bucket with the runic inscription "Sigrid owns [me]," perhaps naming one of the two women buried in the ship.[41]

The carefully excavated Oseberg burial affords us unique insights into the rituals surrounding the burial and how Viking

Age people may have understood what it meant to be buried in a ship. The burial was thoroughly planned and carried out over at least four months. First, a trench was dug from the sea in which the ship could be dragged up on land. The clay excavated from this ditch landed on top of flowers blooming in early spring, so we know that this was done at this particular time in the year. When the ship was in position with the forestem to the south, a grave chamber was constructed just behind the mast. The southern end of the chamber was left open, and the stern of the ship was equipped with utensils for preparing food as well as a slaughtered ox, providing plenty of meat for the two women. Then the back end of the ship, including cooking pots, ox, and all, was covered with soil. The foreship was now left standing in open air while the aft half was covered by half a grave mound. The grave chamber could be seen as a gaping hole in the side of the half-mound. A striking stage was thus provided for the rituals surrounding the burial of the women, and this reconstruction of what the setting looked like moves our imagination. The visible part of the ship had three oars placed in a rowing position, and the forestem was moored to a large stone with a sturdy rope. It looks like a ship ready to set out on the final journey of Sigrid, if that indeed was her name, and her companion. The goal of that journey was clearly visible to everyone who saw the half-finished mound: the ship was quite literally going into the black earth, into the mound. It was at this point that the women were put into their grave chamber, and most of their grave goods were also put there and in the foreship: perhaps as many as ten chests, woven tapestries, down cushions, a wagon, sleds, beds, and much else. The women were given additional provisions in the form of apples and bilberries, revealing that they were buried when those have matured in Norway, late in the summer, at least four months after the trench for the keel of the ship had been dug. The culmination of the funerary rites was the ritual sacrifice when the heads of ten horses and three dogs were cut off. At least some of these killings took place on the foreship, which by the end would have been drenched in animal blood. Perhaps the idea was that the funeral ship might sail the women to the Afterworld on a symbolic sea of blood? Be that as it may, Sigrid and her companion would have arrived there in grand style, in splendid attire, sailing a most beautifully decorated Viking ship fully loaded with all kinds of things that they might need. At the end of the ritual, the mound, including seventy tons of stones, was built up over the rest of the ship, crushing it but also preserving it to be excavated, reconstructed, and moved to a museum in Oslo, Norway, in 1904.[42]

These two examples of ship burials concern women's graves, but men were also buried in ships, probably even more frequently than women. At the archeological site of Valsgärde north of Uppsala in Sweden, fifteen individuals, probably all men, were buried in ships at intervals of about a generation over a period stretching from the late sixth (or possibly the early seventh) century to approximately 1000. The site also contains more than seventy-five other graves. The impression given is that a sequence of political leaders were magnificently buried in ships, while their family members and others were given more quotidian burials without ships or many grave goods. Archeologists have discovered the remains of a large hall built on the top of a hill close by. One assumes that the hall belonged to the chieftains buried in the ships, who after death traveled in an appropriately princely way to the Afterlife.

All of the ship burials at Valsgärde are truly splendid, with a rich assortment of high-status grave goods: a complete set of weapons, horse harnesses, kitchen utensils, rare glass vessels, and board games. They also contain a remarkably large quantity of animal bones, especially grave 66, which contained no less than thirty-one liters of burnt bones. This grave is the only one of the fifteen ship burials that is a cremation: the dead body has been burned together with ship, animals, and all.[43] Cremated ship burials are otherwise not unusual, and we can actually read an eyewitness account of such a burial observed in about 921 by an Arab traveler among the Rus of Russia.

After traveling for almost a year from Baghdad to the town of Bulghar on the Volga, the Arab civil servant Ahmad ibn Fadlan was fascinated by the Rus merchants he encountered there. When he heard of "the death of one of their [the Rus'] great men," he was eager to learn more about their funeral practices, so he traveled to where this chieftain was going to be buried. He wrote down in Arabic what he saw when a great Rus chieftain was cremated in a great conflagration. The exact identity of the Rus is much debated, and we should be careful not simply to take ibn Fadlan's account of the Rus as in any way representative of Viking Age Scandinavian customs. Whatever their ethnic origins, the Rus that ibn Fadlan saw may have been settled in Russia for generations and impulses from many different traditions surely influenced the way they buried their dead leader, but it is clear that Scandinavian rituals stand behind at least some and perhaps most of what happened almost eleven hundred years ago on the banks of one of Russia's many rivers.

When ibn Fadlan arrived at the place where the chieftain's ship was, he "discovered to [his] surprise that it had been beached" (just as the Oseberg ship had been dragged onto land). The chieftain had been temporarily buried in an underground chamber as the funeral was prepared. Wood had been placed close to the ship, and "then the ship was hauled and placed on top of this wood . . . they produced a couch and placed it on the ship, covering it with quilts and cushions of Byzantine silk brocade." At this point, the Rus exhumed their chieftain again from his temporary grave:

> They clothed him in trousers, leggings, boots, a tunic, and a silk caftan with golden buttons, and placed a cap of silk and sable pelts on his head. They carried him . . . on the ship and laid him to rest on the quilt, propping him with cushions. Then they brought alcohol, fruit and herbs and placed them beside him. Next they brought bread, meat and onions, which they cast in front of him, a dog, which they cut in two and which they threw onto the ship, and all his weaponry, which they placed beside him. They then brought two mounts, made them gallop until they began to sweat, cut them up into pieces and threw the flesh onto the ship. They next fetched two cows, which they also cut up into pieces and threw on board, and a cock and a hen, which they slaughtered and cast onto it.

The man had been laid in the ship and provisioned with grave goods and food. Now there remained only to give the chieftain a human companion, and one of his slave girls had, says ibn Fadlan, volunteered to accompany her dead master in death. While the ship was prepared, the girl had gone around to the tents or pavilions of the men on the site. "The owner of [each] pavilion would have intercourse with her and say to her, 'Tell your master that I have done this purely out of love for you.'" In the late afternoon on a Friday, the slave girl appeared next to the ship and performed various rituals. She cut off the head of a hen, and she had visions of the Afterworld, in which she saw her master summon her. She was lifted onto the ship, given alcohol to drink, and was then brought into the pavilion where her master rested. "Six men entered the pavilion and all had intercourse with the slave-girl." Afterward, "they laid her down next to her master and two of them took hold of her feet, two her hands."

A "crone" called the "Angel of Death," who was "a gloomy, corpulent woman, neither old nor young," ibn Fadlan claimed, functioned during the funeral as a kind of master of ceremonies. At this point, she put a rope around the girl's neck, giving the ends to the two remaining men. The Angel of Death "advanced with a broadbladed dagger and began to thrust it in and out between her ribs, now here, now there, while the two men throttled her with the rope until she died."

> Then the deceased's next of kin approached and took hold of a piece of wood and set fire to it. He walked backwards, with the back of his neck to the ship, his face to the people, with the lighted piece of wood in one hand and the other hand on his anus, being completely naked. He ignited the wood that had been set up under the ship. . . . Then the people came forward with sticks and firewood. Each one carried a stick the end of which he had set fire to and which he threw on top of the wood. The wood caught fire, and then the ship, the pavilion, the man, the slave-girl and all it contained. A dreadful wind arose and the flames leapt higher and blazed fiercely. . . . It took scarcely an hour for the ship, the firewood, the slave-girl and her master to be burnt to a fine ash.
>
> They built something like a round hillock over the ship . . . and placed in the middle of it a large piece of birch on which they wrote the name of the man and the name of the King of the Rus. Then they left.[44]

Ibn Fadlan was lucky enough to observe a magnificent shipcremation, at the end of which the wind came and blew away the ashes of the dead chieftain and his ship almost as if it still sailed the seas. Some of what our Arab observer claimed he saw—the sacrificed animals, the ship itself, the mound raised over the ashes, and so forth—can comfortably be set alongside what archeology teaches us about burial customs in the Scandinavian Viking Age, while other observations lack such outside corroboration. In general, ibn Fadlan appears reliable, since he kept a detached distance from what he recounts, although his preoccupation with the sexual mores of the Rus is reminiscent of the ribald stories told at the time in the all-male salons of the Caliphate, which influenced the style of so much medieval Arabic literature. Elements in ibn Fadlan's portrayal of the Rus appear based in racial stereotypes.[45] Not everything he recounted might actually have happened the way he told it, but surely enough of it for us to take his account seriously.

Ships are important in many cultures worldwide and Scandinavia is far from unique in emphasizing the role of ships in the way it did. Still, the geography of the region made ships essential for communication across any substantial distance. In parts of Norway as in Iceland and Greenland, the sea remained the best way to get from settlements in one fjord to the next one until modern aircrafts and infrastructure investments in railroads and roads made alternative forms of transportation convenient in the twentieth century. Denmark is situated on islands and peninsulas around the several sounds between the Baltic Sea and the Kattegat Bay off the North Sea and depended on sea vessels to maintain communications. Sweden's regions are separated by large forests that could be difficult to penetrate in the Middle Ages, when waterways were often better suited for communication. Scandinavians were always skilled at building and maneuvering boats and ships, for good reasons. Their abilities flourished in particular during the Viking Age, when ships also reached a pinnacle of cultural and symbolic importance never since equaled. Scandinavians used their ships not only to raid in western Europe but also to transport trade goods, thus reshaping European commerce and the economy.

CHAPTER 5

COINS, SILK, AND HERRING

Viking Age Trade in Northern Europe

IT WAS PERHAPS NOT AN ORDINARY CLASS OF STUDENTS THAT was camping out for the night at Stavgard on the large Swedish island of Gotland in the Baltic Sea in 1975. They had studied prehistoric Scandinavia for months in school, and now they were going to live like Vikings. The spot they had picked was perfect, full of mysterious ancient monuments: standing stones, inscriptions on rocks, traces of prehistoric agriculture. The students started bonfires, built houses, made and fired pottery, and fished in the Baltic Sea. At dawn on their last day, they prepared "sacrifices" at an old bauta stone, a large upright stone that had been raised there in some ancient time. They sacrificed smoked perch, flowers, and pottery to the gods and wished for good fortune in the harvest, hunting, and seeking and finding money. This last wish had a particular resonance to them, for they had camped on the very spot identified in local lore as the place where the Viking chieftain Stavar had hidden his vast treasure.

It was an idyllic day in the lives of these teens who were pretending to live during one of the most exciting periods in Scandinavian history. A wild rabbit ran across the field, and since all the chores of their trip had been completed, they tried to capture it, just for fun. The rabbit took refuge in a burrow. One of the children was intrepid enough to put his hand down the rabbit hole. Would he pull the rabbit out of its warren by its ears? No, but when he pulled back his hand, he clutched something even more interesting: old coins. Had the rabbit found Stavar's treasure?

The students called the local museum, which sent archeologists to excavate the rabbit's burrow. They found 1,452 Viking Age silver coins that had been hidden around the middle of the tenth century. Of those, 1,440 were Arabic dirhams, the silver currency of the Arab Caliphate, far away on the other side of Europe. The Swedish state paid a finder's fee to the class, which used the money to visit the center for experimental archeology in Lejre, Denmark, where they saw reconstructed early medieval buildings and crafts being practiced as they were a thousand years ago. Their experience made them so enthusiastic about reliving the Viking Age that they decided to create a similar center in Sweden, at the place where they had themselves experimented with Iron Age life and where they had found the Viking treasure. Stavgard still attracts visitors every summer.[1]

The story of the schoolchildren in 1975 may be unique, but finding Viking Age Arab dirhams is far from unusual on the Baltic Sea island of Gotland, or elsewhere around the Baltic Sea. More than seven hundred hoards of such coins have been found in Gotland alone, and typically one is found there every year. Because the school class immediately reported their find to the archeological authorities, the treasure at Stavgard was properly excavated and examined. Other hoards are found by thieves who have no scruples about destroying valuable historical evidence by stealing silver they find in the ground, usually by using metal detectors. A law first issued in 1666 protects Swedish antiquities from such thefts and prescribes jail sentences for those who break the law. In 2011, a Swedish appeals court, as a historic first, condemned three men to prison sentences of fourteen to eighteen months for a particularly egregious theft, but many other similar crimes have gone unreported and unpunished.[2]

In 1999, Swedish television was making a documentary about ancient treasures and the thieves who plunder them. Archeologists had come to the farm Spillings in northeast Gotland to demonstrate the use of metal detectors. A farmer plowing the fields there had over the years found many silver coins and other ancient artifacts, so they had good hopes of making interesting discoveries in front of the television cameras. Unfortunately, they only came across some pieces of bronze, but after the television team had

FIG. 13. A silver hoard found in 1997 in Ocksarve, Gotland, Sweden, contains not only hundreds of coins of varying provenance, mostly German, but also Arabic dirhams, spiral rings, and other artifacts. The treasure was originally hidden in a posthole of a house. The makeup of the hoard, when carefully analyzed, reveals much about the direction of exchange (commercial and otherwise) and the nature of Scandinavian society during the Viking Age. Photo: Raymond Hejdström, courtesy of Gotlands museum, Visby.

packed up and gone home, the archeologists continued to search. After all, they were there with their equipment, and now they found so much metal that the detector overloaded. Excavations revealed the greatest Viking Age silver treasure ever found anywhere, weighing in at more than sixty-five kilograms, including 14,295 silver coins. The treasure had been buried in two separate hoards under the floor of a building in 870 or soon after. This find contains a few coins struck in Hedeby and a few handfuls of Persian coins, but the absolute majority are Arabic dirhams, silver coins produced at the eastern end of the Arab Caliphate, in exotic places like Samarqand and Bukhara.[3] How did these coins come to the countryside of the Baltic island of Gotland?

A crucial clue is provided by the Arab traveler Ahmad ibn Fadlan, whom we met in chapter 4. Caliph Jafar al-Muqtadir (r. 908–932) sent him on a diplomatic mission in 921. The destination of the embassy was the town Bulghar, situated on the banks of the Volga, today a day's journey by train east of Moscow. Ibn Fadlan's assignment was, among other things, to read aloud a letter from the caliph to the king of Bulghar, who had recently converted to Islam and entered into an alliance with the Caliphate. Bulghar was an important trading center in the tenth century, and it was the main town of the Volga Bulgarians who had until recently been a nomadic Turkic-speaking tribe living on the steppes of Eurasia. They were distant cousins of the Bulgarians who settled in what is today Bulgaria. Ibn Fadlan's detailed report of his experiences was rediscovered in an Iranian library in 1921, so we are able to read about his many interesting observations from this trip. He was, for example, intrigued by the shortness of the night during the summer, typical of the high latitude, and absolutely fascinated by his first experience of aurora borealis, the northern lights, a phenomenon that he, naturally, had never observed in his native Mesopotamia.

Ibn Fadlan's report describes a people that he called the Rus. The exact identity of this people, who gave Russia its name, has been enormously controversial for centuries, but most modern scholars agree that they were merchants who were at least partially of Scandinavian origin. Ibn Fadlan described how the Rus arrived at Bulghar, on the Volga, in their boats and then sacrificed to their gods:

> As soon as their boats arrive at this port, each of them disembarks, taking with him bread and meat, onions, milk and mead, and he walks until he comes to a great wooden post stuck in the ground with a face like that of a man, and around it are little figures. Behind these images long wooden stakes are driven into the ground. Each of them prostrates himself before the great idol, saying to it: "Oh my lord, I have come from a far country and I have with me such and such a number of young slave girls, and such and such a number of sable skins . . ." and so on, until he has listed all the trade goods he has brought. [Then he adds:] "I have brought you this gift." Then he leaves what he has with him in front of the wooden post [and says:] "I would like you to do the favour of sending me a merchant who has large quantities

of *dinars* and *dirhams*, and who will buy everything that I want and not argue with me over my price." Then he departs.[4]

So ibn Fadlan saw Scandinavian merchants eager to earn dinars and dirhams (Arab gold and silver coins) through trade in Bulghar. It is easy to conclude that he observed one step in the journey of Arab silver from the silver mines and mints of the Caliphate to the ground of Gotland and the rest of Scandinavia. The Rus would sell their furs and their slaves in Bulghar for Arab coins, which they would then bring west. Perhaps some of the merchants that ibn Fadlan met in Bulghar might themselves have traveled the entire way to Scandinavia and then buried their treasure in their backyards, but it is more likely that the silver passed through many intermediate hands before ending up in a treasure trove on Gotland, where it could be found in modern times by burrowing rabbits, enthusiastic schoolchildren, or unscrupulous treasure hunters.

The silver found in Gotland and ibn Fadlan's testimony from Bulghar provide two snapshots of a significant and wide-ranging network of trade and exchange across northern Europe. Altogether, more than 80,000 Viking Age Arab silver dirhams have been found on Gotland. Another 40,000 come from mainland Sweden.[5] More silver, but generally smaller sums, comes from Denmark, Norway, and the southern coast of the Baltic Sea. Obviously, there must have been an enormous influx of silver from the Arab Caliphate during the Viking Age, especially since one can assume that the discovered silver we know about is only a portion of what was traded, as it does not account for coins melted down to make ingots and jewelry or to strike new coins during the Viking Age, coins held illegally in private hands, and those that have not yet been found. The dirhams obviously came from the Arab Caliphate—which during the Viking Age stretched from the Iberian peninsula, along the southern shores of the Mediterranean, through the Middle East, and all the way to central Asia and the rich silver mines in Shāsh, Uzbekistan, and Panjshir, Afghanistan—but silver reached Scandinavia from other sources as well. More than 51,000 English silver pennies from the period 990–1051 alone have been found in Scandinavia, many more than survive in England itself.[6] Again, this was a huge influx of wealth, bearing witness not only to the success of northern trade but also, and perhaps mostly, to the ability of the Vikings to extort tribute in money from the peoples they attacked.

How and under what circumstances did so much of the currency of the Caliphate and of western Europe make its way to Scandinavia? Some of the transactions that brought silver to the North were commercial, but not all of them, for goods and money often changed hands in many other ways. Coins could, for example, be stolen, plundered, paid as tribute, used as bribes, or given as gifts. Most would have changed hands several times in different ways as they were transported to the North.

The great northern arc of commerce and exchange that tied together the eastern parts of the Caliphate with western Europe via the Baltic region influenced strongly every area it touched. Around the Baltic and North seas, an unprecedented number of trade towns grew up. Those towns flourished for a century or two until fundamental changes in Scandinavian society and economy as well as the decline of the Caliphate meant a restructuring of northern trade, soon leading to its domination in the Middle Ages by the German Hansa League.

The towns served several purposes. They provided outlets for those who wanted to sell the attractive products of the North, such as walrus ivory, slaves, or furs. The chieftain Ottar, who lived in Hålogaland in northern Norway, regularly sailed, for example, to two trade towns: Sciringes healh in southern Norway, identified with the archeological site called Kaupang,[7] and Hedeby at the southwestern corner of the Baltic Sea, then in southern Denmark. Close to his home, he acquired arctic products such as walrus ivory, strong ship ropes made of walrus skins, and various kinds of furs, including pelts of white polar bear. Some he hunted himself; others he collected as tribute from the Sami population of the north.[8]

The exports of northern Europe provided income for chieftains and traders, for trappers and hunters, for middlemen and merchants, but the trading networks and the trade towns were perhaps even more important for what they brought *to* Scandinavia. They served the needs of powerful persons who wanted to become more powerful, by bringing them exotic and prestigious trade goods, which they could use to enhance the aura of power that already surrounded them. Power was visible in the Middle Ages. Powerful people needed to look the part. Chieftains wore splendid clothes of exotic and rare textiles, carried the most impressive jewelry, used the best foreign-made swords, were the most gracious and hospitable of hosts and the most generous of lords. The chieftains of Scandinavia competed to become the most wealthy, the most powerful. One of the ways in which they competed was by importing the most valuable, the most exotic foreign trade goods, with which they decorated themselves and their halls and which they gave away to their followers in an inflationary spiral of competitive gift giving.[9]

Because they needed the trade goods that merchants could bring them, Scandinavian chieftains organized trade and built towns, which grew up like mushrooms after rain all around the North and Baltic seas, mostly at protected natural harbors. The coasts, fjords, and river mouths of those seas are dotted with the archeological remnants of large and small trade towns, from hugely important trade emporia such as Staraya Ladoga in Russia, Birka in Sweden, and Hedeby in Denmark to smaller ports of local significance. Some of the smaller trading settlements were temporary and flourished only during the summer. Scholars know of at least eighty-two Viking Age trading sites around the Baltic Sea and on the North Sea coast of Scandinavia.[10] For example, on the island Gotland, famous for its many Arab dirham hoards, at least five trading sites are known: Visby (which became a real city in the Middle Ages and remains such, still surrounded by its medieval city wall), Paviken, Fröjel, Bandlundeviken, and Bogeviken. None of these sites are mentioned in Viking Age written sources, but all boast remnants that have been explored by archeologists.

Paviken is one example of a minor trade town. Close to the westernmost cape of Gotland, a narrow bay provided an excellent natural harbor where a small settlement grew up. Archeologists have found a stone quay, dwelling houses, a shipyard, traces of a smithy, and remnants of the production of glass beads and jewelry. Except in scale, Paviken resembles the great trading centers of Birka and Hedeby. The settlement at Paviken covered about 1.5 hectares while that at Hedeby extended to about 24 hectares. Like most of the Viking Age trade towns, Paviken ceased to function as a trade town toward the end of the tenth century.[11] The town was never very large or important, and people may have lived there only in the summer. The great trading centers of Scandinavia were, in contrast, permanent settlements of pivotal importance for the kings and chieftains who founded and ran them. Foremost among them all, on a long inlet from the southwestern corner of the Baltic Sea, was Hedeby.

Not every chieftain who wanted his own trade emporium was as determined as the Danish king Godfrid, who in 808 attacked his old enemies the Slavic Obodrites on the southern shore of the Baltic Sea, destroying their town Reric while being careful not to injure the merchants. Those he simply moved to his own town Hedeby. The oldest datable archeological remains there are timbers felled in 811. The two dates are so close to each other that we may take them as approximately when Hedeby was founded. Over the next two centuries, Hedeby would grow considerably, becoming the greatest Viking Age trade town of Scandinavia. Merchants came there "from all directions," wrote Archbishop Rimbert of Hamburg in about 870, and Hedeby is indeed easy to reach from every side.[12] The town is situated on the eastern side of the base of the Jutland peninsula, at the end of a forty-kilometer-long narrow inlet, the Schlei Fjord, leading inland from the southwestern corner of the Baltic Sea. Ships from the entire Baltic Sea region could easily reach the many jetties in the harbor of Hedeby. In addition, overland trade followed the old land route going from Germany and Saxony along the spine of Jutland, crossing over the border fortification known as the Danevirke, not far from Hedeby. Ships from the North Sea might have attempted to reach Hedeby via the long and dangerous voyage around Jutland, about which the German navy still warned sailors in a nautical manual from 1927. It was more convenient to cross the relatively narrow base of the peninsula; navigable rivers brought smaller ships from the west to within a few kilometers of Hedeby.[13]

Hedeby always expanded in accordance with the city plan that Godfrid had laid out on a grid with streets parallel and perpendicular to the shoreline. Its largest extension was about 24 hectares, and there are some twelve thousand persons buried in the cemeteries outside of the town. Building lots were generally fenced in and contained small rectangular wooden buildings, mostly constructed with wattle and daub, used as dwellings or craftsmen's workshops. Some lots in addition contain a well and a small shed. A well-preserved building, slightly larger than average at twelve meters by five meters, has been reconstructed and is a popular tourist destination.

In the tenth century, fortifications were added in the form of a semicircular earthen rampart, up to eleven meters tall, and a palisade of logs around the harbor. That such defensive measures were necessary is clear from the written sources, which make repeated mention of attacks against Hedeby in the tenth and eleventh centuries. A man called Thorulf, who claimed to be a retainer of "Svein" (perhaps one of the Danish kings of that name), remembered his fellow warrior Erik, "who died when men besieged Hedeby."[14] In 1049, the Norwegian king Harald Hardruler attacked his bitter enemy, the Danish king Svein Estridsson. A description of the siege survives in an anonymous piece of poetry attributed to one of Harald's warriors, who reveled in the destruction of Hedeby:

> All Hedeby was burned from end to end out of anger, and that one can call a valiant deed, I believe. There is hope that we will do harm to Svein; I was on the rampart of the stronghold last night before dawn; high flame burst from the houses.[15]

This attack (which probably was not when Erik fell) may have spelled the end of the importance of Hedeby, which soon disappeared entirely. By the eleventh century, the nearby town of Schleswig, with its deeper harbor on a different branch of the Schlei Fjord, had taken over Hedeby's functions.

While Hedeby flourished, it was the greatest trade emporium of the North, where any interested buyer could acquire most things he or she needed. The traders arriving from all directions introduced both utilitarian objects and exotic luxuries, thus enhancing the standing of Scandinavian chieftains, starting with Godfrid and continuing with his successors. Archeologists have found much evidence for long-distance trade of a remarkable variety of goods: small ceramic bottles with mercury, amber, bars of iron, lead, silver, brass, foreign jewelry including carnelian and rock crystal, glass, foreign pottery, silk, a set of counterfeit Arab dirhams, and wine barrels from the Rhineland, which were reused to line well shafts. Among northern products found in Hedeby are walrus ivory, walrus bones, reindeer antlers, Norwegian soapstone, and whetstones. We know from other evidence that fur and most textiles also were traded at Hedeby, but they did not leave much trace in the archeological material, since most organic matter perishes over a millennium. An iron lock from a set of slave fetters, found in the town's harbor, reminds us of Hedeby's slave trade.[16]

An eyewitness report survives from the Arab diplomat Ibrahim ibn Yacoub al-Tartushi, who visited Hedeby on his way to the German emperor Otto I in the middle of the tenth century. He wrote, using the German name for the place, "*Shalashwiq* [Schleswig = Hedeby] is a very large city, on the coast of the ocean. Inside it are many springs of sweet water. The inhabitants worship Sirius [they are pagan], except for a small number of Christians." The text, which is preserved only in excerpts included in a medieval geographical encyclopedia, goes on to talk about several of the customs of the inhabitants of Hedeby: the feasts and religious sacrifices, the inhabitants' poverty in the eyes of a sophisticated man from Arab Spain—"they mostly eat fish," he said—their killing their newborn "to save the cost of raising them," the right of their women to divorce their husbands, their artificial eye makeup or tattoos, and their truly awful singing, "like the baying of hounds, only worse."[17] It is hard to know what to make of this report, which has survived only at several removes from the original, and which gives some rather strange information, which might be based in Ibrahim's ethnic prejudices or those of his copiers. But when his claims are possible to check against other sources, he has correct information. There were indeed Christians in Hedeby; the Frankish missionary Ansgar had built a church there in the mid-ninth century. A stream with fresh water ran through the middle of Hedeby, and the diet of its inhabitants included much fish, although they also ate many kinds of meat, as evidenced by the animal bones thrown away in garbage heaps that have been analyzed by archeologists. Killing newborns appears to have been a custom in Scandinavia; it

FIG. 14. Scandinavian slave trade in the Viking Age was an important part of the economy but seldom leaves recognizable traces in the archeological material. This iron lock from a set of slave fetters was found in the harbor of Hedeby, where in the ninth century Bishop Rimbert of Bremen is said to have observed large numbers of Christians hauled away into slavery. Photo courtesy of Wikinger Museum Haithabu, Schleswig.

is outlawed in the oldest Scandinavian law codes from the twelfth century. Ibrahim has little to tell us about trade and crafts in Hedeby.

Although Hedeby was perhaps the foremost Scandinavian trade town, many others spread out all over northern Europe. The only one that might possibly contend with Hedeby in size and importance was Birka, situated on an island in Lake Mälaren, west of the modern location of Stockholm (which did not exist in the Viking Age). During the Viking Age, Mälaren was a bay of the Baltic Sea. A sea route connected Hedeby and Birka, as we learn from the ninth-century biography of the missionary Ansgar. He and his companion, the monk Witmar, hired passage on a merchant ship going to Birka in 829. Their trip illustrates the danger that merchants encountered regularly: "while they were in the midst of their journey they fell into the hands of pirates. The merchants with whom they were traveling, defended themselves vigorously and for a time successfully, but eventually they were conquered and overcome by the pirates, who took from them their ships and all that they possessed, while they themselves barely escaped on foot to land." A successor of Ansgar, the priest Ragenbert, whom Ansgar (as archbishop in charge of the northern mission) sent to Birka, was not as fortunate. He was attacked and killed by robbers even before he reached the ship awaiting him in Hedeby to take him to Birka.[18]

Birka was well located for trade not only with Hedeby, but also with the rest of the Baltic Sea and especially its eastern and southeastern shores. The German historian Adam of Bremen wrote in the 1070s that it was possible to sail from Birka to Russia in five days.[19] The town was also a convenient meeting place for traders bringing iron and fur from the interior of Sweden. Birka was certainly in existence by 800, but the town was probably founded somewhat earlier. The size of the settlement area has been estimated at about thirteen hectares. About two thousand burial mounds have been found in the vicinity. Like Hedeby, Birka was at least partially surrounded by a defensive wall, and a fort was built at some point before 870 on a height just south of the settlement area. In the late tenth century, Birka was in evident decline. The latest coin found there was minted in 962, and there are very few artifacts that can be dated later than the 970s. When Archbishop Adalbert of Bremen visited the site in the 1060s looking for the grave of his predecessor Unni, who had died there in 936, Birka had been devastated, and the grave could not be found.[20]

Hedeby, Birka, and the other towns of northern Europe were connected by shipping routes crisscrossing the Baltic and North seas. Written sources tell of a handful of traders who sailed in the waters around Scandinavia. We have already encountered Ottar, who sailed first from the north of Norway to Sciringes healh in the Oslo Fjord along the coast of Norway, and then on to Hedeby, still following a coastal route. Wulfstan, another trader who was also at some point the guest of King Alfred in England, told his hosts about sailing from Hedeby due east along the southern coast of the Baltic Sea to Truso, a trade settlement in the delta of the Vistula River, now Wisła in Poland. Both Ottar and Wulfstan sailed between Scandinavia and England, where their stories were recorded.[21]

Runestones occasionally memorialize merchants with enough information to reconstruct at least some of the routes they took. In the eleventh century, for example, Ingibjörg, together with her daughter Ragnhild and her sister-in-law Ulvhild, had two rune-stones made in memory of her husband in Vallentuna, a little north of where Stockholm is now. The man's name is unknown, since the runestone is damaged. "He drowned in the Sea of Holm; his *knarr* [ship] foundered; only three came away [alive]."[22] The "Sea of Holm" has been tentatively identified with the waters around the island Bornholm in the southern Baltic Sea, in which case this runestone testifies to the trade route between the region of Birka, not far from Ulfbjörg's home, and Hedeby, which passes by this island. But the knarr might also have been on its way to or from any of the many trade towns on the southern coast of the Baltic such as Truso or Wollin at the mouth of the river Oder, close to present-day Szczecin/Stettin, or even to the small trading centers of Bornholm itself, such as Sorte Muld. Alternatively, the "Sea of Holm" may refer to the waters of the Bay of Finland on the way to Novgorod, which Viking Age Scandinavians called "Holmgárd." If so, Ingibjörg's stone bears witness to the trade route from Sweden to the trading networks of the Russian rivers.

Someone who we definitely know went to the south coast of the Baltic Sea is Svein from Mervalla in central Sweden, not far from Birka, in whose memory his wife, Sigrid, raised a runestone inscribed, "he often sailed a valuable knarr to Semigallia."[23] Semigallia (Latvian "Zemgale") is a historical region in Latvia on the left bank of the Dvina River, which was one of the several river routes leading into the eastern European landmass. Thus, we can think of Svein as a Scandinavian merchant who traded in eastern Europe. Since Sigrid's runestone mentions only Semigallia, we can conclude that Svein transported valuable goods only across the Baltic and other merchants transported them up and down the Dvina. The trip would probably require a change of ship, in any case, as a knarr, a large and capacious cargo ship, would be more suitable for the Baltic Sea than for river shipping. Svein was one middleman among many who participated in the eastern trade.

The trade towns of the southern and eastern shores of the Baltic Sea were located mainly at the mouths of the great rivers of eastern Europe. Scandinavians began to explore the upland of those rivers in the late eighth century at the latest, brought there by their quest for valuable furs.

Scandinavia always participated in long-distance goods exchange, both before and after the golden period of northern commerce during the Viking Age. By the middle of the sixth century, the Byzantine historian Jordanes reported that the Swedes "have splendid horses . . . [and] send through innumerable other peoples sappherine fur for trade" presumably to Constantinople, where Jordanes lived.[24]

Fur pelts from northern animals were a staple of Scandinavian trade in the Viking Age and beyond. Fur was a very attractive luxury much in demand in all markets. As the moralizing churchman and chronicler Adam of Bremen commented in the 1070s, "We hanker after a martenskin robe as much as for supreme happiness."[25] By "supreme happiness," Adam meant quite literally Paradise after death, suggesting that he thought people would go to Hell because the prospect of owning a fur jacket would make them forget to behave in an appropriately Christian way.

The colder the climate in which the animal lived, the more luxurious its fur, an obvious advantage for traders from chilly Scandinavia. One driving force in Scandinavian trade was to find good sources for the best possible fur and to find the most lucrative opportunities for selling it. The Norwegian chieftain Ottar had succeeded well in both respects in the late ninth century. He recounted at King Alfred's court how he had sailed around the northern cape of Scandinavia and all the way to the White Sea to look for fur as well as other desirable products of the Arctic, such as walrus ivory and reindeer antlers. Ottar was a chieftain and did not need personally to hunt in order to acquire such goods. Presumably using military force, he had persuaded, the Sami nomads of his region of northern Norway to pay him an annual tribute consisting of many things, including "skins of beasts." "Each [Sami] pays according to his rank. The highest in rank has to pay fifteen marten skins, five reindeer skins, one bear skin . . . and a jacket of bear skin or otterskin."[26]

Ottar was in the habit each year of sailing down along the coast of Norway to a trade town that he called "Sciringes healh," which was situated on the western side of the Oslo Fjord, as well as to the great trade town Hedeby in southern Denmark. Every northern trade town would similarly have been a center for fur trade. A curious archeological find from the Swedish trade town Birka gives us another snapshot of this trade. Archeologists have discovered large numbers of claws from foxes and other furry animals, but very few bones. The explanation is obviously that tribute payers, hunters, and trappers roughly skinned their catch, leaving the bodies in the forests (or at home, if the animal was edible), bringing only the skins to town. There, the skins were worked up for sale, meaning that any remaining superfluities, such as claws, were removed.[27]

The furs were then traded from town to town through the hands of many intermediaries, each adding a little profit for himself to the price. Ibn Fadlan witnessed one possible route for the fur, through Bulghar on the Volga, from where much fur went farther south, into the Caliphate, as shown by the writings of several Arab geographers from the Viking Age. Inside the Caliphate, good fur was very high-priced. The Arab writer al-Masudi noted in about 934 that "one black pelt reaches the price of 100 dinars." The dinar was the Arabic gold coin, so this is an enormous sum for the fur of the very rare black fox. Even if al-Masudi may have exaggerated for effect, the point is clear: fur was very attractive, and fur traders could make enormous profits.[28]

That profit drove Scandinavian and other traders to search for new opportunities. It was to find more and better fur that Scandinavians traveled to Russia from at least the eighth century. Northern Russia was made up of vast, sparsely populated forests and marshes that get very cold in winter, ideal hunting grounds for finding the very best furs. We have already seen that Ottar sailed the Arctic Ocean to the White Sea in his quest for valuable furs; other Scandinavians instead crossed the Baltic Sea, approaching inner Russia via the great rivers of eastern Europe. Anyone sailing or rowing up the short river Neva through the site of present-day St. Petersburg to Lake Ladoga would have plenty of alternatives to continue into the interior of the Russian north. One of the rivers feeding into the Ladoga is the Volkhov. Around the middle of the eighth century, Scandinavians participated in founding a market town on the banks of that river a few kilometers to the south of Lake Ladoga. The town is known as Staraya ("Old") Ladoga. From here they had easy access to the vast interior of northern Russia with its rich supply of fur. They appear to have collaborated with the indigenous nomadic populations of Finns and Balts. Like the Sami of northern Scandinavia, many of these Finns and Balts were surely hunters and trappers, and it is possible that Scandinavian chieftains showing up in Russia with a retinue of warriors were able, like Ottar, to force them to pay tribute in the form of fur and other valuable products of the Russian forests. Or perhaps Scandinavians acquired the goods by trading with the Balts and the Finns.

Militarily strong chieftains constantly threatened to impose tribute on the nomads, leading to a custom that fascinated many Arab writers. In silent trade, also practiced in other places and historical periods, the buyer placed his payment for furs or other goods at some suitable, agreed-upon location and then left. The seller would then show up, take the payment, and leave the goods there. In this way, a commercial transaction could take place with little risk of it becoming a robbery or violent in other ways. Obviously, it required trust, but it was in the interest of both sides not to break the trust, so the silent trade actually worked.[29] Archeological evidence shows that artisans in Staraya Ladoga produced a great number of glass pearls, which one imagines were part of the payment for fur. Viking Age Arab dirhams have also been found in the far north of Russia, probably brought in as payment for fur.

When Scandinavians reached Staraya Ladoga and explored the waterways of Russia, they must soon have discovered that they did not need to export their fur across the Baltic; they could sell their wares to the south and east in places like Bulghar and Kiev for export to the Arab and Byzantine markets. Bulghar would have been an important transit port for trade with the Arabs. Ibn Fadlan bears witness to the presence of traders from the Caliphate in

Bulghar, and certainly the fact that the Volga Bulgarians converted to Islam—the immediate reason for the mission of the embassy with which ibn Fadlan was traveling—demonstrates that the contacts between the upper Volga and the Caliphate were strong.

Another branch of the northern trading network reached the Byzantine Empire, centered in its capital Constantinople, now Istanbul in Turkey. The ancient chronicle known as the *Russian Primary Chronicle*, written in Old Slavonic in Kiev in the early twelfth century, discusses the trade routes of the "Varangians," the Slavonic name for Scandinavians. Traders traveled from the "Varangian [Baltic] Sea" through Lake Ladoga and Staraya Ladoga upriver to Novgorod, where archeologists have found a Viking Age trading settlement about two kilometers south of the present city center. From Novgorod, the route continued across Lake Ilmen up the Lovat River to the hilly area now known as the Valdai Hills.

Since European Russia west of the Urals is, by and large, very flat, the rivers on the plain flow slowly and calmly, and thus they are relatively easy to navigate as long as there is enough water. The Valdai Hills constitute the highest spot on the plain, and this is why most of the great Russian rivers have their sources there, which in turn means that the hills are the communication hub of the plains. From them one may, as the chronicler outlines, continue on the Volga toward the east, to places like Bulghar and the Caspian Sea, or on the Dnieper River toward the south, to Kiev and, farther, to the Black Sea and Constantinople. To get from one river system to another, Scandinavian merchants on occasion portaged their ships overland.

The Scandinavian discovery of the eastern route of trade to the Caliphate is clearly reflected in the numismatic record in Scandinavia. By looking at the last datable coin in each dirham hoard, numismatists are able to determine the earliest date at which the hoard may have been deposited. By looking at the composition of the hoard and its size, they can approximate how long after that date it was deposited in the ground. On the basis of such evidence, we know that the stream of dirhams to Scandinavia began as a trickle at the very end of the eighth century and then became substantial around the middle of the ninth century. Toward the turn of the millennium, the stream declined noticeably, which may be explained with reference both to the decline in the production of silver inside the Caliphate and to the fact that strong leaders such as Vladimir the Great (d. 1015) created a Russian principality around Kiev at this time. This meant that much more of the profit from the Arab fur trade stayed in eastern Europe.

The fur trade in eastern Europe is only a fragment of the northern trading network of the Viking Age. It also stretched far into western and central Europe, and many things other than fur were traded between the many market towns of Europe. Ibn Fadlan mentioned another kind of trade good: slave girls. Scandinavians were great slave traders during the Viking Age, exporting slaves to the Byzantine as well as the Arab Empire, and probably elsewhere. Both empires had become dependent on trade to replenish their population of slaves, which earlier they had been able to renew by enslaving prisoners of war. After the rise of the Arabs during the first half of the seventh century, Byzantium no longer was strong enough militarily to be able to take sufficient numbers of prisoners of war as slaves.[30] The same is true of the Arab Caliphate after it had ended its enormous expansion around the middle of the eighth century.

Byzantium and the Caliphate needed slaves because of the way their economies were set up, and Scandinavians as well as other Europeans who had no qualms about selling both Christian and pagan Europeans into slavery supplied at least some of the need. Much suggests that the bulk of the slave trade took place in eastern Europe, in places like Bulghar, where ibn Fadlan observed it, but there was also slave trade passing through the Mediterranean ports of Europe, such as Marseilles and Venice.[31]

During their raids, Vikings not only stole gold, silver, and other valuables; they also captured people whom they sold into slavery. The Viking chieftains Lothen and Yrling in 1048 "took untold booty in men, in gold and in silver" in England.[32] Men were as valuable as gold and silver. When local people in northern Gaul managed to capture a Viking stronghold in 923, they found "a thousand captives" in addition to "an enormous amount of booty,"[33] The number given is more symbolic than exact. The captives were clearly destined for the slave market unless their friends and relatives were willing to pay ransom for them. There were slave markets within the Christian countries of western Europe, and western Europeans themselves held slaves. The chronicle that reports their raid also claims that Lothen and Yrling sold their booty, presumably including the slaves, in "Baldwin's land," that is, in Flanders, a region in modern Belgium.

Scandinavians themselves were not exempt from being made into slaves. The German chronicler Adam of Bremen mentioned in the 1070s that there was much gold on the Danish island of Zealand, which had been accumulated through the plundering of Vikings. He explains that "they have no faith in one another, and as soon as one of them catches another, he mercilessly sells him into slavery, either to one of his fellows or to a barbarian."[34] The biography of Archbishop Rimbert (d. 888) of Hamburg-Bremen throws further light on the slave trade in Denmark. This prelate personally observed slave trade in Hedeby:

> Once when [Rimbert] came to the land of the Danes, to a place called Schleswig [= Hedeby], where he had constructed a church for those newly Christianized, he saw a large throng of captured Christians being hauled away. Among them a nun was seen to bend her knees and to lower her head repeatedly, when she saw him from a distance, not only to honor him, but also seemingly to implore him to be merciful and redeem her. And so that he would understand that she was a Christian, she began to sing psalms in a loud voice.[35]

The bishop fulfilled her wish and freed her in exchange for the horse on which he was riding. Most slaves were not so lucky, and many a European was sold at Hedeby during the Viking Age. Some would have been transported farther north and east. For although many slaves lived and were sold in western Europe, the center for European slave trade was central and eastern Europe. This is evident from the word "slave" itself, derived from the ethnic label "Slav," used for speakers of Slavic languages who lived in central and eastern Europe, east of the Elbe River in western Germany. Most European languages use a word of similar derivation for slave—for example, French *ésclave* and Swedish *slav*. Similarly, the Arabic word for "eunuch" (a particular type of slave), *siqlabi*, is derived from the ethnic label for the Slavs, *saqalibi*. Charlemagne and other Carolingian rulers captured and enslaved Slavs already in the eighth century at the eastern borders of the Frankish kingdom. Arabic sources—ibn Fadlan and others—also talk about substantial slave trade in eastern Europe. During the Viking Age much of that trade would have been managed and organized by Scandinavians.

In addition to furs and slaves, northern Europe exported many other products, luxurious as well as utilitarian. To the luxuries belong the tusks of walruses, which when carved and polished had a sheen very similar to elephant ivory. Magnificent artifacts made of this arctic ivory survive, such as the Lewis chessmen and the hook of several bishops' croziers, including the one found in the grave of a thirteenth-century bishop of Gardar in Greenland,[36] a particularly rich hunting ground for walruses. Whalebones were used in similar ways, as seen, for example, in the delightful but mysterious Franks casket from eighth-century Northumbria, now in the British Museum.[37] The main purpose of the northern trading network was to import southern luxuries for the use of chieftains and kings. We may see how this worked by tracing the history of the walnut in the Viking Age.

The remnants of more than a half dozen early medieval walnuts have emerged out of the soil in Hedeby when archeologists have excavated. The shells of walnuts may be used to color textiles, but it is more likely that walnuts were brought to Hedeby primarily as an exclusive and exotic foodstuff. During the early Middle Ages, walnuts grew in central Asia, where they are native, and in the Balkans, although the monks of St. Gall in Switzerland and Emperor Charlemagne in Aachen planted the tree in their gardens. The great ninth-century ship burial excavated in the early twentieth century in Oseberg, Norway, contains many different luxury goods, including the remnants of a single walnut; the nut was luxurious enough to be included in such a magnificent burial. A poem from the first half of the eleventh century may illustrate the prestige of the walnut. "The famous great king [Olav Haraldsson] sent nuts to me; that prince remembers his fellows," wrote the poet Sigvat Thordarson. He does not specify which kind of nuts King Olav had given him, but one imagines that it would have been something grander than hazelnuts, which grow wild in southern Scandinavia. The most obvious guess would be walnuts, unless Sigvat was poking fun at the king's less than royal gift.[38]

Walnuts are tasty but their greatest value in Viking Age Scandinavia was that they were rare and exotic. Any minor chieftain might eat and give away homegrown hazelnuts, but only the truly wealthy and well-connected had access to walnuts. A chieftain who conspicuously consumed or gave away walnuts enhanced his standing and prestige, persuading more followers that he was a good chieftain and successful leader. Chieftains created trade towns so that they would have access to the goods—such as walnuts—that merchants brought.

The merchants imported a great variety of other exotic things to Scandinavia, to be used by chieftains in similar ways. Archeologists constantly find new examples in prestigious contexts, such as the graves of great men and women, or in the remnants of chieftains' halls. It is, of course, impossible to distinguish luxuries that had been traded from those that had been stolen (for example, during Viking raids). The point remains, however, that the most important function of the many Viking Age trade towns was to bring luxuries to chieftains.

One such desirable luxury was silk, which by the Viking Age was no longer produced only in China, but also in the Byzantine Empire and elsewhere in the Middle East. Archeologists have found pieces of silk in many Scandinavian graves. A grave in Birka, Sweden, for example, contains a small, finely worked silver cone that was once mounted on the point of a cap. Inside this mount, small remnants of silk survive, proving that the cap was at least partially made of this textile. The silverwork of the mount was probably done in the Dnieper region of eastern Europe.[39] One guesses that the cap was made somewhere in the network of trade routes in Russia, which was supplied with silk by the caravans coming across central Asia from China. At one point in his travels to Bulghar in 922, ibn Fadlan joined a Silk Road caravan with thousands of animals and people.[40]

FIG. 15. This conical silver mount carries a granulated pattern typical of the region around the Dnieper River in Russia and Ukraine. Inside, it contains remnants of silk. It would have been attached to the point of a cap at least partially made of silk. The mount was found in a grave in Birka, Sweden. Photo courtesy of Riksantikvarieämbetet, Stockholm.

While the Birka silk cap may have come to Sweden in a peaceful way through trade and certainly on the trade routes of eastern Europe, some other pieces of silk would seem to be booty from Viking raids. One of the great chieftain graves in Valsgärde, Sweden, contains silk cuffs and a silk collar. A careful analysis of the textiles reveals an interesting history. These pieces of silk were woven in the Middle East. They were embroidered with silver threads in a way that brings to mind a western European ecclesiastical context. A border was later added in a manner that suggests that it was done in Scandinavia or in an area influenced by Scandinavians. These silk pieces probably once comprised part of the liturgical vestments of a bishop or other ecclesiastic.[41] It is not too daring to suggest that they became Viking booty in a raid on a monastery or a cathedral, were brought back to Scandinavia, and then retro-fitted to adorn the dress of a chieftain, enhancing his standing as wealthy leader. Many other objects of metal and other materials that have been excavated in Scandinavia were clearly booty adapted for new uses.[42] In any case, if the chieftain in Valsgärde had worn these silk pieces, that would have told anyone seeing him that he had real wealth.

Svein, Ingibjörg's husband, and the merchants that ibn Fadlan met in Bulghar in 922 participated in Scandinavia's internal or eastern trade. Many others took part in Scandinavia's trade with western Europe, as did Ottar and Wulfstan. During the Viking Age, western Europe was full of trade emporia, many of which have been extensively excavated. Dorestad, on the lower reaches of the Rhine River (today in the Netherlands), was a major trading settlement, famous not least for its mint that churned out silver pennies. Its connections with Scandinavia are well attested in the historical record. When the missionary Gauzbert in the 840s visited Birka in Sweden, he met a pious Christian woman named Frideburg. She lived in Birka with her daughter Catla, and she instructed her daughter to hand out all her possessions to the poor in Dorestad after her death, demonstrating that she had some connection to this town. Also, when Ansgar arrived in Hedeby in the 850s to missionize, he found "many . . . who had been baptized in Dorestad."[43]

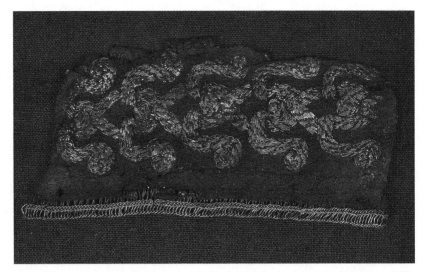

FIG. 16. A grave in Valsgärde, Sweden, contained not only a boat but also this piece of silk, woven in the Middle East. It is embroidered with silver lamella and may originally have been part of the liturgical vestments of a bishop or other churchman, before being reused in the impressive dress of a Scandinavian chieftain. Photo: Teddy Törnlund, courtesy of Museum Gustavianum, Uppsala.

Dorestad was typical of early trade towns in that it was situated in a border region, in this case close to the northern border of the Frankish Empire in the coastal region called Frisia. It functioned as a gateway between the Franks and the peoples of the North. At the same time, it was placed on a major artery of trade, the Rhine River. Traders on the Rhine brought many goods downriver—for example, wine from the valleys of the river and its tributaries, basalt millstones from the Eifel mountains (often found in archeological excavations in Scandinavia), and perhaps also the famous Ulfberht swords, if the conjecture about their origins in the Rhineland is correct. Such trade goods would have passed through Dorestad on the way to their final destinations.

Dorestad was rich and quickly became the target of the Viking raids, which struck there repeatedly in the 830s: 834, 835, 836, and 837, when the "Northmen fell on Frisia with their usual surprise attack." Each time they "exacted tribute"—that is, they made the merchants in Dorestad, some of whom were Scandinavians, pay for their lives. As they were able to come back for more the following year, their raids certainly did not utterly "destroy everything," as the chronicle claims.[44] The merchants thought of such Viking raids as an overhead cost and an occupational risk that they and their business were capable of sustaining. Similar raids also struck trade towns within Scandinavia, many of which, like Birka and Hedeby, were fortified over time. To be a merchant was clearly a dangerous profession during the Viking Age.

There were many other trade towns beside Dorestad in western Europe. Important examples were Quentovic in northern France, and York, London, Ipswich, and Southampton in England. The trading network connecting these towns had grown up in the eighth century. Also the old cities of the Frankish Empire and the English kingdoms continued to function as centers for trade. Vikings founded Dublin in Ireland and made it into a trade town. The settlers of Iceland, Greenland, and the other islands of the North Atlantic traded with Europe.

However disastrous and ruinous any individual Viking raid may have been for those attacked, the overall impact of Scandinavian endeavors was, unexpectedly, to stimulate the economy of western Europe. Trade and commerce had fallen to very low levels after the demise of the Roman Empire but had begun to pick up again before the first Viking ships showed up in the late eighth century. This resurgence was, however, hampered by an acute lack of money. In an economy without money, commerce happens through barter. Such an economy can work surprisingly well, but only up to a point, when the impracticalities become bothersome. Barter requires what economists call "a double coincidence of wants": two persons can barter with each other only when each has something that the other wants. If you have slaves and want an Ulfberht sword, you can barter only if you find a person who is willing to give you such a sword in exchange for slaves. In contrast, a monetary economy allows you to sell your slaves for money and then use that money to pay for the sword. When money was scarce, as in the early medieval economy, trade did not flow as smoothly as it might. Kings and other rulers who were interested in facilitating the exchange of goods needed to provide a means of exchange—money—in order to "grease the wheels of commerce."[45]

Only one kind of money existed in the early Middle Ages: coins containing precious metal—in western Europe from the eighth century, almost exclusively silver. Charlemagne reformed the coinage of his kingdom in 793/794, when he increased the weight of the ordinary Frankish silver penny from 1.4 to 1.7 grams, setting the standard for the rest of the Middle Ages. The medieval penny was a small coin, a little more than a centimeter in diameter and thus slightly larger than a modern American cent or British penny. Charlemagne's reform presupposes that he could dispose of sufficient amounts of silver to increase the standard weight of his penny. This was a problem because his kingdom, as well as the rest of western Europe, suffered from a negative balance of trade. Kings, bishops, and aristocrats demanded expensive eastern luxuries, such as silk, spices, and gems, and the merchants who sold such items demanded to be paid in silver and gold, for they were interested in very few other European products. Precious metals thus flowed from the west to the Middle East and Asia, depleting the western stock of gold and silver. European mines produced little silver and almost no gold, so the metal stock could not be replenished through mining. To be sure, Charlemagne got some of the silver he used for his reform from a mine in Melle in southwestern France, but he probably acquired much of the metal as war booty taken from his neighbors.[46] Still, Europe was starved for gold and silver; European commerce needed an injection of precious metals, and the Vikings provided what was needed.

Before the Vikings came on the scene, much of the gold and silver remaining in western Europe, rather than being made into coins, remained inert in the form of chalices, reliquaries, and other church plate. The treasuries of churches and monasteries were full of precious metals that were not normally available for minting. The Vikings certainly changed that. They stole everything of value they could lay their hands on, and they extorted tributes and ransoms. As an Irish annalist noted with obvious horror, a Viking "shook" the relics of St. Comgall from their shrine in Bangor, Ireland, in 824, clearly valuing the reliquary, made of precious metals and stones, a great deal more than the bones of the saint.[47] Church treasuries typically provided much of the precious metal that was paid out in tribute to threatening pirates. In 858, a band of Vikings led by their chieftain Björn captured Louis, abbot of the Frankish monastery of St. Denis and a cousin of King Charles the Bald. To provide his ransom, "many church treasuries in Charles's realm were drained dry, at the king's command," as complained the chronicler Prudentius, himself bishop of Troyes and surely one of the contributors.[48]

Gold, silver, and money that the Vikings acquired was not lost to the European economy, for the Vikings lived within that economy and they participated in economic exchange just like other Europeans.[49] They would have put the formerly inert gold and silver plate of Frankish church treasuries into circulation after 858, just as they did whenever they got their hands on precious metals by any means. After successful raids, they sometimes set up markets to sell their loot. When, for example, King Charles the Bald in 873 at Angers had defeated a large group of Vikings who had sailed up the Loire raiding, they "requested to be allowed to stay until February on an island in the Loire, and to hold a market there."[50] They clearly intended to sell their booty, and the king granted their request. Some of the precious metal that Vikings gained was, to be sure, buried as hoards in the ground of Scandinavia and some became arm rings and other jewelry, but only a small portion of the loot would have been permanently removed from circulation. Most silver would sooner or later be minted into coins. After some of the members of the great Viking army had settled in the Danelaw in eastern England, in the late ninth century they established well-regulated mints, which produced large quantities of pennies with high silver content.[51] It seems reasonable to assume that the Vikings here minted some of the stores of silver bullion that they had acquired during their piratical raids, which thus was added to the European coinage.

It mattered that the Vikings brought into circulation silver and gold that had been hidden away in ecclesiastical treasure-houses, but we must not exaggerate the impact. Church plate had always been taken to mints and melted down when a bishop, an abbot, or a king needed cash, so it was never permanently withdrawn from the economy when placed in a treasury. More important for the early medieval resurgence of commerce in western Europe was the central Asian silver that Scandinavian merchants brought to Europe. As we have seen, hundreds of thousands of Arab silver coins have been found in buried hoards. Those coins are only the tip of the iceberg; millions of dirhams must have been brought to northern Europe during the Viking Age. Although no exact statistics are available, it seems that Scandinavians and others who exported slaves, fur, and other articles to the Arab Caliphate and Byzantium rectified for some time the lopsided trade balance between western Europe and the East, stopping or perhaps even reversing the flow of silver and gold that had been leaving the western economy. The influx strengthened the European stock of silver, the coinage, and thus commerce. It was during the Viking Age that the European economy slowly began to grow again, eventually, in the modern era, leading to Europe's economic, political, and cultural hegemony. When Scandinavians traded on the northern arc of commerce, they played a small but important role in a world-historical drama.[52]

Goods and money did not change hands in Scandinavian trade towns in the same way as in continental Europe or in the Arab Caliphate, where strong central government guaranteed and imposed the value of coins and standardized pieces of precious metals, which typically were valued higher than the worth of their bullion content. In contrast, coins in the marketplaces of Scandinavia were weighed, not counted. They were valued for their content of precious metals, primarily silver. There simply were no governments strong enough to stand behind a currency until around the turn of the millennium, when local Scandinavian coins began to be struck.[53]

Before that point, traders and others in Scandinavia needed to be able to weigh the metals with which they were paid, normally silver. They used balance scales and sets of weights. Archeologists have found a large number of balances and weights all over Scandinavia, a good indication that the practice was very widespread. In the early eleventh century, the widow Estrid from Såsta was buried with three weights intended for such use; she was, as far as we know, not a merchant, but she ran a large farm, which suggests that farmers also needed to weigh silver.[54] (See the longer discussion of

Estrid in chapter 7.) The Viking Age scales and weights that have been found are surprisingly exact even by modern standards.[55]

In such an economy, coins were considered just another form of silver bullion. A payment might be made up of whole or divided coins, bars of silver, jewelry, and other pieces of metal. Silver coins found in Scandinavia have often been scratched, typically with a knife, in order to check the quality and solidity of their silver. A penny minted for Emperor Henry III in Speyer at the middle of the eleventh century carries no fewer than 118 such test marks. The test marks bear witness to their value as bullion rather than money. If needed, the pieces were cut up into smaller pieces of the right weight. This is the reason why archeologists in Scandinavia often find pieces of dirhams and other coins. Unlike traders from an economy with "real money," Scandinavian traders had no respect for the integrity of the coin, for it was not worth more than its silver content.

The Viking Age trading network of northern Europe, managed and run by Scandinavians in collaboration and competition with others, was a mosaic of sea, river, and land routes connecting markets and trade towns, large and small, which stretched from Greenland to the edge of central Asia. The network was important not only for providing additional income for those chieftains, but also for bringing exotic and prestigious goods to the chieftains of Scandinavia, who used these items, themselves or in the gift economy, to bolster their status among other chieftains, against whom they were always competing for the loyalty of warriors.

Northern European trade saw a new start in the second half of the tenth century. Much of the old exchange of goods (only some of which was, strictly speaking, commerce) functioned to fulfill the needs of chieftains, especially their need for exotic luxury goods to feed into the gift economy system and their need for income to finance that import. Bulk trade (for example, in foodstuffs such as grain and fish) became an important component of trade from the late tenth century. This shift is in complicated ways connected to wide-ranging structural changes in the economy and politics of the North, especially the appearance of royal power. We may with some simplification say that the kind of society, including trading patterns, we think of as "medieval" took form in Scandinavia around the turn of the millennium.

Unlike the prestige goods exchanged under the old system, bulk commodities do not have the kind of cultural cachet that would inspire poets and other writers to sing their praises. The written sources, thus, leave us with few clues to the momentous changes that took place in trade around the turn of the millennium, so our main evidence is archeological. By examining the fish bones remaining in ancient garbage heaps, for example, archeologists are able to track changes over time in the kinds of fish that people were eating. In early medieval England, people ate eel, carp, and other freshwater or migratory fish. At some point close to the year 1000, they started to eat large quantities of cod and herring, both saltwater species. This suggests that those kinds of fish had begun to be caught in large quantities, for example, in the rich waters off Norway and Iceland, conserved by drying or salting, and transported to the consumer. The bulk trade of fish had begun, which would become so very important to the economy of the rest of the Middle Ages (and to the modern economy as well).[56]

That shift to bulk trade is visible also in Viking Age ship technology. The luxury items that had been traded in the early Viking Age did not require much space, nor were they particularly heavy. They could be transported in any kind of ship, so the classic Viking longships were suitable to carry them, and their large crews of warriors in addition protected these very valuable prestige goods. Specialized cargo vessels begin to appear in the archeological record in the tenth century, and they could transport considerably more goods with smaller crews. From loading some ten to fifteen tons in around 800, northern cargo ships in around 1000 might load twenty-five tons, and by the twelfth century, they could carry sixty tons or more.[57] The growth in capacity is in itself evidence of trade in low-value bulk goods—in fish, to be sure, but also in other foodstuffs, such as meat and grain. Whetstones and soapstones from Norway, timber from all over Scandinavia, and millstones of Eifel basalt were also traded.

Most of the old trade towns, like Dorestad, Hedeby, and Birka, declined in importance in parallel to the growth in bulk trade, only to disappear entirely after the year 1000. When, for example,

Archbishop Adalbert of Bremen in the 1060s visited the site of Birka, he found that the town "now was turned into such a wilderness that scarcely a trace of [it] was visible."[58] Hedeby also disappeared at some point soon after 1000, and Dorestad even earlier. These trade towns were functionally replaced by new cities, often situated in the general vicinity of the old towns. Hedeby was replaced by Schleswig on the other side of the Schlei, while Birka's trading functions were taken over by Sigtuna, situated a little more than thirty kilometers to the north. Other similar new cities were Århus in Jutland, Denmark, and Lund in Scania, in what is now southern Sweden. The new cities were royal foundations. The old towns had also been founded by people with power, but the new wave of urban foundations represented a new and much stronger kind of royal power. This was a kingship that had allied with the Church, so the new cities typically contained several churches. The cities were also founded by kings who had learned their craft from European rulers. The new cities often contained mints to provide income for their kings, which meant that real money now began to be used in Scandinavian commerce.

The trade networks that the new cities tapped into had also undergone a fundamental reorientation. From the late tenth century, many more western European coins were brought from England and Germany to Scandinavia, while the flow of Arab silver dried up after about 970. This was also when Scandinavian kings began to produce coins of their own in the mints of the new cities. Mints in Hedeby and perhaps in Ribe had from about 900 produced rather primitive imitations of Carolingian coins with a very low silver content. Other coins produced in Scandinavia were imitations of English pennies, sometimes very crudely produced, to the degree that the Swedish king Olof of the early eleventh century on some of his coins is called "king of the English" in thoughtless imitation of King Ethelred's contemporary coins. The images and lettering on the Scandinavian coins are rougher and less well laid out than on the English originals. The moneyers, the craftsmen who produced the coins, were mostly Englishmen to judge from their names, but they clearly had native assistants who were not as skilled as their confreres in England. Four moneyers moved from England to start the minting on behalf of King Olof in Sigtuna in the 990s:

FIG. 17. This penny struck for the Swedish king Olof in the early eleventh century so thoughtlessly imitated a coin from England that Olof is said to be "king of the English." Olof was the first Swedish king to issue his own coins. Photo: Gabriel Hildebrand, courtesy of Kungl. Myntkabinettet, Stockholm

Godwine, Leofman, Snelling, and Ulfkettil. Perhaps they were identical with four moneyers of the same names who had previously worked for the English king Ethelred in his mint at Lincoln.[59]

The creation of a domestic coinage was a step in the direction of an economy that counted coins rather than weighing them, in which the coins carried value as such, not just the bullion that they contained. But domestic coins were still divided into smaller pieces, suggesting that the practice of weighing coins persisted. Foreign coins also continued to circulate. A king's coinage functioned as a symbol of his royal authority, and this purpose might have been more important than any wish to create a true money economy in late Viking Age Scandinavia.[60]

It is no coincidence that coins began to be produced in Sweden and Norway at the very end of the tenth century. New silver mines had begun to be exploited in Germany, and minting expanded in all of Europe, spreading to regions where silver had not earlier been minted, for example in Poland and Hungary. Even more important, however, was that with the formation of real kingdoms in Scandinavia, the new kings had enough power to begin to control the currency in their territories. Because this is also the time when slow, bulk-carrying cargo ships appear, suggesting that the seas were safe enough that it no longer was as necessary to transport trade goods in warships full of warriors, we might guess that they were also able to control violence, at least to some degree.

CHAPTER 6

FROM CHIEFTAINS TO KINGS

PRAISING HIS DEAD PATRON OLAV HARALDSSON, THE SKALD
Sigvat exclaimed: "The prince subdued every end of Oppland. . . .
Earlier eleven princes ruled them." Olav had arrived in Norway in
1015 after years of itinerant life as a Viking and a mercenary. He had
plenty of warriors and much wealth, and he had proceeded to conquer the country, including the landlocked eastern region known
as Oppland. "Which more outstanding prince has ever ruled the
northern end of the world?" Sigvat asked rhetorically, clearly not
expecting his audience to provide a plausible alternative to Olav
Haraldsson.[1]

Sigvat portrays Olav as a great conqueror who defeated many
competitors to gain sole rule over Norway. We may not want to
accept literally his claim that the region Oppland had previously
been divided up among exactly eleven chieftains (the word for
eleven in Old Norse, *ellifu*, provided convenient alliteration for
Sigvat's verse), but the idea that Olav defeated several petty rulers
is based in reality. The Scandinavian kingdoms came about when
would-be kings consolidated in their own hands the fragmented
power that had earlier been held by many chieftains.

Similar claims show up elsewhere in the history of the creation
of the Scandinavian kingdoms. The skald Einar, for example,
praised his patron, Earl Håkon Sigurdsson, for defeating sixteen
chieftains in Norway.[2] When the Danish king Harald Bluetooth

on his runic monument in Jelling boasted that he had "conquered all of Denmark," he implied that there were parts of Denmark that had earlier been under the control of others. Historians believe that he, for example, subdued the region Scania, which earlier may have been under the control of the chieftains residing in Uppåkra.[3]

Archeological discoveries further illustrate the idea that political fragmentation preceded the high-medieval kingdoms that appeared in Scandinavia around the year 1000. Forests, mountains, and water separate different regions from one another, and those regions were typically different in their material culture. While, for example, the people of the Värend region of Sweden during the Viking Age buried their dead under oval stone settings, the people of the neighboring Finnveden region put them under small mounds.[4] In the sixth century, the Byzantine historian Jordanes mentioned the Finnveden people as one among twenty-eight named Scandinavian tribes.[5] Such evidence clearly suggests that many small but independent-minded areas, including regions such as Finnveden and Värend, were distinctly different regions in prehistoric times.

We may understand the political history of Scandinavia during the Viking Age and preceding periods by viewing it through this lens: successful warrior chieftains fighting one another for political domination. Some were more successful than others and managed to build up greater power by defeating their rivals. That power might fall apart as rapidly as it came together. The general tendency, however, was for more and more power to be concentrated in fewer and fewer hands. Toward the end of the Viking Age, the three familiar Scandinavian kingdoms, Denmark, Norway, and Sweden, appeared, each ruled by a single king, although centuries would pass before they had become truly stable. Something like the old system lived on in the outlying Scandinavian settlements in Iceland and, probably, Greenland until they submitted to the king of Norway in the 1260s.[6]

The preserved sources provide occasional snapshots of this process. When, for example, the great men of the Frankish Empire of Charlemagne and his son Louis the Pious in the early ninth century were for the first time paying serious attention to Danish affairs, we get a glimpse of internal Danish politics. A man called Godfrid had managed to accumulate considerable power by the beginning of the century, dominating at least the Jutland peninsula. He was a thorn in the side of the Franks, attacking their allies the Obodrites, who resided on the southwestern coast of the Baltic Sea. In 810, a Frankish history writer reported that Godfrid had been killed by one of his own retainers. Four years later, we hear of four men fighting over Godfrid's inheritance: Harald, Reginfrid, and two of Godfrid's sons. "In this conflict, Reginfrid and the oldest son of Godfrid were killed."[7] It is tempting to understand this struggle as a battle for the "Kingdom of Denmark," especially since the Frankish chroniclers label the contestants involved "kings," but this is to apply anachronistic categories. There were no stable kingdoms with defined assets and boundaries to fight about in ninth-century Scandinavia. Godfrid had accumulated power in competition with other chieftains, but that power fragmented when he was killed and at least four people competed for a share of it afterward. The conflicts lasted a long time. As late as 826, one of the chieftains/kings involved, Harald, sought out the Frankish emperor Louis the Pious to get his assistance in regaining a foothold in Denmark. He had already received help in 814. Despite the assistance he received, Harald was not able to create a kingdom for himself in Denmark, so he lived the rest of his life as the emperor's pensioner, having been awarded for his upkeep a county in northern Frisia.

We do not know very much about what happened in Denmark during the rest of the ninth century, and much less about Sweden and Norway, for the Frankish recorders of history turn their attention elsewhere and the indigenous material is limited to brief runic inscriptions and archeology. We know the names of some kings, like Björn, whom the Frankish missionary Ansgar encountered in Birka in about 829, and Horik, who was powerful enough in Denmark that the pope sent him a letter in 864 encouraging him to accept Christianity, but we do not know any details about their reigns and we do not know how large their kingdoms were. Archeology tells us about many halls, those focal points of chieftains' power, existing at the same time. Everything points to a situation in which power was fragmented, fluid, and constantly contested by competing warlords.

Godfrid was killed in 810, Reginfrid was killed four years later, and the chieftain buried in the Gokstad ship was, as we have seen, killed in about 900. Many other men and women, chieftains as well as ordinary people, were killed in the competition for power in Viking Age Scandinavia. Competition among chieftains was violent, and each chieftain was a warlord with his own private army. It was, thus, an essential concern of chieftains to recruit as many warriors as they were able. This need for capable warriors is key to understanding how society worked before more regular kingdoms were created around the year 1000.

We learn about some of the most important mechanisms that early medieval Scandinavian rulers employed to recruit and retain warriors, and thereby power, through a poem composed by the same Sigvat who introduced this chapter. He wrote about his lord Olav Haraldsson: "I was with the lord who gave gold to his loyal men and carrion to the ravens; throughout the lifetime of that king he gained fame."[8] A chieftain needed to be generous to his men, he needed to be victorious in battles—to "feed carrion to ravens," in the poetic vocabulary of the time—and he needed fame and a good reputation. If he was not able to achieve all of this, he could not achieve any of it. It was through winning battles that he gained the riches that allowed him to be generous, and his generosity stimulated poets like Sigvat to contribute to his fame by composing and reciting poetry. This, in turn, inspired warriors to seek out the famous king, so that he got more warriors and won battles even more easily, which again gave him a good reputation and more booty to hand out to warriors.

The key feature in this system of political economy was the king's generosity. Chieftains needed above all to be generous, to freely give gold, silver, and other valuables to their followers. We see this already in the quotation from Sigvat's poem with which we began this chapter, if we look at it more closely. The translation given there was simplified and flattened: "The prince subdued every end of Oppland. . . . Earlier eleven princes ruled them." The expression rendered as "princes" toward the end of the quotation is, in the original, a four-word circumlocution of a type that is typical of skaldic poetry, a *kenning*: "the destroyer of the speech of the cave's generous man." The "cave's man" is a giant, for giants live in caves. The "giant's speech" is gold, since Norse mythology has a story of the rich giant Ölvaldi, whose three sons took as much gold in inheritance as each was able to carry in his mouth. Someone who "destroys gold" gives it away, which is the proper behavior for a chieftain or prince, who was expected to "destroy" his own wealth by giving it to his warriors.

Similar ideas lie behind the word that Sigvat used for Olav, simply rendered above as "prince"; Sigvat literally said "giver," which would have been understood as "giver of gold and other gifts." Chieftains, kings, and others who led warriors were the archetypical givers of the early Middle Ages. They needed to give valuable gifts to their warriors, which inspired those warriors to be loyal followers. This gift-giving system was such a deeply engrained component of early medieval ideology that it was thoroughly embedded in the very language of poetry.

The archetypical gift was an arm ring. Money did not exist as such in early medieval Norse society. Wealth was simply gold and silver bullion, or land or natural products. The normal way of storing wealth was in the form of more or less weighty arm rings of gold and silver. Archeologists have found many such rings in graves and in treasure hordes, some simple loops of metal, others beautifully worked jewelry. Literature and poetry devote a lot of attention to rings, and kings were often referred to as "ring-givers" or "ring-breakers," for the rings could be broken apart to be shared among several retainers.

At some point in the early eleventh century, the poet Arnorr composed a partially preserved poem, probably about King Cnut of Denmark and England. The poem illustrates the importance of arm rings:

> Fire of the stream [= gold] was set
> between the wrist and shoulders of the Danes;
> I saw men of Scania thank
> him for an arm-ring.[9]

The fragment begins, typically, with a kenning for gold, one of very many kennings that existed for that metal. Gold was alluded to as watery fire, since according to Norse mythology the sea god Ægir once invited the gods to a meal in his underwater hall, which they found illuminated solely by radiant gold. Cnut set his gold as arm rings on the Danes. Arnorr pointed out that the men of Scania were grateful to the king. Either the Scanians in the poem are simply representative of the Danes in general or, more likely, Arnorr wanted to emphasize that they were loyal to the king since Cnut could not always take for granted the reliable allegiance of the region, probably subdued with arms by his grandfather Harald Bluetooth. In any case, the poem shows that Scanians and other Danes wore their gold on their arms.

Another ring-breaker was the Scandinavian king Erik Bloodaxe of York (d. ca. 954), whose generosity is a theme in a celebrated poem by the legendary Icelandic Viking poet Egil Skallagrimsson:

> The breaker of arm fire [= rings]
> offers arm gems [= arm rings].
> The ring-breaker will not praise
> the tardy handing-out of treasure.
> The pebbles [gold] of the hawk-beach [= arm]
> are highly alienable to him [the king, giving away golden arm
>   rings].
> The lot of men are happy about the
> meal of Froði [= gold].[10]

Line after line of the poem drives home the point that Erik is a very generous king, quick to break (i.e., hand out) rings and offering ornaments for the arms of warriors. His generosity makes his throngs of fighters happy, and that was the purpose of giving away wealth. The warriors of an early medieval Scandinavian ruler were not simple mercenaries fighting for pay; they were independent-minded and proud warriors who would fight alongside those they were bound to in honorable relations of friendship. If they accepted a gift from their chieftain, they knew that this meant that they owed their loyalty and fighting prowess as a countergift.

The warriors who accompanied the Norwegian king Harald Hardruler on his failed attempt to invade England in 1066 understood that they owed him loyalty unto death. They died alongside their prince at Stamford Bridge, at least if we may believe the hyperbolic lines the poet Arnorr wrote about the battle:

Spear-points inlaid with gold
did not protect the slayer of robbers [= just ruler = Harald].
All the retainers of the gracious prince chose
much rather to fall beside the battle-swift commander
    [= Harald]
than wishing quarter.[11]

Harald had given his warriors gilded spears, which did not protect him sufficiently, although it did inspire them to fight on, rather
being killed next to their leader than suing for peace. The connection between the chieftain's gifts and the warrior's loyalty, unto
death if necessary, as countergift is spelled out in a famous passage
of the Old English poem *Beowulf*, written at some point during the
Viking era. Beowulf's loyal follower Wiglaf, "mournful at heart,"
upbraids other warriors who were slow to join their leader in fighting a fearsome and fire-spewing dragon:

I remember the time that we took mead together,
when we made promises to our prince
in the beer-hall—he gave us these rings—
that we would pay him back for this battle-gear,
these helmets and hard swords, if such a need
as this ever befell him. . . .

———

It seems wrong to me that we should bear shields
back to our land (= survive), unless we first might
finish off this foe.[12]

Wiglaf here outlines a warrior ethic in which every gift required a
countergift. Those cowardly followers of Beowulf who did not give
him their loyalty forfeited their honor. Wiglaf scolded them, "those
ten weak traitors," now "shamefaced," after the end of the battle,
when both Beowulf and the dragon lay dead: "Death is better for
any earl than a life of dishonor!"[13]

Given the unusually fearsome nature of his fiery enemy in this
battle, we should perhaps not be surprised that Beowulf's gifts
were not successful in inspiring total loyalty among his warriors.

The sense of the passage is, however, that loyalty and warrior bravery was the expected countergift, as it indeed was among King
Harald's warriors in 1066. Or as another Norwegian king, Håkon
the Good (d. 961), expressed it in a poem that was put in his mouth
by a high-medieval Icelandic saga composer recounting the king's
last, fatal battle: "Well do my men repay me . . . for gold and inlaid
spears."[14] The men repaid the king's gifts by continuing to fight,
even in a doomed battle.

Successful chieftains not only gave their followers gilded spears
and golden arm rings but also inspired them in other ways—for
example, by inviting them to great celebrations in the chieftain's
hall. Those banquets could carry a religious accent if they happened
in conjunction with pagan sacrifices or with Christian rituals,
which added a sacred tinge to the relationships that were created
there. We often hear about chieftains who were generous with food
and drink, like King Hrothgar, whose hospitality in his "mead-
hall" Heorot in the *Beowulf* poem is legendary. Many runestones
commemorate great men with some variation of the formula "he
was generous with food." With a stone erected during the first half
of the eleventh century close to the southern tip of the Scandinavian peninsula, the widowed Tonna memorialized her husband
Bramr, who "was the best of householders, and generous with
food."[15] Great chieftains were famous for being great hosts, like
Earl Thorfinn of the Orkneys, who, according to his skald Arnorr,
was much more hospitable than other chieftains. They feasted with
their retainers only over Yule (the midwinter holiday) itself, whereas
Thorfinn offered ale ("the swamp of malt," in Arnorr's kenning) all
through the winter. "The ruler exercised bounty then!" the poet
exclaims happily.[16]

The great feasts took place in the halls of the chieftains, which
were spaces devoted to establishing and maintaining friendships between chieftains and their followers. Then as now, lively
and boisterous parties with food and drink were ideal settings in
which to build close-knit communities, and more than eating and
drinking went on there. It was in the halls that skalds recited their
poetry, praising and celebrating the chieftain who presided at the
festivities, and thus making it even more desirable to be his friend.

FIG. 18. The great halls of Scandinavia were large, impressive buildings with open interiors intended for feasting and camaraderie. Here chieftains and their warriors planned and celebrated Viking raids. This careful computer reconstruction of the large Viking Age hall at Lejre, Denmark, is based on the archeology of the site. Courtesy of Nicolai Garhøj Larsen, EyeCadcher Media, and Roskilde Museum.

The hall was also the site where the chieftain might hold forth, proving his eloquence and persuasive powers, to encourage his followers to fight alongside him and to persuade other chieftains to ally with him. Chieftains distributed gifts to their followers in many places—for example, on the battlefield—but perhaps most typically inside their halls. The *Beowulf* poet tells us as much when he imagines King Hrothgar giving Beowulf wine and gifts after his defeat of Grendel: a famous historic sword, a ridged helmet, a golden banner, a mail shirt, and eight horses with ornamented bridles and a "skillfully tooled" saddle "set with gemstones."[17] The chieftain's hall was also a sacred space where chieftains used religious rituals to bind his followers even more tightly to himself. A sumptuous banquet was useful to inspire community among those invited, but if it was not just a dinner but also a sacrificial meal, then that community took on an added sacred dimension. This applies to both pre-Christian and Christian religions. A Viking Age ruler celebrated not only for his hospitality but also for his religious zeal

FIG. 19. This set of Roman wine utensils, found in Öremölla in the province of Scania, Sweden, contains a large mixing bowl, a ladle, and a sieve of bronze, as well as two glasses. A chieftain who was able to prepare his wine with such equipment would consider himself fortunate. Photo courtesy of Riksantikvarieämbetet, Stockholm.

was Earl Sigurd Håkonsson in Lade (d. ca. 962). He was hospitable, so his guests did not need to bring boxed food and drink to his feasts, as the poet Kormakr expressed it. Kormakr characterized the earl as the protector of a sacred place.[18] The poet thus reminds us that religious rituals were closely linked to eating and drinking, perhaps so that the meat of any sacrificed animal was cooked and eaten after the gods had received their share. Later in the Viking Age, some enterprising chieftains replaced the old pagan religion with the "new" religion of Christianity, with which they had come in contact on their travels in Europe. Just as resourceful chieftains impressed their followers the more strongly by inviting them to drink their mead—or, even better, imported wine—from wondrously beautiful glass vessels, they would awe them with the rituals and customs of an exotic religion that was embraced by some of the most powerful people in Europe.

A good chieftain needed not only to be generous and victorious in battle but also to be eloquent, to be able to persuade with honeyed words. Runestones and skaldic poetry often praise men for eloquence. The eleventh-century Swede Holmbjörn, for example, advertised on a runestone at the main road close to his home that he was "generous with food and eloquent," obviously trying to lure warriors and other followers to join him in his hall.[19]

When Magnus, the son of the Norwegian king Olav Haraldsson, was coming back from exile in Russia to take back his father's kingdom, he needed troops. Olav's queen Astrid Olofsdotter had been a Swedish princess, so she had returned to her family in Sweden when her husband had fallen in the battle of Stiklestad (Trondheim) in 1030. Magnus was not her son; his mother was Alfhild, one of King Olav's mistresses (or that is how she is characterized by the high-medieval sagas, which employed then-current ideas about marriage and concubinage that may not have applied in Viking Age Norway). Astrid nevertheless helped Magnus to recruit troops in Sweden by speaking persuasively to an assembly of people. She impressed those who heard her to the degree that Magnus got a large enough army to conquer Norway. She particularly impressed one of Olav's old court poets, now composing for Magnus, Sigvat

Thordarson, who wrote a poem in her praise, of which three stanzas are preserved.

Astrid was a "good advice-giver," Sigvat said, who could not have dealt better with "the daring Swedes, had bold Magnus been her own son." It was thanks to her that Magnus was able to claim his rightful inheritance, for "a substantial army of Swedes assembled . . . when Astrid announced the cause of the son of Olav." So "generous Magnus owes Astrid a reward for her bold deed."[20]

Sigvat portrays Astrid as a woman of deep counsel and eloquence, and she must have enjoyed good relations with the Swedish warrior circles from which she originated. This kind of praise of a woman for her political skills is all but unique in the skaldic corpus, the male-oriented poetry that typically praised the battle deeds and the generosity of kings and chieftains. Sigvat was a poet who was not afraid of breaking new ground, as he did when he praised Astrid.

Chieftains gave gifts and persuaded warriors to follow them. Together with their warriors, they sailed and rowed to the European continent and to the British Isles to raid and plunder, so as to be able to give more gifts. Some of them were better at their jobs or had more luck than others, who were knocked out of competition, so over time there were fewer and fewer chieftains with larger and larger followings. We discern a hint of this process when the European writers who chronicled the Viking raids on Europe tell us that the raiding parties became ever larger and larger. The disappearance of chieftains' halls in Scandinavia, which we can study through archeological surveys, tells the same story from a different perspective.[21] The chieftains became fewer and fewer, meaning that the remaining ones each had more power. The distinctions among chieftains, petty kings, and kings are not very well defined, but at some point during the Viking Age, it becomes appropriate to talk about kings rather than chieftains. These kings met new and different challenges from those faced by their chieftain forebears. Their power over people extended so far that they could no longer maintain the kind of personal friendships that the gift economy of previous centuries promoted. Instead, they needed military and administrative structures to run what increasingly looked like older

European kingdoms. The Church was the best organized institution in Europe at the time, and kings received help from clerics to build up their royal administration. Chieftaincy based on charisma and friendships yielded to organized and administrative kingship, although for a long time both "systems" existed in parallel.

As late as in the preamble to the earliest preserved Norwegian law book, *Gulatingslov*, the text expresses a wish that the ruler of the land "be our friend, and we his," just as in the old gift economy.[22] The date of this law book is much debated; it survives in manuscripts from the thirteenth century but claims to be based on texts from the early eleventh century. Whatever its age, the book bears witness to the old system, when the king or chieftain was seen more as the first among equals, a friend of his friends, than as a ruler in a hierarchical system. This idyllic state of affairs changed radically with the end of the Viking Age. In about 1277, King Magnus Håkonsson of Norway issued a law book for the aristocracy of his kingdom, the *Hirdlov* or *Law of the Retinue*. The title refers to the king's retainers, the group of warriors that followed the Viking chieftains of old. But these thirteenth-century warriors had a very different relationship with their king, who here lets his men know that they should "serve him personally . . . in unbreakable fidelity and complete loyalty" as the king's "servants."[23] The word here translated "servant" (*þjónn*) used to be applied only to slaves and thralls. In the Viking Age, it would have been an unforgivable insult to libel thus any of the king's warriors, and a chieftain calling his warriors "servants," as King Magnus did, would quickly lose their loyalty. New uses of language had, however, come into Scandinavia with Christianity, which characterized all Christians as servants or slaves of God. With the new language came also new ideas about social relationships. The king became a ruler appointed by God and his followers became his servants.

The organization of the Church was strictly hierarchical, and kings learned to organize their kingdoms in a similar way. The retinue that appears in the *Hirdlov* is no longer a band of drinking buddies and fellow warriors; they are officials serving their king, and it is appropriate that they should fall to their knees in front of their king, as the law book demands. The memory of the great festivities in the mead halls survive in the *Hirdlov*'s rules for appointing high-born officials called table page, cup-bearer, and steward, although these were distinguished titles that should not lead us into assuming that their bearers were simple waiters. Otherwise, the law book portrays a hierarchical society in which even the greatest aristocrats were, in the last analysis, the king's servants. The chancellor, often a cleric, attended to issuing and preserving documents, while the marshal spoke on the king's behalf and organized his travels. Each official had his defined assignment in war, but also in peace, which is very different from Viking Age retainers, whom the king or chieftain gathered for the primary purpose of fighting wars.

If the retinue had metamorphosed from being a proud warrior elite into an aristocracy of service (and that change began long before 1277), the role of the king had changed even more radically. After the end of more than a century of civil war, off and on, the Norwegian king sat securely on his throne after 1240. There were no more wars about succession. Each king was succeeded by his son, as is stipulated by the *Hirdlov*, until 1319, when King Håkon Magnusson died without sons and his grandson Magnus Eriksson took over the kingdom.

The Norwegian kingdom to which the *Hirdlov* bears witness encapsulates the most important changes that took place in Scandinavia with the end of the Viking Age and afterward. Hierarchically organized "feudal" kingdoms with defined territories and a more or less bureaucratic administration replaced looser confederations of warriors. Kings strove to organize an ordered succession to the kingdom, be it as an elective monarchy or a hereditary one, in sharp contrast to the free-for-all of the Viking Age, when warlords fought for the unstable loyalties of people not defined territories. The medieval kingdom attempted to control violence within its territory, and to some degree it succeeded. Instead of plunder and raiding in foreign lands, taxes, fines, and other fees claimed from the territorial population provided the stable economic basis for rulership, which was exerted in close collaboration with the Church.[24]

Scandinavia's transformation into the medieval kingdoms was a long, slow process, and it happened at different speeds in different parts of Scandinavia. It was fastest in Denmark, whereas Sweden was particularly slow in getting organized. The process had two aspects. On the one hand, the kind of bureaucratic and hierarchical kingdoms described in the Norwegian *Hirdlov* came into being everywhere, although exactly how this happened is mostly hidden in the mists of history. On the other hand, kings succeeded in pulling together the different regions that made up each of the three medieval kingdoms of Scandinavia, and that process is better known.

In Denmark, it seems clear that kings like Godfrid (d. 810) and his more shadowy predecessor Sigifrit (r. ca. 780) were powerful rulers, since they constituted enough of a threat to the Carolingian Empire that Charlemagne's court paid close attention to their doings. Sigifrit's supposedly intransigent paganism was a matter for banter among the court's intellectuals, while Godfrid's attacks on the Obodrites, allies of Charlemagne, were carefully recorded in official Frankish history writing.[25] Since the latter source tells us that Godfrid forced the merchants of Reric, the main Obodritian trade emporium, to move to Hedeby close to the base of the Jutland peninsula, we may conclude that Godfrid held power at least over Jutland, as did Sigifrit, probably. It remains unclear and unlikely whether we really should think of their power in terms of territory, and whether, if so, it extended also to the Danish islands between Jutland and Scania.[26]

Archeology tell us about even earlier powerful people on Jutland. In 726, someone had a canal built across the small island Samsø, east of Jutland. An observer on this island would be able to spot any ship heading toward or coming from the Great and Little Belts, the two best and most important passages between the Baltic Sea and the North Sea. The Samsø canal made it possible to sail quickly from the protected harbor at the island in any direction toward any passing ship. The chieftain who organized the building of the canal would have been powerful enough to command the work of many, and he would probably have been able to maintain enough ships and warriors on Samsø to be able to stop, rob, or demand a toll from any but the largest fleets that would sail through either of the Belts. This would have been a lucrative business.[27]

A decade or so later, in 737, a chieftain built a great earthen wall with an interior timber structure, the so-called Danevirke, across the center of the base of the Jutland peninsula. Whether this was a defensive military measure (it was used as such in the Danish–Prussian war of 1864) or a way to control and tax (merchant?) traffic, this large construction project demonstrates that a chieftain in southern Jutland in the 730s was able to command a large workforce.[28]

Was the chieftain behind the Danevirke identical to the chieftain behind the Samsø canal? Or, to express it differently, are the two construction projects evidence that a single person ruled over at least the southern half of Jutland in the early eighth century? The answer is often assumed to be yes, and that a single kingdom responsible for both the Samsø canal and the Danevirke extended from the Danevirke to Samsø and that this was the kingdom later ruled by Sigifrit and Godfrid. This is possible, but probably an overinterpretation; the canal and the wall might well have been built by chieftains in competition with one another.

King Godfrid was murdered in 810 by one of his own retainers, whom we should think of as a competitor for power who must have broken the bonds of friendship. A period of intense competition followed the murder, with at least four persons, including two of Godfrid's sons, competing for the power that he had held. Two of these competitors were killed in the process, and a third, Harald, took refuge with Emperor Louis the Pious. But not even with the emperor's help was he able to take power in Denmark.

Meanwhile in Denmark around 850, a King Horik gives the missionary Ansgar permission to build a church in Hedeby, so his power extended at least over southern Jutland, and probably farther. Over the following century, Danish history is only spottily known, which did not prevent later medieval historians, such as the influential Saxo Grammaticus (d. ca. 1220), from constructing an unbroken series of Danish kings from grey antiquity through Godfrid and on to their own contemporaries. Saxo and his colleagues did not do so on the basis of information that we now lack, but because they took it as self-evident that something like the Danish kingdom they themselves experienced had "always" existed. They simply made up a list of names for those kings, including a prehistoric King Amleth, whom William Shakespeare later made world-famous as Hamlet. The story told by contemporary sources is rather of constantly contested power during the early Viking Age, but a contest in which a few families tended to return generation after generation, at least for some time, showing a tendency to form dynasties, a characteristic of the mature medieval kingdom. This may well be, but we should remember that family and kinship in the early Middle Ages were not necessarily based in biological fact. People made up familial relationship where none, strictly speaking, existed. A famous example is the rebel leader Sverre, who fought his way to becoming the king of Norway (r. 1184–1202). Ostensibly the son of a Faroese comb-maker, Sverre claimed that he was the love child of an earlier Norwegian king, Sigurd Munn (r. 1136–1155). At this point in history, one could not become king of Norway without royal blood. Sverre won the kingship and his genealogical claims, which most likely are fictional, were widely accepted, although opponents continued to contest them. If we accept that people are likely to have similarly made up kinship in the Viking Age, we must admit that what may look like Viking Age dynasties in the sparse source material are not necessarily that. Genetic examinations of bodies buried in prestigious graves in central Sweden reveal, for example, an open family structure; genetically unrelated persons were able to reach positions of high status and be buried in what are usually seen as dynastic cemeteries.[29] In other words, a new chieftain in central Sweden was not necessarily the biological kin of the old chieftain he replaced; we have no reason to expect that things would have been different in Viking Age Denmark.

Danish political history emerges from the mists of prehistory when a splendid royal compound was constructed during the second half of the tenth century at Jelling, a central location on Jutland, from which the entire peninsula and the Danish islands could be militarily controlled. The great variety of features and their unprecedented size and magnificence make Jelling stand out, far surpassing any similar site elsewhere in northern Europe. Someone with much to prove and resources to match stood behind it all: King Harald, the first man that we know with certainty was king of all of Denmark. Later in the Middle Ages he was nicknamed

"Bluetooth" (and this nickname, in turn, inspired the name of a much-used wireless communication technology standard developed by history-savvy Scandinavian computer scientists and symbolized by a combination of the runes H and B).[30] King Harald himself tells us, in runes inscribed on a large boulder inside the Jelling compound, that he "won for himself all of Denmark, and Norway." Through the runestone, Harald dedicated his "monument" (probably referring to the entire compound and not just the inscribed stone) to his parents, Gorm and Thyre.

The compound in Jelling was surrounded and protected from prying eyes by a wooden palisade, perhaps three meters tall, in the form of a slightly skewed square 360 meters on a side. Several magnificent structures were constructed at different times inside this stockade, including the two greatest Danish grave mounds, standing almost nine meters tall, and the largest ship setting (large rocks placed to outline a ship) anywhere, about 340 meters long. The ship setting was pulled down when the second, southern mound was constructed. Harald's magnificent runestone rests at the exact midpoint between the two mounds, with a smaller runestone raised by his father Gorm close at hand. The eleventh-century stone church of Jelling stands between the runestones and the northern mound. Various postholes under the present church suggest that at least one wooden church preceded it, but it remains unclear exactly when this church might have been constructed and how large it was. It is attractive to imagine Harald as the builder of the first church in Jelling, for he claims in his runic inscription to have "made the Danes Christian," and he reinforced this message by having a magnificent image of the crucified Christ sculpted into the stone. Archeologists have found the remnants of several other buildings within the palisade, but not yet the king's residence.

Among the most fascinating features of Jelling are two Viking Age graves. A disarticulated skeleton rests under the present church together with few grave goods. It appears to have been put in the grave inside precious textiles including gold threads. This grave cannot be dated exactly and may not even have been inside the church when the skeleton was buried. Another grave chamber is found in the northern mound at the exact midpoint of the palisade enclosure. This chamber contains no human remains at all but plenty of grave goods, including a horse. This grave is situated also at the midpoint of the ship setting and was constructed with timber felled during the winter of 958/959. The grave chamber of the northern mound must have contained the body of a very important person, and many scholars agree that this must have been the grave of Harald's father, Gorm (or possibly his mother, Thyre), as suggested by Harald's runestone dedicating "this monument" to his parents.

Why have no bodily remains been found in the northern mound? If the body had been cremated, it would have left ashes. It is possible, but not very likely (given how well wood has survived in the grave), that any body once in the grave has completely disintegrated since 959. What complicates the mystery is that someone clearly broke into the grave chamber at an early point, perhaps as early as in the 960s. We may reasonably guess that the body was removed at this point from the grave in the northern mound. An attractive but unprovable theory suggests that the body was removed from the mound to be put into the grave under the church floor, thus Christianizing in retrospect the burial of King Gorm (if it indeed was he who once rested in the northern mound). Harald's large runestone with its depiction of Christ would have had a similar effect, Christianizing the entire compound with its large "pagan" grave mounds and its ship setting.[31] Other explanations for the graves in Jelling are also possible. The skeleton in the church may be Harald Bluetooth himself; he was deposed and driven into exile by his son Svein Forkbeard, and it is possible that his body was transported back to his own royal compound after first resting in foreign lands.

We will probably never know for certain exactly who rested in each Jelling grave, but this matters little for the big picture. The Jelling compound as a whole was intended to tell a powerful story: Harald Bluetooth was a splendidly mighty and resourceful Danish king. That story becomes even more obvious if we place Jelling into context. In about 978, Harald had a long wooden bridge constructed across the swampy valley surrounding the Vejle River, a little south of Jelling. The Ravning Enge bridge was five meters broad and extended about 760 meters. It allowed the king to move quickly, with his army if necessary, between southern Jutland and the central parts of the peninsula around Jelling. In this way, he avoided a long detour around the river valley.

Harald also constructed fortifications all around Denmark. In 964–968, he extended by 3.5 kilometers the Danevirke, the old wall that marked the southern border of his power on Jutland.[32] In about 980, he had built four or five circular fortifications, so-called *trelleborgs*. Two of them are on Jutland, one on Fyn, and one on Zealand. A fifth was most likely in Scania. They were all constructed on the same plan, with a circular palisaded wall (having an inner diameter of 120 or 240 meters, which interestingly corresponds with the 360-meter-long sides of the Jelling fence). The walls of the trelleborgs had gates at the four cardinal points of the compass. The interior was divided by two wood-paved streets into four quarters, each with four or twelve buildings, which were about thirty meters long. The buildings had different uses: dwellings, workshops, storage buildings, and stables. At least two of the trelleborgs also contained cemeteries. Harald constructed these fortifications as permanent military strongpoints, and clearly also as demonstrations of his power. With the help of troops stationed in the trelleborgs, Harald was able to dominate Denmark militarily, thus striving to control violence within his kingdom. He clearly was not lying when he claimed on the Jelling runestone to have "won all of Denmark."

Since Harald claimed that he had won *all* of Denmark, he must not have started out with all of the country. His home base was clearly Jutland, where Jelling, with its runestones, mounds, and ancient church, is situated. Jutland also appears as a political unit a little earlier, in 948, when the first three bishops with sees in Danish towns were consecrated; they all resided in Jutland. We guess that Harald's father, Gorm, at this point dominated Jutland, and was not hostile to Christianity (despite his ostentatiously pagan burial, if indeed it was he who rested in the northern mound in Jelling), considering that he welcomed bishops within his kingdom. The fact that no bishops at this time were appointed on the Danish isles or in Scania suggests that Gorm's kingdom did not include these regions. Harald's investments in military infrastructure allowed him to suppress the power of chieftains that might have competed with him. They did not help much against his son Svein Forkbeard, who rebelled against his father in the 980s, taking over power. Harald died in exile.

King Svein appears not to have cared for his father's military fortifications, the trelleborgs and the Ravning Enge bridge, which he allowed to decay. Perhaps he felt strong enough without them. Svein was active as a Viking raiding in England. In the early 990s, he plundered in England together with the Norwegian chieftain Olav Tryggvason. The English king Ethelred paid them a danegeld of sixteen thousand pounds of silver in 994 to make them go away. With a windfall like that, Svein might have been able to keep Danish chieftains and warriors happy with gifts. He came back for more two decades later, when he even drove Ethelred out of the country and succeeded in making himself king of England. He was proclaimed king on Christmas Day, 1013, but died suddenly only a few weeks later. His younger son Cnut managed to repeat his father's feat in 1016 and conquered England, acquiring power also in Denmark a few years later when his brother Harald died. He would rule England for almost two decades, to be followed by his two sons. When his last son, Harthacnut, died in 1042, the old Anglo-Saxon royal family returned in the person of Edward the Confessor.

Meanwhile in Denmark, Cnut's nephew Svein Estridsson (d. 1074) became king after an interlude with a Norwegian ruler. Svein was succeeded in turn by no less than five of his sons, most of whom fought one another bitterly. Their fratricidal strife proves that there now was a kingdom of Denmark to fight about. Denmark had definitely become more than a geographical concept, something that the papacy also recognized in 1103, when it awarded Denmark an archbishop residing in Lund. It is also at this time that we first hear of royal servants similar to those mentioned in the Norwegian *Hirdlov*: a marshal in 1085, a chamberlain in the early twelfth century, and royal notaries by the mid-twelfth century at the latest testify that Denmark had become a hierarchically organized society in which the king's servants, aristocratic or not, served the needs of the kingdom.

Danish kings had long cultivated their contacts along the southern shore of the Baltic Sea, and they turned later to military conquest. King Valdemar I conquered the island of Rügen, including its famed pagan temple, in 1169, and his son Valdemar II conquered Estonia in 1219.

The "way to the north" that has given its name to Norway was a sea route following the long coast with its many deep indentations and fjords. It took the chieftain Ottar, who claimed to live the farthest north of any Norwegian, about a month to sail the entire way down to the Oslo Fjord in around 900 (if his statement about this trip, preserved in Old English summary, has been correctly recorded and understood). The great span of the country plus the fact that tall mountains separate the fertile valleys, which in most places were narrow, means that Norway was more difficult to unify than Denmark. The unification often came about piecemeal with the areas around the Oslo Fjord and those around the Trondheim Fjord being controlled by different rulers for the longest time. The history of Norway is both enlightened and confused by native history writing, which began at least as early as the twelfth century and attained high literary standards with the sagas of thirteenth-century Iceland, especially the *Heimskringla*, a splendid narrative in Old Norse of history from hoary antiquity through the twelfth century. Like Saxo in Denmark, these writers projected back in time the unified Norway they themselves experienced.[33]

Heimskringla and other late history works celebrate Harald Fairhair (d. 930) as the first king to unify all of Norway under the rule of a single man, but contemporary sources and other shreds of evidence vaguely suggest that he may have ruled only parts of western and southern Norway. Be that as it may, it is clear that whatever lands he was able to pull together did not stay together after his death. Several of his sons held power in Norway, including Erik Bloodaxe, who became king of York in England, and Håkon the Good, who had been brought up as a Christian at the court of King Ethelstan of England. Håkon is claimed to have attempted to introduce Christianity in Norway, but his history is very poorly known.

Harald's sons and grandsons had to compete with other Norwegian chieftains, especially the earls of Lade, and the kings of Denmark were in the habit of meddling in Norwegian affairs. Harald

Bluetooth claimed in the 970s on his great runestone in Jelling, as we have seen, to have "conquered Norway." We cannot know exactly what that means, but his influence is not likely to have extended far beyond the Viken region (the area around the Oslo Fjord), and he probably controlled Norway indirectly through Norwegian clients. His son Svein Forkbeard and grandson Cnut the Great treated Norway similarly, Cnut even placing his own son Svein as king there for a few years in the early 1030s. The earls of Lade were traditionally the most important clients of the Danish kings—some of them also served King Cnut in England—although they could also be independent-minded. Two Viking adventurers, both named Olav, inserted themselves into this mix, and each was able to take control of Norway for some time around the year 1000.

Olav Tryggvason used the fortune he had made as a Viking chieftain as well as his Christianity to defeat Earl Håkon of Lade in 995 and become king. A coalition of the Danish king Svein Forkbeard, the Swedish king Olof Eriksson, and Håkon's son Erik in turn defeated Olav in 1000 in a grand sea battle at Svölðr, an otherwise unknown location that probably was in the sound between Zealand and Scania. Another Christian Viking chieftain, Olav Haraldsson, took power over Norway in 1015 but was eventually defeated and killed in the land battle of Stiklestad (at Trondheim) in 1030. The two Olavs, who may (wrongly) have claimed descent from Harald Fairhair, became famous as missionary kings. Their hostility to the kings of Denmark also earned them posthumous praise and renown in indigenous medieval histories as heroes in the struggle for Norwegian independence. Olav Haraldsson even became a Christian saint—the most famous Scandinavian saint—and his family provided the kings of Norway for more than a century after the demise in 1035 of the Danish client king. Olav's son Magnus took advantage of a power vacuum in Denmark to become king there as well for five years in the 1040s. Olav's half-brother Harald Hardruler served successfully in the Byzantine emperor's elite body guard, the so-called Varangian guard of Constantinople—the only identifiable such Scandinavian recruit to be mentioned by name in Byzantine sources—before coming back to Norway with enormous riches and a large army to share power with his nephew. Harald is famous for his attempt to conquer England in 1066, being defeated and killed at the battle of Stamford Bridge just a few weeks before the arrival of William the Conqueror.

In the High Middle Ages, Norway was a strong kingdom that was able to expand its rule to the North Atlantic islands thanks to its seafaring traditions. The Orkneys, Hebrides, and Isle of Man submitted to the Norwegian king around 1100, with Iceland and Greenland following in the mid-thirteenth century.

We do not know how much of Sweden beyond the town of Birka itself was ruled by the kings whom the missionary Ansgar met there during his two visits in around 830 and 850. A merchant called Wulfstan reported in the late ninth century at the court of the English king Alfred that the *svear* (Swedes) dominated the western coast of the Baltic Sea through the province of Blekinge. The svear were a seafaring people, perhaps mentioned as such already by Tacitus in the first century CE, and their basis was the region around Lake Mälaren in eastern Sweden. The fertile areas around the two large southern Swedish lakes Vänern and Vättern, known as Västergötland and Östergötland, were mostly landlocked and thus not easy for the svear to dominate. Competition and tension between the svear and the residents of the two Götaland regions remained a central theme of Swedish history for centuries.[34]

The first king known to have ruled both the svear and the Götalands is Olof Eriksson, who was a Christian and fought against Olav Tryggvason at the battle of Svölðr in 1000. His descendants were important rulers in the history of Sweden into the twelfth century, but they also had competition from other chieftains who were able to seize power, at least regionally, now and then. The Danish kings meddled here, too, and at least Cnut the Great claimed to rule over parts of Sweden. The details of all this escape us, since the sources are unhelpful in the extreme. It appears clear that religion, both pagan and Christian, played a great role in the eleventh century to rally the forces on either side. From the middle of the twelfth century, two new families fought for power in a now mostly unified Sweden, which also began to look like a feudal and administrative monarchy. The country was, however, not a stable monarchy with ordered succession to the throne; most kings throughout the twelfth century were murdered or fell in battle. Only with the accession of the Folkunga dynasty in the mid-thirteenth century did Sweden become a more stable kingdom, and the country now also displayed the expected feudal and administrative features that we saw in Norway at the same time. Already in the twelfth century, Swedish kings expanded their power to the other side of the Baltic Sea, especially to Finland. Gotland submitted to the Swedes through an agreement in the late thirteenth century.

The Viking Age not only brought Scandinavia into concrete and direct contact with the rest of Europe, it also took the region into the European mainstream. When Charlemagne's courtiers jested in the 780s about converting "impious," "brute," and "impenetrable" Danish kings to Christianity, Scandinavia was still far outside European civilization and culture, and the Franks could only joke about the region. Their attitude became outright hostile when the Vikings began to attack, when learned clerics learned to contemplate God's words to the prophet Jeremiah (1:14): "From the north an evil will spread out upon all the inhabitants of the land." Scandinavia belonged to the realm of barbarians.

After the end of the Viking Age, in the twelfth and thirteenth centuries, Scandinavia was a part of Europe, no longer an alien region beyond civilization but a region that was organized and structured along the same lines as the rest of the continent. For example, the Scandinavian population began to pay taxes and fees to their kings and other feudal overlords, just as in France, Germany, or England. This was part of a bargain through which they received protection from raids and plundering, at least in theory. During the Viking Age, kings and chieftains secured the income they felt they needed by looting and pillaging away from their own lands, which were thus left undefended and vulnerable to similar raiding by other chieftains and their warriors.[35]

To provide protection, medieval kings in Scandinavia as well as in the rest of Europe built up military resources as well as a bureaucracy to administer those resources and to collect and manage taxes and fees. The Church played a pivotal role in the process, providing education as well as administrative know-how, in addition to an ideology that promoted the idea that kings ruled with divine sanction at the top of a hierarchical bureaucracy. All of Europe went through a similar transformation during the centuries after the turn of the millennium, but it was most revolutionizing in Scandinavia, which started at a very different stage of societal development. Western Europe already had kingdoms with some centralized power in the early Middle Ages, when power in Scandinavia still was fragmented and localized.

The processes that brought about the three medieval kingdoms of Scandinavia were long, complex, and violent. Many of the details are lost to history, but the main outline of events is clear. The formless but dynamic society of the Viking Age, when many chieftains competed violently with one another, was followed by the early kingdoms, where power continued to be violently contested and unstable. When such kingdoms matured, as they did in Denmark in the twelfth century and in Norway and Sweden in the thirteenth, kings enjoyed largely stable rules, and the system of taxes, fees, and hierarchy was not seriously questioned. Thus Scandinavia entered the mainstream of European history.

CHAPTER 7

AT HOME ON
THE FARM

THE MATRIARCH OF THE FAMILY WAS DEAD. SHE HAD DIED AT the farm of her long-dead first husband, at Såsta, about seventeen kilometers north of where, a century or so later, Stockholm would be built. She died in the late eleventh century at a great age for the time, older than sixty, and she had outlived two husbands, three sons, and her stepson. None of them had been Vikings plundering around the shores of Europe, as far as we know, but they lived in the Viking Age and were no strangers to traveling far. Estrid Sigfastsdotter had always taken care of feeding and clothing her family, of bringing up the children; she carried the keys of the farm (one key followed her into the grave) and she managed the storehouses. But as the men around her died, Estrid took on an even more central role in the family, managing farms and thralls, running the family business, making the important decisions. Her influence and wealth are still discernible in the Swedish landscape through the many runic inscriptions that she decided to create to memorialize the dead of her family. But when we read the inscriptions, we are perhaps less fascinated by the men of the family than by Estrid herself, the matriarch, who stands out in unusually vivid colors.[1]

Estrid died and was buried on the farm in Såsta that she had been running for decades. Her skeleton was found in the 1990s, helping us form a basic idea of what she looked like so we may imagine her in life and death. She was 165–170 centimeters tall, lithe, and had

FIG. 20. When a road was widened close to two runestones in Såsta, Sweden, archeologists found a well-preserved female skeleton from the Viking Age. She has persuasively been identified as the matriarch Estrid Sigfastsdotter, who sponsored the runic inscriptions. Photo: Lars Andersson, courtesy of Stockholms läns museum.

gracious features. She had been married twice, but now she was buried next to the monument to her first husband, Östen, and the grave of their first son, Gag. Perhaps it was her decision to rest here rather than at the farm of her second husband, Ingvar; perhaps she liked Östen better. Or it could be that her surviving sons decided her final resting place. One does, however, get the impression that Estrid was used to making decisions, so I suspect she had determined her own final resting place.

Estrid did not have the satisfaction of resting next to Östen's body, for his burial mound was empty, as she explained on the runestone that she had had erected on the site decades earlier: "Estrid had these stones raised in memory of her husband Östen. He traveled to Jerusalem and died in Greece." Östen had made a pilgrimage to the most holy place in Christendom, the place where the Church of the Holy Sepulcher enclosed not only the tomb of Christ, but also the hill on which his cross had stood. Östen had died in transit somewhere in the Byzantine Empire—whether on the way there or on his way home we cannot know—and his widow had created a cenotaph (an empty, symbolic grave mound) for him close to his farm at home. Did they bring any part of his body home with them? That would at least be possible, although we cannot check, for the mound was removed when a road was broadened in the nineteenth century. When Archbishop Unni of Bremen died in Birka in 921, his companions brought his head home to Bremen, where the priests in the twelfth century were still able to point out the small, squarish grave in the cathedral where it had been buried.[2] Perhaps Estrid (if she had accompanied Östen) similarly brought home Östen's head, heart, or some other part of his body.

Estrid, Östen, and their family were Christians, and they put crosses on their runestones to let everyone know it. Christianity was still so much in its infancy in Sweden that consecrated cemeteries were rare, so Estrid was buried close to home, as had been the custom for centuries before the conversion. A generation or two later, the inhabitants of Såsta would be buried at the local church in Täby, but that tradition had not yet established itself in the eleventh century. Estrid and Östen were wealthy and could afford the expensive pilgrimage to the Holy Land. It makes sense that she would have accompanied him, for when she was buried, a small shrine, probably made of lindenwood and covered with painted linen, was placed in her grave. The shrine contained two coins, one of which came from Basel in Switzerland. Perhaps this was a souvenir from the trip.

On an island in Lake Constance, now on the border between Germany and Switzerland, the old monastery of Reichenau maintained lists of its benefactors. This "Book of Life" contains thousands of names and the monks would have prayed for the persons listed. The list includes the names "Östen, Estrid," written consecutively in the eleventh century. Are these the names of our Swedish pilgrims who would have rested in the monastery before their arduous crossing of the Alps on their way south? The name immediately before theirs was "Sven," a name carried by one of their sons. Other Scandinavian names follow immediately afterward: Esbjörn, Åskatla, Tor, Torun. One gets the distinct impression of a group of Scandinavian pilgrims stopping at Reichenau and making

the appropriate donations to have their names remembered. One
of the best ways to get from Scandinavia to Reichenau was to travel
upstream on the Rhine. If this was the way Estrid and Östen went,
they would have passed Basel on the way, where Estrid might have
picked up her souvenir.[3]

Also in Estrid's shrine were three weights of the kind used by
those who needed to weigh silver and other precious metals. They
symbolize Estrid's responsibility for managing family affairs; she
paid and received money and silver, which she may have stored in
the small lindenwood shrine, which could be locked with a key. The
Scandinavian economy was only partially monetized in Estrid's
time, meaning that coins typically were weighed, not counted,
when used as a means of exchange. Together with the evidence of
the runic inscriptions, the contents of her grave portray Estrid as an
independent and active woman. She sponsored, alone or together
with her close relatives, five runic inscriptions to commemorate her
dead relatives—her husbands Östen and Ingvar, and her sons Gag,
Ingefast, and Ingvar.[4]

Estrid must have been born a decade or two after the turn of
the millennium, and she was given a name that was unusual in
Scandinavia at that time. The king of the Swedes, Olof Eriksson,
was married to a woman from the Mecklenburg area of northern
Germany. Her name was Estrid, and it is possible that our Estrid
got her name from the queen. Scandinavian chieftains and kings
used Christianity and especially the relationship-creating ceremony of baptism to create and confirm alliances with the great
men and women of their kingdoms. Perhaps Queen Estrid was the
godmother of little Estrid, giving her an unusual name associated
with royalty. That would mean that Estrid's father, Sigfast, a local
chieftain residing on the farm Snåttsta, fifteen kilometers to the
north of where his daughter was buried, was one of King Olof's
loyal men. That relationship would have been so important to
the king that he tied Sigfast closer to himself by having his queen
sponsor the baptism of Sigfast's daughter. We know of a similar
event from about the same period in Norway, where King Olav
Haraldsson was the godfather of the daughter of his warrior and
poet Sigvat Thordarson.[5]

Whether or not Estrid's name was given her by the queen, she belonged to the richest and most important class in Swedish society, and it is hard to argue that her life in general was typical for Viking Age women. But aspects of her life certainly were. For example, it is typical that we know the names of seven of her sons but not of a single daughter. It is hard to believe that she would not have had any daughters. The fact that we do not know of any must be because nobody, not even Estrid, saw any reason to memorialize the names of daughters with a runic inscription. Or perhaps the woman Åskatla mentioned in the Book of Life at Reichenau shortly after Estrid may have been a daughter who accompanied her parents on the pilgrimage.

The names of women were less important than the names of men in early medieval society. We discern this phenomenon in the Old Norse poem *The List of Rig*, in which a god taking on the name Rig visited representative homes of the three social classes of early medieval Scandinavia: slaves, farmers, and magnates. The poem gives the names of the twelve sons of the representative magnates, Jarl and his wife Erna, but it does not mention any daughters, an omission that a recent editor understands as deliberate.[6] This was a patriarchal society, in which, essentially, only men were important enough to be commemorated by having their names chiseled into stone. Women were subordinate to men.

This uncompromising image of male domination is, however, considerably tempered when one looks more closely at the evidence—for example, the three thousand or so runestones we know of from Scandinavia. Estrid was, to be sure, an exceptional woman to be so very active in erecting runestones, but many other women also appear in the runic record. We actually know the names of Estrid's sister Gudrid and her sister-in-law Inga, the latter also appearing in more than one inscription. Estrid was able to create runic monuments because, as the person in charge of a large farm, she had the economic resources to do so. Many women in fact had such resources. Almost 12 percent of the runestones known from Scandinavia were, according to their inscriptions, erected by women acting alone. An additional 15 percent were commissioned by women together with men. These statistics warn us against drawing glib conclusions about the relationship between women and men in Viking Age Scandinavia.[7]

Another way in which Estrid's experience is typical of women of her time is that some of her children died before she did. Her son Ingefast was an adult, a married man with at least two sons, when he died, but her first-born son (as far as we know), Gag, was only about ten when he died, if archeologists are correct in identifying him with a boy's skeleton found in a grave close to Estrid's. Gag had suffered from diseases such as a severe ear infection. The uneven growth of the enamel on his teeth suggests that he was malnourished during at least three periods when he was between one and five years old. We should remember that even rich people, as Estrid's family clearly were, could suffer from malnutrition during years of extreme famine. But it is also possible that Gag suffered from some disease that made it impossible for him to eat properly or to absorb the nutrition in the food he ate.

It is a cliché that children died in devastatingly large numbers before the invention of modern medicine. In Sweden's oldest reliable population statistics, from the period 1751–1800, for example, about 40 percent of children died before they were four years old. The Viking Age appears to be different, though. Archeologists have examined many Scandinavian grave fields from the period, including fields used by the agricultural population, and thus not just by elite groups such as warriors and merchants, where one would not expect many graves of children. Only about 10 percent of the graves in the grave fields of Swedish Viking Age farms were occupied by children. This number should be compared to the corresponding figure from the early Iron Age (roughly 500 BCE–500 CE), when 30 percent of the graves were dug for children. Similarly, a large inventory of 320 Viking Age graves in Denmark showed that only 9 percent contained the remnants of children.

Such evidence may suggest that during the Viking Age Scandinavia experienced low child mortality, but it does not seem very likely that the graves are telling the whole story. Other explanations for the relative and unexpected lack of children's graves have been sought, but there is no agreement among specialists.[8] Perhaps the bodies of dead children were disposed of in some way other than burial in the usual grave field. A Viking Age cemetery in Fjälkinge, Scania, which has been carefully examined, provides a more representative image of child mortality. Of 128 burials, 79 were of children, most of whom died in their first year. If a child survived to five years old, she had a great chance of reaching forty. Few reached sixty, as Estrid did.[9]

A reason to think that the Viking Age was not a period of relative health with low child mortality is that those who lived to an adult age were not as tall as people in previous and later periods. A person's adult height depends partially on the quality of the nutrition she received as a child. In the Fjälkinge grave field, adult males were 160–185 centimeters tall while women measured 151–171 centimeters. Estrid, 165–170 centimeters, was thus a little taller than average. The average height of Viking Age skeletons found in Denmark is 171 for men and 158 centimeters for women. That is shorter than for the previous period (175 and 162, respectively) and for the following high and late Middle Ages (173 and 160). The man, more than sixty years old, buried close to Estrid at Såsta (nobody has come up with a plausible identification for him, but it is likely that he was one of her relatives, perhaps even her second husband, Ingvar) was a stately 180–185 centimeters tall. This is in accordance with another finding of the Danish height study: there is a correlation between wealth and being tall. The man buried at Såsta clearly belonged to the upper stratum of the agricultural population.

Archeological investigations of the graves tell us a great deal about the life and death of ordinary families. Husband and wife appear buried next to each other, just as Estrid was buried next to Östen's symbolic grave. There are few differences between the graves in which men were buried and those of women. Men's graves are typically a little larger and more prominent, while women were attired for burial with more jewelry and dress details of metal. Men's graves from before the conversion to Christianity (which outlawed grave goods) contain bones from more animal species than women's graves. Bones from dog, sheep, and roosters appear often in graves for both sexes, whereas horse and pig bones typically are found only in men's graves. A few women's graves contain these kinds of animal bones and are also prominently situated. A reasonable interpretation of such graves is that they contain the bodies of women who, like Estrid, had a prominent position in society (for example, as owners and managers of important farms).

What men and women had in common, irrespective of social class, was that they were much affected by disease. Both Estrid and, to an even higher degree, the tall man who was buried close to her had severe problems with their teeth, as did everyone who survived to mature age in the Viking Age. Their teeth were infected to such a degree that it is visible in their skeletons, although caries was seldom the cause. The molars (grinders) in their mouths were worn down almost to the gum, because they ate bread, porridge, and other products made from grain that had been threshed on the ground. Dust and sand thus were mixed in with the grain, which wears down the teeth. In the cemetery from Fjälkinge with 128 carefully examined Viking Age skeletons, people over age sixty had lost, on average, two-thirds of their teeth. A fifth of the adults and almost all children buried in the Fjälkinge cemetery suffered from iron deficiency, probably because of parasites or bacteria that gave their hosts persistent diarrhea. Almost half of the adult individuals from this cemetery had suffered from some health problem that is still visible on their skeletons or teeth. Broken bones are legion; Estrid had once broken her arm, but it had healed nicely. Older women have many knee injuries, and a few persons who were buried at the edge of the Fjälkinge cemetery suffered from leprosy. The usual image of the Vikings as able-bodied, strong, and healthily virile men has an important corrective in the skeletons surviving from actual Viking Age Scandinavians.

Some historians have suggested that women played an important role in Scandinavia during the Viking Age, for they would have stayed at home managing the farms while their husbands sailed out to raid as Vikings. This conclusion is based on the idea that, during the Viking Age, all or most able-bodied men in Scandinavia were Vikings and left home for months or years on end. This is a gross exaggeration. The Viking raiding parties were small and, as far as we know, to a large part made up of young men who did not own much, if any, landed property, and who were typically not married. The reason they went out raiding was that they had no farms to manage at home. They were men like the Norwegian Bjor, who "died in the retinue when Cnut attacked England," according to the runestone that his father, Arnsteinn, erected in his memory.[10] It is possible that Bjor could have expected to inherit something from his father, who must have been a wealthy man since he could afford a runestone, but if there were many sons in the family and Bjor was one of the younger ones, he could not have expected to get much landed property. He may have opted to try his luck with the Danish king Cnut, who in 1018 conquered England. Bjor appears to have been a typical Viking: a younger son with few prospects in life except those he could create for himself. He may have hoped for a piece of land in England to cultivate, or a sufficient share in Cnut's booty that he could live comfortably for the rest of his life. A few generations earlier, the Viking chieftain Halvdan provided such opportunities to his followers when he "divided up the land of Northumbria." His Vikings then "plowed and provided for themselves."[11] They were not men who had much to return to in Scandinavia.

Women in any case played important roles that had nothing to do with their husbands being away on Viking raids.[12] In premodern agricultural societies, the daily work of farms required the constant participation of both men and women. A farm could not really function if it was not headed by a couple, which is the reason why widowed family heads typically remarried very quickly, as Estrid did after the death of her first husband, Östen. The loss of a wife or a husband was a catastrophe, as the Swedish farmer Holmgaut felt acutely after his wife Odindisa died in the late eleventh century: "No better housewife ruling the farm will come to Hassmyra," he inscribed sorrowfully in the Old Norse poetic meter of fornyrðislag on her memorial runestone.[13]

In Viking Age Scandinavia, women and men had relatively clearly defined domains in which they worked, domains later specified in law, and that we hear about in literature and see in grave goods. The medieval Icelandic law book *Grágás* specified that the wife was responsible for affairs "within the threshold" (that is, inside the house) while the husband was in charge of everything outside.[14]

Notable in women's graves are the many tools for textile work, such as spindles for spinning and warp weights from looms. The work of producing clothes was women's work in the Viking Age, as in many other periods of history. Textiles were made both from animal fibers, especially wool, and from vegetable fibers such as flax and hemp. The processes that made clothing from sheep's wool and growing flax plants was long and time-consuming. The sheep had to be sheared of their wool. Scissors had been introduced to Scandinavia in the first century CE, but the old method of tearing the wool from the sheep with one's hands was still in use in the Viking Age. The wool then had to be cleaned, sorted, and combed to produce the long fibers that could be spun into worsted yarn. By the Viking Age, the sheep of Scandinavia had been bred to produce white wool (before the Common Era, they had been black, gray, or brown).

The harvesting and preparation of flax to make linen was similarly labor-intensive. The combed wool or flax was put on a distaff and was spun by hand with a spindle. When the god Rig wandered around the world (according to the Old Norse poem *The List of Rig*), he met the ancestress of all the stout farmers of the world:

> On it sat a woman, spinning with a distaff,
> stretching out the thread, preparing for weaving.[15]

The thread was then woven, typically on a vertical loom with weights keeping the warp straight, producing twill fabric. We can count on this being done in every homestead of Scandinavia, requiring a great deal of work from the women of the family. It was laborious indeed to weave the cloth needed to produce the huge sails of the ships used by Vikings, merchants, and others, and it was women's work, as Ottar the Black, a court poet of King Cnut of England and Denmark, admitted when praising the ship the king commanded:

> You cut the high, engulfing waves
> with a smoothed rudder;
> the sail, which women had spun,
> played against the mast-top
> on the reindeer of the roller (= ship).[16]

The cloth was colored with dye from a variety of vegetable sources: for example, woad (blue), madder (red), and perhaps walnut shells (brown).

By the Viking Age, well-to-do families no longer needed to produce their own cloth; high-quality wool and linen fabrics were produced commercially in several Scandinavian centers, in western Norway, on Gotland, on Zealand, and in Finland. For anyone who could afford to purchase such ready-made textiles (and they appear only in the graves of the well-to-do), it would be an enormous saving of work. Women cut the fabric and made it into clothes. Early medieval clothes in Scandinavia were mainly made of wool and linen. No complete article of clothing survives for either men or women, and wool survives better than linen, but many fragments help give an idea of the typical dress.[17]

Both men and women used brooches to hold their clothing in place. Their clothes were layered—perhaps to be expected in a highly variable climate like Scandinavia, with warm summers and bitterly cold winters. Women wore a long shift under a long, tight-fitting dress that reached from the armpits to midcalf. Straps that were fastened at the front by two large oval bronze brooches held the dress up. These brooches are typical of women's dress and are found all over Scandinavia as well as in areas that have been culturally influenced by Scandinavia, such as Russia. They must have been mass-produced and their decoration is rather stereotypical. Most women also wore a scarf or a cloak, fastened with another brooch, on top of the dress. An almost obligatory part of female attire during the Viking Age were strands of beads of glass, metal, amber, and other materials, which a woman wore as a necklace or hanging from her dress.[18]

Men typically wore trousers, which could be of different lengths and cuts, and a shirt, which could be loose- or tight-fitting (the man Rig encountered in the peasant farmhouse wore a "close-fitting shirt").[19] Over the shirt, men wore a cloak of heavier material, fastened over the right shoulder with a brooch or with ties. This kept the right arm free for handling a sword, a knife, or another tool. Men and women wore shoes or boots, which could have long or short shafts. Clogs with soles made of wood were also used.

Shoemaking was a very common craft in the trade towns of Scandinavia, and archeologists have found a lot of Viking Age shoes in excavations.

The dress I have described is the "Sunday best" worn by wealthy, or at least well-to-do, women and men. The wealthier they were, the more luxuriously their dresses might be adorned. The man buried toward the end of the tenth century in Mammen, Jutland, was clearly a very wealthy man, and his dress included bands of silk, marmot fur, sequins, and embroidery depicting leopards.[20] The decoration of the dress of wealthy people could include silver and gold threads. Of course, less wealthy people would wear less luxurious variants of the standard dress. Common to all, however, was that every one of the many steps in the process of making clothes, from shearing the sheep and reaping the flax to cutting and sewing, was a female task (with the possible exception of making shoes).

Another especially female task was preparing food for the family. In the Viking Age as in many other time periods, it was women who managed the dairy products, baked the bread, cooked the meals, and prepared the drinks. They cooked food over the fire hearth in the farmhouses, in cauldrons of iron or soapstone that hung on chains, or they fried it on spits or in frying pans. In graves, both men and women were often accompanied by utensils for food preparation. The production of milk, butter, cheese, and other dairy products belonged entirely to the women's domain, even if they sometimes milked cows and sheep "outside the threshold." In the winter, they cared for the animals inside the longhouses of the homesteads, but in the summer, the animals would be grazing farther away from the farms, being watched over by male and female shepherds, who would also milk them. After milking, it was the women's task to sieve the milk, probably in the perforated ceramic vessels that archeologists have found at many Viking Age farms. Similar vessels were used when separating the curds from the whey in the cheese-making process.

Bread was often given as grave gifts, and when they were included in cremations, they carbonized, which meant that they have a greater chance of surviving until today, when scholars can analyze them. Viking Age bread was, leavened or not, made in different sizes, from smallish round buns, five centimeters in diameter, to larger loaves reaching eighteen centimeters. They were mostly thin, from 0.5 to 1.5 centimeters thick, and typically round (though occasionally oval and rectangular loaves are found). The main ingredient in the breads was hulled six-row barley, which during the Viking Age was the most commonly cultivated grain in Scandinavia. Other grains such as rye, spelt, oats, and flax, or even peas, could be mixed into the bread. Sometimes the ground inner bark of pine has been mixed into the bread, which contributed vitamin C to the diet, preventing scurvy. Another additive to bread could be blood, producing various kinds of black pudding. The bread was baked in ovens, which existed in Scandinavia for centuries before the Viking Age. Grain was also an ingredient in beer and other brewed drinks. Brewing took place in the kitchen and was a female task.

The grain obviously grew outside the threshold, so it was a male task of managing the fields—to fertilize, plow, sow, harvest, and thresh—although all able members of the household would help during the particularly labor-intensive stages of the process of producing grain, especially during the harvest. The cycle of grain production began with plowing. In the Viking Age, Scandinavian farmers mostly used the ard (also known as the scratch plow), which was a nearly vertical spike. It produces a deep scratch in the soil, breaking it up, but not turning it over (as with later medieval and modern plows provided with a moldboard). For this reason, farmers typically cross-plowed their fields, meaning that they went over the same ground once or twice again, plowing across the scratches they had previously made. The ard was typically pulled by oxen, but in the absence of such animals slaves would do.[21] The ard was originally made entirely of wood. Its cutting edge would quickly become dull with use and would have to be replaced every other day or so, as scholars have discovered in modern experiments. Beginning in the early Middle Ages, the ard's edge would be made of less destructible iron, saving much time and effort.

More advanced plows, including moldboards, show up already in the Scandinavian Viking Age, at least in Denmark, where some fields thus plowed have been examined by archeologists. Fields

plowed with moldboard plows are recognizable because they produce broader furrows than the simple ard, plus these plows move
soil a little to one side. Since one tended to plow long and narrow
fields (presumably because it was difficult to turn the moldboard
plow, which typically was drawn by oxen), going back and forth
on different sides of the field, those fields tended over the years to
become convex: higher in the middle than on the sides. They are,
thus, easily recognizable—for example, when archeologists remove
layers of wind-blown sand lying on top of them, as often must be
done in western Denmark.

Viking Age farmers saved dung from both animals and humans
to be spread as fertilizer on the fields. In addition, they, or at least
some of them, practiced crop rotation, alternating different crops
and letting the soil sometimes rest by leaving it fallow, practices
that replenish nutrition in the soil. When the grain was ready to be
harvested, the farmer cut it with a scythe and typically the women
of the farm raked. Threshing was men's work and was probably
done with clubs and pokes, not with flails, since archeologists have
not found any flail datable to the Scandinavian Viking Age. What
was then done to the grain was the task of the women, who might
grind it on hand mills and bake bread, as we saw. Or they might
make porridge or gruel (probably more often than they made
bread), or they might brew beer and ale from it.

Hand mills could be found at most Viking Age Scandinavian
farms, but water-powered mills were beginning to appear also in
the North at this time. They were already common in England and
the Frankish Empire, where they were investments made by lords,
who used them as a means to get greater income from the farmers
who wanted to grind their grain. It is likely that the few Scandinavian water mills that archeologists have examined (mainly in Denmark) were constructed for powerful people.

Grain had long been cultivated in Scandinavia, but it had not
been the main source of nourishment. The acreage devoted to grain
was comparatively small. This changed during the Viking Age,
when the typical medieval diet was introduced into Scandinavia,
as in the rest of Europe, with a much greater focus on cultivation
and consumption of grain than previously. Pastures and meadows

were put to the (improved and thus more productive) plow and made into grain fields. The shift began in southern Scandinavia and moved slowly north.

In most of Viking Age Scandinavia, much farmwork focused on animal husbandry. Animals were used primarily to produce milk and wool and as a source of power as draft animals and riding horses, rather than as livestock for meat. In fact, it was during famines when all other food had been consumed and farmers were facing starvation that they would actually kill and eat their animals. The traditions of keeping cattle, sheep, and horses go back a long time in Scandinavia. Pigs had always been raised, as in the rest of Europe. In the eighth century, however, pigs became much more common in Europe, and this happened to some extent in Scandinavia, although not on nearly as large a scale. The reason for this shift appears to be the intensifying focus on grain production, which removed much of the pasture land where sheep and cattle might graze. The diet of pigs is different from those animals, since they thrive on household waste as well as acorns and other forest products. The osteological evidence of animal bones as household waste reveals that during the Viking Age pork appeared on the table of the wealthy; pig bones have been found predominantly at magnate farms and in the towns. People who could afford it ate beef, chicken, and venison. Fish was on everyone's table and was an important part of the diet.[22]

Also changing, and first among the wealthy, was the layout of the farms themselves. The center of the farm was the longhouse, a type of house that by the beginning of the Viking Age had dominated in northern Europe for hundreds of years. Two Viking era farmhouses in Vorbasse on Jutland, Denmark, measured thirty-three meters in length. Longhouses had three naves. A double row of interior wooden posts, connected in pairs by beams, carried the weight of the roof. Other posts were placed along the walls, and they were connected by beams with the double post rows in the middle of the building. The roof was covered with whatever suitable material was available in the region, such as straw, water reed, heather, or wood shingles. The walls were at first constructed by weaving thin wooden reeds between upright wooden stakes and then daubing the resulting lattice with clay or other sticky materials (wattle and daub). Later on in the Viking Age, planks were used instead for the walls. The floor was probably simple stamped earth, although there could be raised areas covered with planks. A hearth somewhere in the middle of the living quarters provided heat, light, and plenty of smoke, since there were no chimneys. The smoke would seek its way out through small openings in the walls and perhaps the roof, which must have been provided with shutters. There was not a lot of furniture in the houses of ordinary farmers, although the wealthy would have had beautifully carved chairs and beds with soft bedding stuffed with feathers and down, as demonstrated by the items buried in Oseberg in 834. Benches along the walls as well as chests provided places to sit. The walls sported rugs and tapestries that not only were decorative but also protected against drafts. The farmer's longhouse must in addition have contained a lot of equipment, especially for the women's work "within the threshold": cooking utensils, storage jars, a hand mill, and looms.[23]

When archeologists excavate longhouses, the only thing remaining typically is traces of the postholes, which gives a basic idea of the architecture of the house but little information about its height. Only once have almost intact wall posts been discovered. They had been reused to line the walls of a well in Vorbasse in Jutland, which served to preserve them. Those posts are 180 centimeters long, suggesting that the walls of longhouses, at least of those belonging to the well-to-do, may have been about that tall. Since Viking Age people seldom were taller than that, most would have been able to walk straight through the door opening. Chieftains' halls could certainly stand taller than the one in Vorbasse. Judging from the angle of the raking timbers on the great hall at Lejre, Zealand, the side walls would have been three to four meters tall, which would allow for the ridge of the roof to be some ten meters above ground. That was a stately house built to impress, much like Hrothgar's hall Heorot described in the *Beowulf* poem: "The hall towered high."[24] The chieftain's hall had better be an impressive building; it was the center of his world. It was here that he feasted with his followers and that he sacrificed to his gods. People came to see him in the hall, and he gathered his warriors here before going out to plunder as a Viking in Europe or before attacking the chieftain in the next valley.

Unlike the chieftain's hall, the farmer's longhouse was divided by interior walls into several rooms, which each would have had its own designated use. Originally, people lived in one end of the house, typically in the western end, and the animals in the other, at least during the winter (so the women's work of milking the animals really was "within the threshold"). The longhouses could be up to forty meters long and thus truly deserved their name.

Building traditions changed fundamentally during the Viking Age. The longhouses no doubt survived in some places much as they had for centuries, including the space for animals at the eastern end. Two significant developments took place, however: the great halls of chieftains developed from the ordinary farmer's longhouse at the same time as most ordinary farmers built smaller dwelling houses and began to house the animals in separate buildings. Farms began to consist of several houses, each with its own designated use— for example, for different kinds of crafts, such as weaving, baking, and carpentry. Outbuildings used for such purposes were typically pithouses, partially dug into the soil. The excavated farm Lillinggården, close to Herning in western Jutland, Denmark, consisted of five buildings. The dwelling house was a longhouse of almost twenty-five meters, including at least one inner wall and a fireplace. A smaller building stood close by and may have been a workshop, a storage house, or an extra dwelling house. A little farther away were the barn and the stable. Unusually, at Lillinggården archeologists have been able to identify a pole barn, that is, a shedlike structure, mainly used for storage, that consists of four poles carrying a roof. This shed may have had simple walls, but no traces of them survive.

Viking Age farms were surrounded by fences, which kept animals away from grazing in the farmer's cultivations, just as in more recent times. Doors on residences may have been decorated with woodcarvings or iron fittings, and they may have contained locks made of wood or iron. The mistress of the house would normally have carried the keys to the houses. Many women were buried with their keys, made out of iron or bronze. The museums of Scandinavia contain many Viking Age keys.

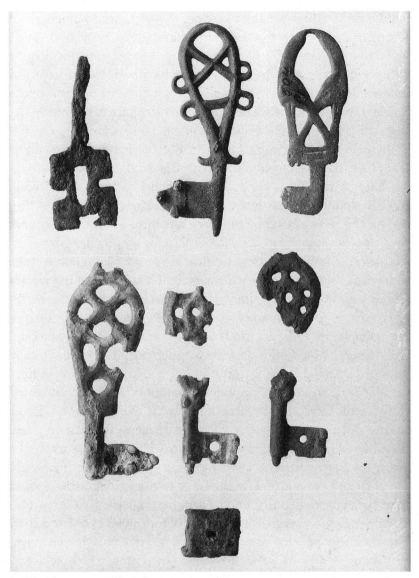

FIG. 21. Medieval women carried the keys to the important buildings at their farms, and many of them, including Estrid Sigfastsdotter, were buried with at least one of their keys. These examples come from several women's graves in Sweden. Photo courtesy of Riksantikvarieämbetet, Stockholm.

The architecture of the dwelling houses of ordinary farmers changed in ways similar to those of the chieftains' halls. More and more of the interior posts were removed, creating large interior spaces, but it also meant that more of the weight of the roof rested on the walls, which became buttressed by raking timbers. New types of constructions also appeared, such as timber houses standing on stone sills, which would become typical in the Middle Ages and beyond.

Farms were either found alone in isolated locations or clustered in villages, especially on the plains of southern Scandinavia. While the farm buildings during the Iron Age often were rebuilt at new locations close by when the old buildings needed to be replaced, they became stationary during the Viking Age. Not uncommonly, farms are still to be found in the same spots as a thousand years ago, or at least they remained in those spots until they were moved in the eighteenth and nineteenth centuries, when many villages were reapportioned. Farmers who lived in villages performed some of the agricultural work, such as sowing, harvesting, and fencing, in collaboration with one another, and they would also share some more expensive equipment.

When thinking about Scandinavian farms during the Viking Age, it is easy to imagine each farm as self-sufficient and isolated, simply sustaining the people living on the farm by producing just enough food, so there would be no reason to be in contact with the greater world around each individual homestead. But this is not how Viking Age agricultural society worked in Scandinavia. Many would have had brothers and sons, and perhaps also daughters, who participated in Viking raids, served as mercenaries in Constantinople and elsewhere, went on pilgrimages to the holy places of their religion (like Östen in Såsta going to Jerusalem), or traded furs, slaves, and silver in foreign countries. Farmers did many things that connected them to the outside world, even when they stayed at home on the farm. They had not personally manufactured every tool they used. The soapstone pots many used for cooking had been transported from Norway. The iron of the plow bill had been transported from the iron-producing regions of Sweden and sold on a market. Of course, some farmers supplemented their agricultural work by mining soapstone and making pots, while others shoveled lake ore out of lakes, streams, and marshes, and then smelted the ore to make iron. All of them would have been tied into a commercial network that appears to have functioned well, even though for most of the Viking Age Scandinavia had no money economy. That is why household managers like Estrid needed scales to be able to carefully weigh the silver (or other precious objects) used for payment. Scales and weights are often found in Viking Age graves, and not only in merchant graves.

We should remember that there were substantial groups in the population of Viking Age Scandinavia who did not produce food but still needed to consume it. The great men and women of the halls surely owned large farms where they had slaves and employees who produced food for them, but they may still have needed to buy more than they produced, since a great chieftain needed to entertain many, many followers with food. Likewise, trade towns such as Hedeby and Birka had large populations that needed to be fed. Many more people lived there than could be fed with the produce of the immediately surrounding area, so food must have been brought in from the outside, even from far away. Archeologists have found some hints about how food might have been provided for these towns.

The farm at Sanda lay in Sweden not far north of the current site of Stockholm. The settlement expanded strongly just before and during the Viking Age. A large three-aisled hall remained on the same spot for five hundred years, although it was rebuilt at least twice. When it was reconstructed at some point between 850 and 950, it was twenty-five meters long and six meters wide. This was clearly the residence of rich people. Three other archeological finds make Sanda stand out among other farms. Unexpectedly, much burned grain, mainly the unusual high-status variety of wheat (*triticum aestivum*), was found. Several of the outbuildings contained ovens. A lot of worn-out millstones had been used to build hearths in some of the houses, starting in the tenth century. Taken together, these findings suggest that Sanda was a center for the production of wheat flour and also for baking bread. What the millers and bakers produced was high-status stuff, far more than would have been consumed on-site. These products were probably transported to and consumed at some high-status location where much food was needed. The most likely candidate is the trade town Birka, some thirty kilometers to the southwest. It seems that at least the wealthier people in Birka got their bread or their flour from Sanda.

Further exchange of goods is implied at Sanda, for the surroundings are marshy and unsuitable for growing much wheat, so it must have been grown elsewhere and transported there. The millstones also come from elsewhere, farther north in Sweden. This single site reveals itself as a node in a network of goods exchange that brought in millstones and wheat and sent on flour and bread. The owner of Sanda must have been able to make a good profit on providing food to Birka: he or she constructed a hall with a surrounding stone terrace as a visible manifestation of wealth and power.[25]

When considering life at home on the farm in the Viking Age, we must be careful not to idealize and make peasant life in former times seem idyllic. Farmwork was (and is) unpleasant, laborious, and backbreakingly hard. In the early Middle Ages, almost all work had to be done manually with what even hobbyist gardeners today would consider inadequate tools, mostly made of wood. In the absence of moldboard plows, for example, farmers would need occasionally to turn the soil with a spade. If they, as was common, had to use a wooden spade, they would quickly wear it down and have to manufacture a new one. To make a dress from growing flax or sheep wool was a process in many steps, each of which required both skill and hard work. It is difficult for modern people living in the West to imagine how hard life was for medieval peasants, although we might get some idea if we study farmers in the developing world.

During the Middle Ages, the upper classes knew how hard farmers worked. The old Scandinavian poem *The List of Rig* imagines how hard work deformed the physical features of an agricultural thrall:

On his hands there was wrinkled skin,
crooked knuckles,
thick fingers, he had an ugly face
a crooked back, long heels.

The poem tells us something about what this thrall and his family worked with:

> They put dung on the fields, worked with swine,
> looked after goats, dug the turf.[26]

More details are filled in by a school text written in England in about 1000, which is framed as a conversation between a master and his student. The text is in Latin with an Old English translation between the lines. The student takes on the role of people at different stations in society. When he plays the role of the plowman, he says: "Oh, my lord, I work too hard. I go out at dawn, driving the cattle to the field, and I yoke them to the plow. The winter weather is never so bad that I dare to hide out at home . . . but when the oxen are yoked, and the plowshare and coulter attached to the plow, I must plow one whole field a day, or more." When asked what more the plowman does, the student answered: "I must fill the manger of the oxen with hay, and water them and carry out the dung." "Oh, oh, that is really hard work," responded the master.[27]

Not only was agricultural work hard, the farmer was also always threatened by natural disasters as well as willful destruction by hostile bands of warriors. If the harvest failed, perhaps several years in a row, poor people might simply starve to death, or die of any of the many diseases that often accompany famines. Medieval chronicles and other records of contemporary events often describe famines in Europe. No such sources are preserved describing famines in Viking Age Scandinavia, but there is no reason to believe that Scandinavia escaped the disasters that afflicted Europe. After all, the climate is colder to start with in Scandinavia than in the more southerly latitudes of Europe for which we have sources. Since it has been established that periods of bad weather (often implying crop failure and famine) could occur globally as a result of, for example, volcanic eruptions spewing ash into the atmosphere, such episodes would certainly affect Scandinavia as well; indeed, they are discernible in the ice cores taken from the glaciers of Greenland.[28]

One of the most eloquent descriptions of a European famine was written by the loquacious French monk Rodulfus Glaber, whose description of the great famine of the years surrounding year 1000 is probably exaggerated but still suggestive:

> A famine raged in the whole Roman [= Catholic] world for five years. It was so terrible that there was no region which was not destitute and without bread. Many people died for lack of food. In many parts of the world the dire famine forced people to eat not just the flesh of unclean animals and reptiles, but also that of men, women, and children; not even family relationship could prevent it. The famine had become so savage that grown sons ate their mothers while mothers did the same to their babies, lost to all maternal love.[29]

Of course, farmers of every time period develop strategies for managing failed crops and bad weather, to avoid starving. When the grain harvest was small, they would mix grain with other edible products of nature, such as roots and the inner bark of certain trees. Those who lived close to the sea or other bodies of water would fish more if land crops failed. For most farmers, the animals themselves, mostly kept for their milk, fur, or as sources of power, were a food of last resort. People would also eat the fodder set aside for the animals to eat during the winter when they were kept in barns. Even as late as the nineteenth century, cattle were often so starved by the end of the winter that they were unable to walk out of their barns when spring finally came.

Not only nature visited farmers with disasters. War and violence were manmade tragedies for the population. The Vikings are, of course, infamous for inflicting such suffering on the population of Europe, but we should not imagine that the warlike chieftains and their warrior bands remained peaceful within Scandinavia itself. Before being united into the three kingdoms Denmark, Norway, and Sweden in around 1000, many chieftains in Scandinavia would inflict violence on their major competitors. There were no states to check them; only the threat of other chieftains and their warrior bands could stop them.

We have every right to expect that Scandinavian chieftains fought one another at least as often as they attacked Europeans, and we should not think that any farmer who happened to be in the way would have been spared, or that his crops and animals would not have been destroyed. Farmers would probably look to local chieftains for protection, but they had little recourse if those chieftains lost the competition with other chieftains. Written sources seldom or never tell us about such "collateral" damage, although they make abundantly clear that Scandinavia was not a peaceful place during the Viking Age.

The *Beowulf* poet had an acute sense of people's suffering in war. King Beowulf had been able to protect his Geatish people (who were Scandinavians) from raids by hostile forces, but he died at the end of the poem. On the poem's last page, a Geatish woman (her hair was bound up, which means that she was old) lamented the death of her people's protector and foretold a terrible future:

> And a sorrowful song sang the Geatish woman,
> with hair bound up, for Beowulf the king,
> with sad cares, earnestly said,
> that she dreaded the hard days ahead,
> the times of slaughter, the host's terror,
> harm and captivity.[30]

It was dangerous to be a Viking, to sail out to Europe to raid and pillage, since the intended victims might at any point fight back, injuring or killing attackers. But to stay at home on the farm was not necessarily a much safer alternative. All your diligent work to grow grain, care for your animals, fish, and harvest might be for naught if nature sent bad weather, or if your chieftain's enemies from the next valley showed up with an armed band of warriors.

PLATE 1. Magnificent multicolored glass vessels equipped the halls of the richest chieftains. This well-preserved example comes from a grave in Birka, Sweden. Photo: Gunnel Jansson, courtesy of Statens Historiska Museum, Stockholm.

PLATE 2. Arabic dirhams (silver coins) and gaming pieces made of glass, including a "king," were found in a rich grave in Birka, Sweden. Photo: Sören Hallgren, courtesy of Statens Historiska Museum, Stockholm.

PLATE 3. The ruins of Erik the Red's farm Brattahlid, Greenland, are still clearly visible as the icebergs slide by on the fjord. Photo: Werner Forman/CORBIS. Reproduced with permission.

PLATE 4. Ships played a prominent role in the life and imagination of the Vikings. The Scandinavian countryside is dotted with thousands of ship settings, where large rocks have been placed to form the outline of a ship. They are typically associated with graves and may represent the vessels that brought the deceased to the Afterworld. This example is from Djupvik on the island Gotland, Sweden. Photo: Bengt A. Lundberg, courtesy of Riksantikvarieämbetet, Stockholm.

PLATE 5. Hundreds of picture stones survive from the Viking Age on Gotland in Sweden. One of the most magnificent shows several battle scenes, at least one of which includes a woman. The large ship at the bottom dominates the composition. Stora Hammars 1, Lärbro, Gotland. Photo: Bengt A. Lundberg, courtesy of Riksantikvarieämbetet, Stockholm.

PLATE 6. The Viking Ship Museum in Roskilde, Denmark, used medieval shipbuilding techniques in creating a reconstruction of one of the grandest Viking longships ever found by archeologists. "The Sea Stallion of Glendalough" has proven eminently seaworthy and has sailed from Denmark to Dublin and back; volunteers have the opportunity to man the oars every summer. Photo: Vikingeskibsmuseet, Roskilde. Reproduced with permission.

PLATE 7. Viking chieftains who sought to strengthen their relationships with their warriors handed out generous gifts, such as splendid swords with decoration in gold and silver. This sword with its discreet but graceful pattern produced with silver inlay comes from a grave in Sollerön, Sweden. Photo: Gabriel Hildebrand, courtesy of Statens Historiska Museum, Stockholm.

PLATE 8. This exquisite pearl string with twenty carnelian beads, twenty-two pieces of rock crystal, and a blue glass pearl was found in a grave at Hedeby. Whereas rock crystal might be found in several locations in Europe, the carnelian probably came from either the Caucasus region or India. Photo courtesy of Wikinger Museum Haithabu, Schleswig.

PLATE 9. When Estrid Sigfastsdotter became a widow in the eleventh century, she erected this runestone in memory of her husband Östen, close to their farm at Såsta, Sweden. In the text, she announces that Östen died on a pilgrimage to Jerusalem. Photo: Bengt A. Lundberg, courtesy of Riksantikvarieämbetet, Stockholm.

PLATE 10. This exquisitely carved animal head from the ninth-century Oseberg burial probably decorated a chair or some other piece of furniture. It would not have been out of place on the high seat of a powerful chieftain. © Kulturhistorisk museum, Universitetet i Oslo.

PLATE 11. This eleventh-century runestone in Altuna, Sweden, depicts the god Thor, hammer in hand, having captured the Midgard Serpent on his fishing line and pulling so hard that his foot has pushed through the bottom of the boat. Photo: Bengt A. Lundberg, courtesy of Riksantikvarieämbetet, Stockholm.

PLATE 12. This statuette depicts the god of fertility Frey. According to the eleventh-century Christian writer Adam of Bremen, Scandinavian pagans fashioned Frey's image "with an immense phallus." Photo: Gabriel Hildebrand, courtesy of Statens Historiska Museum, Stockholm.

PLATE 13. *Flateyjarbók* is one of the greatest surviving medieval manuscripts collecting the stories of ancient Scandinavia, including many sagas about rulers in Norway and elsewhere, which often quote skaldic poetry praising kings and chieftains. Four stanzas are included on this page. In medieval manuscripts, poetry is typically not copied line by line, as in modern books, but in the same way as prose. Photo courtesy of © Stofnun Árna Magnússonar í íslenskum fræðum, Reykjavik. From GKS 1005, fo. 131v.

PLATE 14. Two treasure troves found close to each other in Erikstorp, Sweden, contain almost two kilograms of gold, including seven elegant arm rings. The round brooch, also of gold, was produced using a mold excavated in Hedeby, many hundreds of miles away. Photo: Ulf Bruxe, courtesy of Statens Historiska Museum, Stockholm.

CHAPTER 8

THE RELIGIONS
OF THE NORTH

THE CHRISTIAN KING HARALD OF NORWAY, DESTROYER OF ancient temples, was dead. The new ruler, Earl Håkon, returned to the old rituals, and, see! suddenly "the earth was growing again." When the old king had "dared to damage temples," he angered the gods, who answered by sending bad weather to spoil the grain crop and expelling the herring from their usual spawning grounds. Norway had been starving. Now, in the 970s, with pagan Earl Håkon Sigurdsson in charge, the temples were reopened, and the gods responded happily by providing good weather and plentiful herring catches. That is the message Håkon wanted people in Norway to hear: that he, in his wisdom, reaffirmed the old gods, in contrast to recent rulers who had been trying to introduce this foreign new religion, Christianity, to Norway. As Håkon's poet Einar skálaglam put it:

> The wise one [Håkon] enabled
> honor of all Einriði's [Thor's]
> ravaged famed temple grounds,
> and the gods' sacred places.[1]

The Norwegians would do best keeping to their old gods and rallying around their new ruler, Håkon Sigurdsson—not only a true and devoted pagan but also one who claimed descent from the chief god Odin, Thor's father.

Håkon used pagan religion to counter the old kingly but Christian-leaning family as well as their relative, the Christian king of Denmark, who were contesting Håkon's power in Norway. Håkon may well have been a true devotee of the old Norse religion despite having received Christian baptism; we cannot really know his personal feelings in the matter. His embrace of paganism led, however, to a short-lived pagan renaissance around his court in Lade (today a suburb of Trondheim), producing one of the last real flourishings of pagan culture and literature in Scandinavia.

Håkon employed an unprecedented number of poets and skalds at his court—at least nine—and they embraced pagan imagery in their poetry, which of course was a part of Håkon's propaganda effort. The image that they strove to conjure was of Håkon in collaboration with the gods stimulating good harvests and general prosperity as well as gaining victory in battle:

> He piled the fields with corpses,
> the lord of Froði's storm [= warrior = Håkon],
> the son of the gods [= Håkon, descendant of Odin] rejoiced in
>   victory,
> Odin received the slain.
> What doubt can there be but that
> the gods control the destroyer [Håkon] of the race of princes?
> I say that the most powerful gods
> increase the might of Håkon.[2]

These words are, again, those of Håkon's skald Einar, who wrote a long poem known as *Vellekla* in praise of the earl. (The title *Vellekla* means "Lack of Gold" and is probably meant to suggest the necessity of giving the poet a suitably valuable reward.) In particular, Einar extolled Håkon's prowess in war, as in this stanza. The poem ranges from battle to battle, and Håkon appears, according to Einar, to have battled victoriously almost everywhere in Scandinavia, even as the Danish king's ally at the Danevirke, on the southern border of Denmark. At home in Norway, he defeated neighboring princes—"Who has ever heard of one chieftain dominating the lands of sixteen princes?" Einar asks rhetorically—gaining dominance over Norway because "the gods desire it." It is thanks to Odin, the god of war, and the other gods that Håkon was so successful in battle and that Norway now enjoyed prosperity and fertility.

Håkon was not only a friend of the gods and their favorite; he was also said to be their blood relative, descending from a union between Odin himself and a giantess called Skadi. That union had produced Earl Semingr, Håkon's twenty-seven-generation ancestor. The story of Håkon's family was retold in the poem *Háleygjatal* by another of Håkon's skalds, Eyvind the Plagiarist: "The descendant of the Æsir [= Odin], shield-worshipped, begat the bringer of tribute [= Semingr] with the denizen of Ironwood [= Skadi]."

Eyvind received his epithet because he cribbed much of this poem's content from the older poem *Ynglingatal* by Thjodolf of Hvini, which similarly described the descent of a Norwegian ruler (in his case, the petty king or chieftain Ragnvald) from a god, Frey, through twenty-seven generations. Eyvind's borrowings go beyond plagiarism, however, to appropriate an older tradition that Håkon's opponents and his ancestors' opponents had used for their own propaganda. It is as if Eyvind were subtly pointing out that the family of Håkon's opponents, once proud of descending from the gods, had forfeited that inheritance by embracing Christianity while Håkon remained true to his divine ancestors.

Eyvind emphasized this point with repeated allusions to pagan myth and cult in *Háleygjatal*, for instance in the passage quoted above when he refers to Odin as "shield-worshipped." Although it is difficult to pinpoint the exact meaning, "shield-worshipped" must refer to a pagan cult practice involving some kind of protective incantation like that mentioned in another old poem, *Hávamál*: "If I have to lead loyal friends into battle; under the shields I chant, and they journey inviolate, safely to the battle, safely from the battle, safely they come everywhere."[3] The incantation would serve to protect the friends of the leader who has such good relations with the gods, especially the warrior god Odin, that they deign to hear his "shield-worship." When Håkon's skalds and other propagandists emphasize his good relationship with the gods, they emphasize that he is able to summon divine protection for his friends. We see Håkon using religion to inspire people to follow him and to be loyal, just as he and other chieftains gave valuable gifts to attract followers.

Håkon, his skalds, and his warriors lived during the Viking Age in the midst of religious turmoil when the old pagan religion of Scandinavia was being replaced by Christianity, a key moment in the development of northern society.[4] While Einar was praising the Norwegian Håkon for his devotion to Thor, the German monk Widukind was saluting King Harald Bluetooth of Denmark for becoming a Christian. Håkon had defeated a Norwegian king who embraced Christianity, and in 996 Håkon himself would be defeated by the former Viking Olav Tryggvason, who became famous as a pioneering missionary king converting Norway.

Earl Håkon, reasserting paganism and resisting conversion, provides a snapshot of the religious movements of Viking Age Scandinavia: pagan mythology and cult, Christian conversion and organization. We will examine these facets of Scandinavian religion in turn. A common thread will be that Scandinavian kings and chieftains used their religion, whether paganism or Christianity, to elevate their status and to bolster loyalties among their followers.

Norse pre-Christian mythology is not as well known as we would wish. What we think we know comes from sources produced sometimes centuries later by Christian writers, so our information is colored by Christian influence as well as the writers' systematizing tendencies and desire for a coherent narrative. They sometimes invented stories and even gods to spice up or polish their narratives. Still, the stories we have continue to exert a strong pull on us with all their fascinating and mysterious detail; indeed, there are today several groups of religious reconstructionists that embrace the old religion of the North. We will have a closer look at the god who seems to have been Earl Håkon's favorite, the strong and choleric Thor, and move on to the end of the world, Ragnarök, in the process examining the problems found in our sources.

Earl Håkon's court saw a late flowering of pagan culture in Scandinavia and thus helped preserve it for posterity. His skalds celebrated the pagan gods in their poetry. This may, for example, have been where the poet Eilífr Godrúnarson composed the exceedingly difficult *Thórsdrápa*, celebrating feats of the god Thor in such exaggerated and baroque language that the text to this day continues to baffle its interpreters.[5]

Thor was the son of Håkon's putative ancestor Odin, and he was popular over vast swaths of Scandinavia. Several Viking Age rune-stones invoke Thor ("May Thor hallow these runes!"). Some ninety place-names that include his name (Thorshov, Torslunda, etc.) are found almost everywhere in continental Scandinavia.[6] Thor's popularity is also suggested by the many models of his hammer, Mjöll-nir, with which he was thought to create thunderclaps. Hundreds of miniature hammers survive from the Viking Age, some very simple amulets made out of iron or some other base metal. The simple but elegant hammer amulet of the woman buried in Vatnsdalur in Iceland (see chapter 4) is an example. Others are sophisticated works of art in silver and gold, with filigree and other decoration.[7]

Thor was (like the Roman Mars) portrayed as a red-haired and red-bearded god, quick to anger and enormously strong. Many stories circulated about him, for example about his long enmity with the great serpent Jörmungandr (Mighty Monster), or Midgard Serpent, who lay coiled around the world. This giant snake grasped its own tail and thus held the world together; when it let go, the world would break apart and end.

Thor is, in this story as in so many others, matched with a giant, in this case named Hymir, and he gets plenty of opportunity to demonstrate his enormous strength, which stands out even in comparison with Hymir's. Thor is the giant's guest and eats two of the giant's oxen for dinner before the odd pair decides to go out fishing the next day to catch their dinner. When Thor asks for bait, Hymir tells him to look for it in his pasture, probably expecting Thor to dig for earthworms. Thor instead finds Hymir's black ox and tears off the head to use it as bait. They row their boat out to sea, considerably farther than Hymir wishes, and Thor "[baits] his hook with the ox's head," according to the old *Hymir's Poem*, written down in the thirteenth century in the *Poetic Edda*, a collection of poems that treat mythological and legendary topics.

We can see Hymir and Thor out fishing on a Viking Age picture stone from the island of Gotland. Next to a large Viking ship with raised sails, a smaller boat is outlined with two figures in it. One of them holds a fishing line with a large bait. Another depiction of the same scene appears on a fragment of a large stone cross from Gosforth in a part of England where many Scandinavian immigrants lived during the Viking Age, and here one can very clearly see that the bait is an ox head surrounded by curious fish.[8]

The giant Hymir "caught two whales on his hook at once," but Thor, ever competitive, aimed for an even greater catch: "He whom the gods hate, the girdle of all lands," that is, the Midgard Serpent, "gaped at the bait." So Thor's hook captured it and "very bravely" he attempted to "pull in the serpent, gleaming with venom, up on board." Thor pulled so hard and the serpent was so strong that both the god's feet pushed through the bottom of the boat, and he braced himself against the seafloor. This scene is depicted on a Swedish eleventh-century runestone in Altuna, which commemorates a father and son who died in a fire. The stone depicts a large snakelike creature having taken the bait, and the sole fisher in the boat, Thor, struggling so mightily to pull in his catch that his foot has pushed through the bottom of the boat. In his other hand he holds an ax.[9]

Hymir's Poem portrays the same scene in very dramatic terms: "The sea-wolf [Midgard Serpent] shrieked and the underwater rocks re-echoed, all the ancient earth was collapsing." Another Viking Age poet, Bragi the Old, instead employed typical Scandinavian understatement when describing the same scene: "The fishing-line of Viðrir's [= Odin's] son [= Thor] did not lie slack on the ski of Eynæfi [= sea king; his ski is a boat], when Jörmungandr was dragged on the sand [= seafloor]."[10] Thor fought the serpent courageously, not caring about the consequences. The giant Hymir, in contrast, "grew pale and feared for his life"—in Norse literature giants are portrayed as physically strong and boastful but cowards when the chips are down—and when Thor raised his hammer to strike the Midgard Serpent dead, Hymir cut off Thor's fishing line. The serpent sank back into the sea and was safe for the time being (but Thor would later kill him in the chaos that preceded the end of the world, Ragnarök). As reported by the Icelandic politician and antiquarian Snorri Sturluson (1179–1241) in the thirteenth century, Thor became so annoyed with Hymir that he threw him overboard, but in other versions of the story the giant survives to foil Thor in new adventures.

The story of Thor and the Midgard Serpent was very popular in the Viking Age and shows up, as we have seen, in many different contexts, both pictorial and literary, but typically as fragments. When we in modern times study the different representations, we want to combine the various surviving fragments into a single, coherent story, but if we do that, we miss the richness of the tradition. The poet Ulfr Uggason, for example, alludes to a story in which the Midgard Serpent dies after Thor has caught him on a fishhook—how else should we interpret Ulfr's words that Thor "loosened the head of the serpent"?[11] Bragi the Old, in contrast, alludes in his poetry to Hymir cutting off the fishing line, saving the serpent's life. Clearly, different versions of the story circulated, and we should resist the temptation to harmonize their differences to get a single neat narrative. Snorri Sturluson did exactly that when he retold pagan traditions in his book known as the *Prose Edda*. Since he knew from other sources that the Midgard Serpent would fight Thor again at the end of the world, he opted for the variant of the fishing story in which the monster survived, thus suppressing the other stories also circulating. In this case, Ulfr's version of the story still survives, but in many other cases Snorri's is the only version we have.

When Snorri Sturluson was writing his handbook, the *Prose Edda*, on how to interpret old poetry, he was disturbed by the great variety among the old stories. He wanted to be able to tell straightforwardly what he thought was the "real story," so he spent a lot of energy on combining and harmonizing the different stories he found. Sometimes he simply misunderstood his sources.[12] Snorri's *Edda* presents a compendium of stories about the Norse pantheon, but it is a collection of flattened stories, whose complexity has been suppressed in favor of consistency and simplicity. Even when scholars study the fragmentary stories preserved in Viking Age poetry or images, they tend to fit those fragments into the whole as conveyed by Snorri hundreds of years later. This often disfigures the authentic pre-Christian traditions of Scandinavia.

A Christian himself, Snorri lived in a country that had been Christian for a couple of centuries. He would never have met any pagans, and his portrayal of paganism is the product of a scholar's efforts to interpret books in his study. His writings are valuable because he had access to many books and stories that are now lost to us, but he purveys distorted images of pagan beliefs. We should, for example, not be surprised that we can trace Christian influences in the stories he tells. This Christian coloring might come from Snorri himself, who may have more or less consciously introduced Christian themes and ideas into his book, or it might have come into paganism while it was still a living tradition. Before Scandinavians definitively became Christian around the year 1000, their paganism did not live in isolation from the Christian parts of Europe. Merchants, mercenaries, and raiding Vikings traveled in Christian Europe and would have picked up ideas and ideals there, with or without becoming outright Christians.

The story of Thor's fishing expedition is, for example, clearly influenced by Christian myths and ideas. A god fighting a serpent living in the ocean is paralleled in stories about Christ catching the great sea monster Leviathan. A plethora of legends arose around the question posed in Job 40:20: "Can you draw out Leviathan with a fishhook?" Jewish exegetes took the fisherman to prefigure the Messiah, and Christians applied the verse to the cosmic contest between Christ and Satan, in which Christ on the cross allegorically was the bait that Satan/Leviathan would take. In Norse versions of these medieval Christian legends Leviathan is sometimes replaced with the Midgard Serpent. Similarly, Snorri's account of Thor's fishing adventure is heavily suffused with Christian myth and legend. It is very hard, if not impossible, to identify any authentic pre-Christian myths in his story.[13]

Another example is how the Judeo-Christian story of Noah and the Great Flood got into Snorri's account of pagan religious beliefs. In the old Eddic poem known as *Vafthrudnir's Sayings*, the anonymous poet tells us about the giant Bergelmir, who lived long ago:

Uncountable winters before the world was made,
then Bergelmir was born;
that I remember first when the wise giant
was first laid in his coffin.[14]

These lines are uttered by the giant Vafthrudnir in order to prove that he knows much that is hidden to ordinary mortals, including esoteric lore such as the story of Bergelmir. The last line has caused trouble for interpreters because the poet uses an unusual word of uncertain meaning, *lúðr*, the basic sense of which appears to have been "hollowed-out log." Most modern readers agree that here the word means "coffin" (as reflected in the translation quoted above), so Vafthrudnir remembers both Bergelmir's birth and his death. When Snorri read the text, however, he understood *lúðr* to mean "ark, ship" (another way a hollowed-out log could be used; see chapter 4), which he related to the biblical story about Noah and the Flood. Early in the history of the world, so Snorri narrates, the giant Ymir was killed and "when he fell, so much blood gushed from his wounds that . . . all the race of the frost giants drowned except for one who escaped with his household . . . Bergelmir. He, together with his wife, climbed up on to his *lúðr*, and there they kept themselves safe. From them come the races of the frost giants, as it is said here: 'Uncountable winters . . . .'"[15] Snorri then goes on to reproduce the stanza quoted earlier from *Vafthrudnir's Sayings*. We might compare Snorri's words to those of Genesis 7:7: "And Noah and his sons, his wife and his sons' wives with him went into the ark." Just as Noah became the ancestor of all humans after the Flood, Bergelmir became the ancestor of all the giants after the flood of Ymir's blood.

The story of Bergelmir illustrates how Snorri more or less consciously strove to cast a Christian light on the stories of pre-Christian mythology, how he looked for evidence that his pagan ancestors were aware, however dimly, of the true history of the world as revealed in the Bible. Like every medieval Christian, he knew that the Flood had literally happened, and when he perceived an allusion to it in an old poem, he pounced on the opportunity to harmonize the pagan story with what he believed to be true history.

One of the most fascinating tales in Norse mythology is about the end of the world or, as it is called in Old Norse, Ragnarök (Fate of the Gods). Snorri retells the story with bravura, but it is also known from two older poems. In one of the grandest Old Norse poems ever composed, the *Völuspá* (*The Seeress's Prophecy*), a *völva*—a sibyl or seeress born before the world began—outlines a cosmographic vision of the history and the future of the world. The preserved copies we have of this poem come from the thirteenth century, but they are generally thought to reflect a composition from the late Viking Age.

In the vision of the völva, the world carries the seeds of its destruction from early on, at least since three giantesses, "filled with cruel might," arrived there from the demon world. When the world then grows old, disaster follows on disaster. Freyja is given (or promised; the poem is unclear) to the giants, but oaths and promises are broken. "From the east falls, from poison valleys, a river of knives and swords." The good god Baldr is shot by his own brother Hod with an arrow made out of mistletoe, "that plant which seemed so lovely." Snorri explains, or imagines, the story to which the poem alludes. Baldr is the chief god Odin's second son: "He is the best, and all praise him. He is so beautiful and so bright that light shines from him. . . . He is the wisest of the gods."[16] One night he has a dream suggesting that his life is threatened. Since he is so beloved, his mother, Frigg, takes oaths from everything in the world not to kill him: metal, stones, wood, animals, diseases, and so forth. Baldr thus becomes impervious to injury, so the gods, ill-advisedly, take to amusing themselves by shooting or throwing things at Baldr, who is never affected, thanks to the oaths.

But Loki, portrayed as a trickster who often causes trouble for the gods, finds out that Frigg has overlooked the unassuming mistletoe plant, which seemed too young to do any harm. Somehow fashioning an arrow out of the mistletoe's flimsy stems, Loki gives it to Baldr's blind brother, Hod, encouraging him to shoot at Baldr. When he does, Baldr falls down dead. The gods capture Loki and tie him with his own sons' guts to a stone, where a poisonous snake ever after drops its venom in his face. Loki's wife, Sigyn, catches the poison in a bowl, but when the bowl is full and she goes to empty it, Loki's pained convulsions shake the world as earthquakes.

It is impossible to know how much of this story we should ascribe to the imagination of Snorri (or his predecessors) and how much was actual pagan myth that had been passed down to him. It is likely that the story as we have it preserves only some details, at best, of any real pagan myth, while Snorri's learned speculation is clearly apparent, for example, in Baldr's Christlike innocent death, killed by a person who was "blind" to his divinity, just as Christ's killers were.

After the seeress retells her prophecy about the death of Baldr, the tempo of her tale of doom increases. The wolf Garm gets loose from his bonds in front of Gnipa-cave. "Brother will fight brother and be his slayer, brother and sister will violate the bond of kinship; hard it is in the world, there is much adultery, ax-age, sword-age, shields are cleft asunder, wind-age, wolf-age, before the world plunges headlong; no man will spare another" (*Völuspá* 45). Three of the most important gods fight duels with monsters. Odin is killed by the wolf, who in revenge is killed by Odin's son Viðar, while the giant Surt murders Frey. Thor again fights his archenemy, the Midgard Serpent: "In the air gapes the Earth-girdler, the terrible jaws of the serpent yawn above; [Thor] must meet the serpent." After killing the monster, Thor manages to walk only nine steps before he also falls down dead, killed by the lingering effects of the serpent's venom.

This is the end of the world; this is the fate of the gods, Ragnarök. "The sun turns black, earth sinks into the sea, the bright stars vanish from the sky; steam rises up in the conflagration, a high flame plays against heaven itself" (57). But this end proves a new beginning: The seeress "sees earth coming up a second time from the ocean, eternally green; the waterfall plunges, an eagle soars over it, hunting fish on the mountain" (59). After the great conflagration of Ragnarök, a better world grows anew. Baldr comes back and lives happily together with his innocent killer, Hod. "A hall she [the seeress] sees standing, fairer than the sun, thatched with gold . . . there the noble lords will live and spend their days in pleasure. Then the powerful, mighty one, he who rules over everything, will come from above, to the judgment-place of the gods" (64–65). The poem *Völuspá* is a brilliant and powerful vision of the end of the world couched in the voice of a female prophet. Its author (whose exact dates elude us) clearly knew a great deal about pagan beliefs and ideas in Scandinavia but was eclectic and often relied on Christian traditions. The bare outline of the story of the end of the world is almost identical to that in the Revelation of St. John and other places in the Bible. The *Völuspá* poet predicted fratricidal strife, just as Jesus did: "And brother will deliver up brother to death" (Mark 13:12). The poet foresaw fights between individual gods and various monsters, such as Thor and the Midgard Serpent, just as John saw the archangel Michael fight the great dragon (Revelation 12:7).[17]

The paganism of *Völuspá* has been deeply influenced by Christianity, and other sources, such as Snorri's *Edda*, are even more Christianized. Poets promoting paganism for political ends, such as Einar skálaglam and Eyvind the Plagiarist, both working for Earl Håkon, pushed for paganism in conscious emulation of Christianity and were thus bound to pick up aspects of the religion against which they polemicized. Older sources may contain more "pure" paganism, but then we run into the problem that those sources are too brief to provide evidence for much more than the names of gods. "May Thor hallow these runes" on a runestone in Danish Sönder Kirkeby, or "May Thor hallow" on a stone in Velanda, Sweden—these tell us that a cult of the god Thor was current at those locations, but we find out nothing about Thor himself.[18]

Many gods are, indeed, little more than names—like Heimdal and Tyr—that even Snorri just mentioned in passing, but they may at one point have been important. Tyr, at least, is one of only four gods who have given their names to days of the week (in his case, Tuesday), so he must have been of more than passing interest. The other three are the warrior god Odin (Wednesday), the weather god Thor (Thursday), and the fertility god Frey (Friday). Of course, Sunday and Monday have their names from the Sun and the Moon, but there are few hints, if any, that those natural phenomena were the subjects of cults in the Viking Age, as they were in many other premodern societies.

Even the more developed stories of Scandinavian myth do not tell us much of lived religion, how people in Scandinavia related to their gods and religious beliefs, how the cult of the gods was carried out. One of the most exciting archeological discoveries in recent years is a building that surely was some kind of pagan temple, an extremely rare find in the archeological material of Scandinavia. The temple stood in Uppåkra in the province of Scania, in what today is southern Sweden. The building, measuring 13 × 6.5 meters, contained a single room with four posts inside, which, to judge from their size, may have supported a tower riding on the roof. The building was in continuous use for hundreds of years from 200 CE on, being rebuilt on the same spot and with the same layout at least seven times, until it was finally torn down, probably in the ninth century. It was used for lavish feasts; a glass bowl and a decorated pitcher have been found there, both of which were imported prestige goods. More than 110 so-called *guldgubbar* have also been discovered inside the building along the walls and in the corners. These are thin gold foils with images imprinted on them, usually two persons who stand facing each other. Their posture, subject to interpretation, can be seen as embracing and kissing, in which case the guldgubbar appear to have been part of a fertility rite. But they may also be seen as wrestling with each other, pointing to a more martial purpose. Most interpreters are, however, agreed that the guldgubbar had some kind of religious significance and function. Perhaps they are best understood as representations of a sacrifice, a kind of substitute sacrifice in place of a real animal. Judging from where they are typically found at archeological sites, they would have been placed on the walls or the corner posts of the building.

Be that as it may, there are plenty of animal bones at Uppåkra to suggest that real animals were sacrificed. Some human bones may even be evidence of human sacrifice. Weapons that have purposely been destroyed testify to the sacrifice of weapons, probably those of vanquished enemies. In the period before the Viking Age, weapon sacrifices were very common, but they then took place in lakes, where the destroyed weapons were thrown into the water. It is characteristic of the Viking Age that the sacrifices move from lakes at a distance from human settlement to the settlements themselves, and often into buildings. Sacrifices continued, however, to take place outdoors. Excavations under the church of Frösö on a lake island in northern Sweden have revealed exciting evidence of such outdoor sacrifices.

Under the floor of the medieval church at Frösö, archeologists found the burned stump of a birch. Bones of dead animals, including at least five bear crania, mostly from young animals, surrounded it. Before the place became a Christian ritual site, a church, it clearly was a pagan ritual site, where grand sacrifices were made. The bear is much feared in Scandinavia. Down into modern times, the Sami people of northern Scandinavia carried out a bear cult, which at least in some of its variants included displaying bear heads in trees, as the pagans in Frösö appear to have done. The Sami cult and the bear sacrifices at Frösö obviously share some characteristics, although the details are lost.

Written evidence about Scandinavian pagan cults also focuses on trees, but this evidence is intrinsically problematic, since all of it was produced by foreign Christians who had never seen any pagan rites and in any case had all kinds of reasons to embellish their stories. The historian Adam of Bremen, for example, recounts in the 1070s a story about pagan rituals at Uppsala in Sweden, where he claims that a grand sacrifice takes place every nine years. "Of every living thing that is male, they offer nine heads, with the blood of which it is customary to placate gods of this sort. The bodies they hang in the sacred grove that adjoins the temple. . . . Even dogs and horses hang there with men." As his source, Adam refers to "a Christian, seventy-two years old," who had seen the bodies hanging in the trees.

Adam also describes the temple at Uppsala, which he claims is "entirely decked out in gold." In it, "the people worship the statues of three gods." The mightiest, Thor, occupies a place in the middle of the hall, surrounded by Wodan (Odin) and Frikko (Frey) on either side. Thor, Adam claims, "presides over the air, which governs the thunder and lightning, the winds and the rains." Odin "carries on war and imparts to man strength against his enemies," whereas Frey "bestows peace and pleasure on mortals." Frey's statue "they fashion with an immense phallus."[19]

Another German historian, Bishop Thietmar of Merseburg, writing between 1013 and 1018, tells of "remarkable things" that he "has heard" about Lejre on the island of Zealand in Denmark. "Here all of them [the pagan Danes] come together every ninth year during the month of January, after the day when we celebrate the Epiphany of the Lord [January 6], and then they sacrifice to their gods ninety-nine persons and as many horses, together with dogs and hens (instead of falcons)."[20]

It is hard to know exactly what to do with testimony of this kind. On the one hand, the accounts of Thietmar and Adam appear to support each other: both report the nine-year intervals between grand sacrifices and similar numbers of sacrifices (nine or ninety-nine). But the correspondences might reflect the common clerical culture shared by Thietmar and Adam, which included certain expectations of how pagans behaved. Or Thietmar's writings may have inspired Adam. Either Scandinavian paganism attributed some sacred value to the number nine or European Christians attributed some special pagan value to it.

Some details of what Thietmar and Adam say is confirmed by archeology. A small statuette of the god Frey with a large phallus was found in 1904 in central Sweden. And what Adam says about hanging sacrificial animals in trees is to some degree supported by the Frösö find, and also by what is known about Sami bear sacrifices from as late as the eighteenth and even nineteenth centuries.[21] On the other hand, archeologists have not found in Lejre the masses of bones one would expect if ninety-nine individuals of several kinds of animals and people were sacrificed there every ninth year. Uppsala has not produced any remnants of a pagan temple. Archeologists have, however, recently uncovered a straight line of tall wooden posts standing at six-meter intervals, which apparently ended on the banks of a river, suggesting some kind of road possibly used for processions to sacrifices deposited in the river. The road was built well before the Viking Age.[22] Uppsala also possessed several great halls, just as at Lejre. Sacrifices probably were performed inside those halls, but the temple as described by Adam can hardly have existed in Uppsala. Overall, both Adam's and Thietmar's stories of pagan sacrifices are probably better read as stories meant to alarm and inspire their colleagues among the Christian clergy who made up their main audiences than as factual reports of pagan rites. In general, there is little reason to think that early medieval pagan rites in Scandinavia took place in any special buildings. Guldgubbar are often found inside halls (that is, the residences of chieftains and other great men and women), and on that evidence we can conjecture that religious rituals were carried out inside such residences. One might extrapolate that conjecture to ordinary farmhouses, as the halls are really only splendid versions of such ordinary buildings.

A single Viking Age writer is able to tell of pagan sacrifices from his own experience, even though he did not get a chance to directly observe the rites themselves. In the 1020s, King Olav Haraldsson of Norway sent some of his retainers on a diplomatic mission to Sweden. One of the envoys was the poet Sigvat Thordarson, who afterward composed a diverting poem about the hardships of the trip. The roads were unreliable, his horse limped, night quarters were abominable if they could be found at all. At one point, Sigvat and his companions sought lodging in a building but their reception was not friendly; in Raymond I. Page's amusing translation:

"No farther can you enter,
You wretch!" said the woman.
"Here we are heathens
And I fear the wrath of Odin."
She shoved me out like a wolf,
That arrogant termagant,
Said she was holding sacrifice
To elves there in her house.[23]

It is likely that the Christian Sigvat, composing his versified travelogue for the Christian court of Olav Haraldsson, exaggerated this story for effect, but some details stand out. The sacrifices took place in what at least from the outside must have appeared to be an ordinary residential building since Sigvat sought lodging there. A woman claimed to preside over the sacrifices, and Sigvat implies that she owned the house. Most historians of Scandinavian religion believe that sacrifices took place in homes—grander sacrifices in grander homes like the chieftains' halls—and that they were performed by the owners of the houses. As Sigvat's story suggests, there were no prohibitions against women performing sacrifices, unlike in Christianity.

The Arab traveler Ibrahim al-Tartushi, from Tortosa in Spain, recounted what he had learned about pagan religion when he visited Hedeby in southern Denmark in the tenth century: "They gather together for a religious festival to honor the gods, at which they eat and drink. Those that intend to sacrifice an animal set up a pole in front of their house from which they suspend a piece of the animal whose sacrifice they are offering: beef, mutton, goat or pig. In this way everyone can see how they plan to honor the gods."[24] As Ibrahim understood it, sacrifices happened at home and were associated with food and drink. We may compare this display of the sacrificed animal both with the bear heads displayed in the Frösö birch and the animals and humans mentioned by Thietmar and Adam.

Pagan rites were widespread all over Scandinavia, not just concentrated in a few places, as Adam of Bremen and other writers imagined. In the stanza before the one just quoted, Sigvat tells his audience that he came to a *hof*. This common noun has been defined as "a farm where cult meetings were regularly held for more people than those living on the farm." According to the Eddic poem *Völuspá*, the *æsir*, that is, the pagan gods (singular *ás*), at the beginning of the world "built altars (*hörg*) and high temples (*hof*)."[25] Both words are common components of place-names. Twenty-two places in Norway have names that are compounds of the name of a pagan deity and *hof*; for example, Vidarshov, outside Hamar in Norway, combines *hof* with the name of the god Viðar, Odin's son. Eighty-five other Norwegian places are simply called *Hof* or *Hov*, and forty-one combine *hof* with something other than a god's name. Such place-name evidence gives the impression that pagan cults were widespread indeed.

By mapping the hundreds of Scandinavian place-names that include divine names, one can get an idea of the spread of the cults of the different Scandinavian gods. The gods Thor, Frey, Freya, Njord, and Ull appear in place-names everywhere in Scandinavia. Odin's name, in contrast, is more common in eastern Scandinavia. There are no place-names derived from Odin in Iceland, and he never personally visits Iceland in Icelandic sagas, despite so much of their action taking place there. He does appear in the sagas in the rest of Scandinavia—for example, in Norway to tempt Olav Tryggvason to apostatize from Christianity.[26]

Taken together, the evidence for pagan cult in Scandinavia suggests great variation and diversity. Odin was perhaps more popular in the east than in the west, and some scholars have also suggested that his popularity grew over time. Archeological sites such as Frösö and Uppåkra as well as what contemporaries wrote about Lejre and Uppsala convey an image of sacrifices and other cult acts on a grand scale, important for at least the regional communities. In contrast, Sigvat's encounter with sacrifices to "elves" in a farmhouse show pagan cult on a more modest scale. The meager sources hint at a diverse and rich landscape of beliefs and cult practices. Christian practices and beliefs entered into this landscape, at first making it even richer and more diverse, but eventually Christianity with its strict requirement of exclusivity suppressed other religious expressions. We turn now to the long and multifaceted process through which Scandinavia became Christian.

Scandinavia converted to Christianity through a slow and prolonged process that played out on many different levels over several centuries. The end result was the high-medieval Christian monarchies, under which much of the population regularly participated in Christian rituals such as baptism, funerals, and the Eucharist, and the Church strove to teach congregations to embrace correct beliefs. At least initially, however, religious conversion was more about changing how people behaved, about which religiously significant acts they carried out, than about changing beliefs.

The immediate reasons for conversion were the needs and goals of Scandinavian chieftains and kings. We usually think of conversion as coming about through the fervent and patient work of missionaries converting through preaching and persuasion. That romantic model does not, however, apply to the large mass of conversions in early medieval Europe. Missionaries were few, and it took a long time before a network of parish churches had built up any real coverage for the population at large. Missionaries and preachers could have reached and tried to persuade only a small minority even if they could make themselves understood in the Scandinavian languages, which were foreign to them. So missionaries' work cannot explain why every informed observer, including the pope, thought of Scandinavia as a Christian region by the twelfth century at the latest. A close reading of the sources reveals a different and more likely explanation: kings and chieftains used religion as a community-building tool in their political economy. In the gift-exchange system, exotic artifacts were particularly valued as high-status gifts; the gift of religion and its ability to enhance and deepen relationships among people made it particularly suitable for chieftains building loyal followings. Any religion works for such purposes—indeed, we have seen Earl Håkon using Norse paganism—but Christianity works particularly well, because of its prestigious associations with the great rulers of Europe and because, unlike paganism, it can be monopolized.

A soapstone mold from northern Jutland in Denmark conveys an instructive image of how Christianity slowly entered Scandinavian culture without immediately driving out previous religions. The artisan who owned the mold was able to cast either a Christian cross or a model of Thor's hammer, Mjöllnir, or even both at the same time, in the three spaces of the mold. He or she lived in a time when Christian and pre-Christian religions existed side by side in Scandinavia. This would have been the normal state of affairs during most of the Viking Age.

The Danish metalsmith was not an isolated case. Others embraced both Christian and pre-Christian symbolism in a kind of syncretistic approach to different religions, like the man who in the eleventh century was buried in Eura in western Finland with a Thor's hammer amulet alongside a Christian cross hanging around his neck. Similarly, in the tenth century a woman was buried close to Hedeby accompanied by a silver cross amulet but in a casket decorated with hammer symbols.[27]

Perhaps these persons were similar to Helgi the Lean, a man who supposedly was the original settler of the Akureyri region in northern Iceland toward the end of the ninth century. By the late thirteenth century, he was imagined as a man who "believed in Christ, invoked Thor when it came to voyages and difficult

FIG. 22. This soapstone mold from Trendgården in Jutland, Denmark, demonstrates that the conversion of Scandinavia from paganism to Christianity was a slow process. An artisan could use this tool to cast either a Christian cross or a model of Thor's hammer, the most important symbols of the competing religions. Photo courtesy of Nationalmuseet, Copenhagen.

matters." Thor had showed him where to beach his ship and claim land, but he still called his land Kristsnes, "Christ's point."[28] The stories about Helgi the Lean may have been embellished or even invented to entertain Icelanders during the High Middle Ages, but they still catch a basic truth about conversion. Most Scandinavians of the conversion era did not accept Christianity as a readymade package of beliefs and practices; instead, they accepted a few ideas at a time. We can see this, for example, in Swedish burials, which already in the ninth century began to be oriented west–east, as was the custom when Christians were buried. No one would argue that all who were thus buried in ninth-century Sweden were Christians. They had simply accepted and adopted a new burial custom, whether or not they knew that it was inspired by Christianity. The same can be said about the fashion for inhumations (burials of the unburned body) that spread in Scandinavia during and around the Viking Age, replacing cremations as the most common mode of burial. Christians frowned on, and even outlawed, cremations.

That Scandinavians began to inhume their dead does not mean that they had become Christians; it simply means that they had come into contact with the custom of inhumation and had adopted it, perhaps unaware of the religious implications of their choice. Estrid's grave (discussed in detail in chapter 7) illustrates the same tendency to accept some Christian practices without abandoning at once everything that Christianity condemned. Estrid, who clearly was Christian, was buried with her lindenwood box, weights, and a knife, despite Christianity's command that the faithful be buried without grave goods.

Christian practices, ideas, and beliefs may have begun creeping into Scandinavia quite early, perhaps as soon as the Roman Empire converted to Christianity in the fourth century. Scandinavians served as mercenaries in the Roman army and may have picked up Roman culture, including religion, and brought it with them if they returned home. When the Vikings from the very late eighth century began to capture people in western Europe, bringing them to Scandinavia to serve as slaves, they brought Christians into their households, and some Christian ideas certainly came that way. When Ansgar, one of the first missionaries known to have visited Scandinavia, arrived in the Swedish trade town Birka in 829, he encountered captives who were Christian.[29] That Christian ideas and practices penetrated Scandinavia before the region converted in any real sense is vouched for by the tenth-century historian Widukind of Corvey, who, when he begins to tell the story of how the Danes converted, informs us that "the Danes were of old Christian." They still needed conversion. The pre-Christian religions of Scandinavia had little problem accepting new religious practices and new gods into their open pantheon. Widukind in fact had heard about preconversion Danes who accepted "that Christ certainly was a god, but claimed that other gods were greater than he, since they revealed themselves through greater signs and omens."[30] Christianity was already there in some form, however irregular, when the first missionaries arrived in Scandinavia.

The missionaries, thus, did not so much introduce Christianity into Scandinavia as they brought a powerful idea: the Christian idea of conversion, which insisted on exclusivity and radical change. The Christian convert must "put off the old self" (Ephesians 4:22), including the Norse open pantheon of gods and any ritual or custom deemed pagan, and "put on the new self" (4:24), accepting the entire package of Christian beliefs and practices at once. This was what missionaries preached when they began to show up in Scandinavia in the early ninth century. They directed their message primarily to kings and powerful persons, who, reciprocally, desired the attention of missionaries as representatives of both a prestigious faith and powerful earthly rulers, their royal and imperial patrons.

Intellectuals in the Carolingian kingdom had discussed the possibility of converting the Scandinavians even before the Viking attacks began in earnest in the late eighth century. For example, in 789 the grammarian and theologian Alcuin wrote, from Charlemagne's court, a letter to an unnamed friend who was abbot in the eastern border regions of Charlemagne's realms, asking him "if there is any hope about converting the Danes."[31] Unfortunately, no response has been preserved. Alcuin and others at the court were interested in the prospects of converting the Danes for political reasons, and the topos of intransigent Danish paganism often turns up in their writings.[32] By conquering Saxony (corresponding to today's western Germany), Charlemagne had for the first time brought his Frankish kingdom into closer contact with the Danes, who became his neighbors to the northeast.

The Danes were becoming a political headache for the Franks; they sheltered political refugees from Saxony and were hostile to some of the Franks' allies beyond their borders. For such reasons, Charlemagne and his successors continued to meddle in Danish affairs, for example by supporting the friendly Danish chieftain Harald, one of several who fought for power in Denmark after the death of King Godfrid in 810. They also sent missionaries to Denmark. In 823, Emperor Louis the Pious demonstrated the importance of his relations with Denmark by putting the Scandinavian mission in the hands of a great churchman, Archbishop Ebo of Reims, whose mother may have been the emperor's wet nurse. Ebo personally went to Denmark several times, but we do not know any details of what he did there. We do know that King Harald was not very good at holding on to power in the fluid politics of Denmark, and the emperor had to assist him several times. In 826, Harald again fled into exile in the Frankish Empire, and this time he cemented his alliance with the Franks by accepting baptism at the imperial palace of Ingelheim outside Mainz, the emperor himself serving as his godfather. Harald was the first Scandinavian king known to have been baptized, but his kingship never became more than an empty title, for despite the emperor's help, he was unable to take back power in Denmark. He lived the rest of his life as the emperor's pensioner. His nephew Roric similarly carved out a lordship for himself within the Frankish Empire, as we saw in chapter 3.

When Harald tried to return to Denmark following his baptism, Christian clerics accompanied him. Among them was a young monk from Corvey named Ansgar. After Harald failed in his purpose to take back power in Denmark and settled with his followers inside the Frankish Empire, Ansgar set up a school for their children and for Scandinavian slave boys he had bought. The idea was to educate them to become effective missionaries who spoke the native language. While Ansgar was thus occupied, Emperor Louis received messengers from a Swedish king requesting that priests be sent to him. Ansgar and another monk, Witmar, were selected to go, while Gislemar stayed with King Harald. Ansgar and Witmar arrived in the trade town of Birka after an adventurous voyage, during which pirates attacked their ship. The two monks swam ashore and had to walk the rest of the way without their books, which they lost in the attack. In Birka, King Björn received them kindly.

Ansgar and Witmar settled in Birka for a year and a half, ministering to the Christians among the population and attempting to win new converts. Ansgar's pious biographer, Rimbert, mentions a single convert by name, the city prefect Heriger, in addition to vague phrases about "many" seeking to be baptized. Such formulations damn with faint praise; it does not look as if Ansgar's mission was brilliantly successful. Otherwise, the two monks ministered to Christian slaves who had been captured during Viking raids in Europe.

Until then, the mission to the North had been led by Archbishop Ebo, but he had picked the wrong side in the 833 rebellion against

Emperor Louis, so when the emperor came back from captivity in 834, Ebo was summarily dismissed and imprisoned in a monastery. Now Ansgar and his colleague Gauzbert became leaders in the work of converting Scandinavia, dividing the mission area between them. Gauzbert was in charge of Sweden, where he traveled to be honorably received by the king. Ansgar, meanwhile, was in charge of Denmark, but there is no evidence that he was able to return there after the Harald fiasco of 826 until around 850.

Ansgar built the first churches in Scandinavia, in Birka and Hedeby, according to Rimbert. Ansgar and Rimbert were also responsible for creating the first ecclesiastical structure that encompassed Scandinavia. The mission that Ansgar and Gauzbert led encountered serious difficulties in the 840s. Gauzbert was expelled from Sweden, and one of his priests was killed there. Ansgar's mission station in Hamburg, which at the time was a border fortification, was wrecked in a Viking attack in 845, when Ansgar himself barely escaped with his life. Even worse was the death of Emperor Louis the Pious in 840 and the subsequent division of his empire into three portions for his three sons. Ansgar and Hamburg ended up in the kingdom of Louis the German, while the monastery Turholt in Frisia, which the old emperor had given him as a source of income, was in the portion allotted to King Charles the Bald, who had no intention of allowing Ansgar to continue to collect revenue within his kingdom. After some uncertainty, in 848 Ansgar became bishop in Bremen in northern Germany, while Gauzbert became bishop in Osnabrück.

Ansgar had greater ambitions, however. He craftily succeeded in creating an archbishopric for himself in northern Germany with the official assignment to convert all of Scandinavia, through a combination of political maneuvering and outright forgery. He sent clerics to Sweden and returned there himself in about 850, when he also traveled to Denmark. We know of Ansgar's activities through the biography that his successor, Rimbert, wrote about him, which was primarily meant to disguise Ansgar's forgeries and a few new ones that Rimbert himself added. He made it appear that in 864 the pope had joined together two bishoprics in Hamburg and Bremen and, in the process, freed Bremen from obedience to its superior archbishop in Cologne. Thus was the foundation laid for the combined archbishopric of Hamburg-Bremen, which after a few decades became an accepted feature of the northern Church. The archbishopric inherited the assignment first given to Ansgar of converting Scandinavia, which became part of its territory until the early twelfth century.[33]

Beginning around 850, Ansgar visited the Danish king Horik frequently both as a missionary and as a diplomatic envoy from King Louis the German. Rimbert's claim that Ansgar became a friend and confidant of the king probably exaggerated how close Horik and Ansgar were, but it nonetheless captures something essential about the missionaries in Viking Age Scandinavia: they came to Scandinavia because Scandinavian kings and chieftains wanted them to come, and they typically stayed close to those who invited them. Ebo's original mission was closely related to the ambitions of King Harald, and Ansgar and Gauzbert went to Sweden at the request of the king.[34]

There are many other examples of collaboration between kings and missionaries from later Scandinavian history. The Norwegian kings Olav Tryggvason (d. 1000) and Olav Haraldsson (d. 1030) brought with them bishops and other clerics from England when they conquered Norway, including the bishops John, Grimkel, and Sigfrid. The Swedish king Emund (d. ca. 1060) had brought to Sweden a bishop Osmund who had received consecration in Poland although he seems to have been an Englishman educated in Germany. The missionary Poppa, later archbishop of Cologne under the name Folkmar, was Danish king Harald Bluetooth's guest at a feast in the 960s, when he reportedly proved the superiority of Christianity to the king and his court through a miracle, thus converting them. Scandinavian kings and chieftains embraced missionaries as bringers of a prestigious religion and as representatives of truly powerful European rulers, thus adding luster to their courts. They used that splendor to build up their own power.

Olav Tryggvason was a Viking before he became a king, and he led Viking bands on raids in Europe. In 994, he joined forces with the Danish king Svein Forkbeard to attack England, wreaking havoc, as Vikings tended to do, and famously defeating an

Anglo-Saxon army under the ealdorman Byrhtnoth at Maldon in 994, among other feats. The English king Ethelred offered to pay a huge tribute of sixteen thousand pounds of silver if the Vikings would stop their plundering. Olav and Svein agreed, and as a part of the settlement, Olav was invited to King Ethelred's hunting lodge Andover, where the king gave him royal gifts and "received him at the hands of Bishop" Alfheah. That Ethelred received Olav at the bishop's hands means that he was his godfather at baptism. Gifts obliged the recipient to give countergifts. Ethelred's gifts meant that Olav was obliged, as a countergift, to keep his promise never to return to plunder England. When Olav was baptized with Ethelred as his godfather, the agreement was sealed by their entering into religiously sanctioned kinship. After gift giving and baptism, Olav and Ethelred were bound to each other with multiple bonds of honor and obligation. The Anglo-Saxon chronicler notes that Olav in fact was true to his word and never returned, thus preserving his honor.[35]

After the ceremony at Andover, Olav was able to return home to Norway bringing two kinds of capital. First, he had his share of the silver that Ethelred had given to him and Svein, some of which he would have generously handed out to his warriors. Second, he returned home with valuable cultural and political capital. He returned as kin of powerful King Ethelred, his spiritual father, and as someone who was able to offer to his followers the most prestigious religion of Europe, for he brought clergy with him from England.

Olav built his prestige and power and bound his followers to him by sharing all these forms of capital. He was successful in winning Norway because he was able to recruit sufficient numbers of warriors and to persuade enough people to join him. Here we see how missionaries came to Scandinavia because kings and chieftains needed them to help meet political goals.

In 995, Norway was dominated by Earl Håkon Sigurdsson in Lade, the man who used his paganism as a rallying point for his followers. He simply could not match Olav's resources, either material or spiritual. He was a devotee of the old indigenous religion, which certainly was also useful to create religiously sanctioned bonds.

Håkon had, as we have seen, worked hard to use this religion to create a community focused on himself. But Christianity was more powerful for building communities. With its associations to the great rulers of the time, the kings of England and France, the emperors of Germany and Byzantium, Christianity carried with it much more prestige than the old Scandinavian religion. Earl Håkon realized that he was outmatched, and he did not seriously contend Olav's invasion. Olav quickly became the undisputed ruler of Norway and began to call himself king.

As king, Olav attacked pagan religion. His contemporaries praised him as a destroyer of temples and a breaker of *horgs* (outdoor stone altars for sacrifices). Later storytellers, active in the twelfth and following centuries, filled in the story with fictions about how Olav Tryggvason traveled around Norway to persuade people to accept the new religion, using torture to force some recalcitrant magnates to convert. At meetings of entire regions, Olav supposedly preached so persuasively that hordes of people decided to accept baptism then and there. In other words, Olav conformed to the standard image of a missionary. We might perhaps wonder how Olav became such a good preacher; his previous life as a raiding and marauding Viking scarcely would have trained him in homiletics. The historian Oddr Snorrason, who lived in northern Iceland toward the end of the twelfth century, had an answer: Olav had in a dream been visited by the great missionary St. Martin of Tours, who promised to provide the words Olav needed when he preached. Oddr and his colleagues constructed with hagiographic elements an image of an appropriately behaving missionary king. This image has very little to do with what actually happened.[36]

As a great missionary hero of Christianity, the king, when converting Norway, was portrayed as carrying out the injunction of Christ, "Go ye, therefore and teach all nations, baptizing them" (Matthew 28:19). Olav's religious convictions, if any, may indeed have played a role, but political considerations must have been decisive. By destroying temples and pagan altars, Olav strove to remove his competitors' ability to organize resistance to his rule around the pagan religion. At the same time, Olav used the Christian religion to gain followers. Some of Earl Håkon's followers abandoned him to follow Olav instead. One of them was the skald Hallfred Ottarsson, who himself tells us that he was baptized with Olav as his godfather and that he then received many gifts. In other words, Olav re-created his own baptism under Ethelred's sponsorship.

The story of Olav Tryggvason's namesake Olav Haraldsson (d. 1030) is in many ways similar. This Olav had gained a great fortune as a Viking and by serving as a mercenary for King Ethelred of England. He had accepted baptism in Normandy from Ethelred's brother-in-law, Archbishop Robert of Rouen, himself the brother of Duke Richard of Normandy. Olav Haraldsson shared his religion and his material wealth with those he wanted as allies or followers, to persuade them to join and to remain. "I became very happy that day, when [King Olav] lifted my daughter home from heathendom," composed the skald Sigvat Thordarson when remembering how the king had been his daughter Tofa's godfather.[37] In other poems, Sigvat recalled the magnificent material gifts the king had given him, including a gold-wound sword and golden arm rings. Sigvat appears, in turn, to have been the godfather of Olav's son, the future king Magnus.

The Norwegian magnate Eyvind in Oddernes, similarly, remembered Olav Haraldsson's godfatherhood years afterward, when he had a runestone raised next to his church. He identified himself as "St. Olav's godson."[38] In so doing, Eyvind claimed a share in the spiritual network centered on Olav Haraldsson, including his links to the rulers of Normandy and England. Eyvind must have been a chieftain in his own right (as suggested by his ability to build a church) and was himself, through his runestone and his church, promising those who wanted to follow him a connection to that prestigious spiritual network.

The examples of the two Olavs demonstrate how kings and chieftains used religion and especially its community-building capabilities as means to achieve their political goals. Our sources are full of examples of kings who strove to eradicate pagan religion. In Widukind's story about the conversion of Harald Bluetooth of Denmark, for example, the most important result of the conversion was that the king "decided that Christ would be the only god to be worshipped, and he ordered that his people should reject the idols." ("Idols" was the normal term used in Christian writings for any kind of non-Christian deity.) We have already seen that Olav Tryggvason pushed hard to eradicate paganism in Norway. It would be ill-advised to attempt to argue that these kings' hostility to pagan religion had nothing to do with their personal religious convictions and beliefs, but the political expediency of preventing competitors from using paganism as a rallying point would have been of utmost importance.

Christianity became established in Scandinavia during the Viking Age. This period witnessed the step-by-step construction of an institutional Church, with regular bishoprics and parishes, church buildings, and hierarchies of bishops, priests, and other clerics. This institutional Church lived in Scandinavia under the control of the king at least until the twelfth century. This institutional process was, as we have seen, paralleled by the Christianization of customs and beliefs, which, however, was a slower process, beginning long before the Viking Age and continuing long afterward.

The archbishops of Hamburg-Bremen continued Ansgar's work of converting Scandinavia and cultivating contacts with the rulers there. They also strove to build up a regularly organized Church with cathedrals and parish churches in the North. The process began in Denmark in the middle of the tenth century, even before King Harald had converted. When a meeting of Church leaders was held in Ingelheim, Germany, in 948, three bishops from Denmark appeared for the first time: Horath of Schlesvig/Hedeby, Liafdag of Ribe, and Reginbrand of Aarhus.[39] These first regular Scandinavian bishops all resided in important trade towns on the Jutland peninsula. Over the following centuries, regular bishoprics were instituted everywhere. An administrative survey from the first decades of the twelfth century lists some twenty Scandinavian bishoprics.[40] Iceland got its first bishopric, in Skalholt, in 1056, and Greenland was provided with its own bishop at Gardar in 1124. The organization of the medieval episcopacy in Scandinavia was completed when a bishop was appointed for Finland in the early thirteenth century. He was soon to reside in Turku (Åbo) on the west coast.

The Scandinavian Church was subordained to the German archbishop in Hamburg-Bremen, which was a thorn in the side of

Scandinavian rulers, since they might thus be thought of as subjects of the German emperor. They preferred a church independent
of foreign powers and worked with the pope to accomplish this.
The many schisms between the pope and the German emperor
(often supported by the archbishop in Bremen) in the late eleventh
and twelfth centuries helped their cause, and Pope Paschal II promoted the bishop of Lund in Denmark to archbishop in 1103. The
Scandinavian Church had thus come of age and become independent of Hamburg-Bremen.

Cardinal Bishop Nicolaus Breakspear, an Englishman educated
in France, visited all three of the Scandinavian kingdoms in the
early 1150s, and his trip signaled that the region had become a regular province within Christendom, newly converted to be sure, but
no longer a mission area. The pope had given Nicolaus the job of
creating an archbishopric for each of the two kingdoms that lacked
it. Denmark already had a leader for its church in Lund, while the
cardinal now promoted Trondheim in Norway to an archiepisco-
pal see. The cathedral stands only a few kilometers from where Earl
Håkon only 160 years earlier had presided over his pagan sacrifices
and mythographical poets. When Nicolaus came to Sweden, he
found the country in the throes of a violent civil war, and he judged
the time not right for creating any archbishopric there. The cardinal still managed to organize a meeting of the Swedish church in
Linköping in 1153, where he presumably told the warring Swedes to
make peace and then agree on which bishop should be promoted.
On his way home, the cardinal left with Archbishop Eskil of Lund
the pallium (a liturgical woolen vestment looking a little like a scarf
that the pope traditionally gave to each archbishop) that he had
brought for the new head of the Swedish church province. When
the Swedes finally were able to make peace, Eskil was to give it to
a new Swedish archbishop. This happened in 1164 in Sens, France,
when Eskil in the presence of Pope Alexander III consecrated the
Cistercian monk Stephen the first archbishop of Uppsala.

Scandinavia was still sparsely populated and far away from
Rome, and its inhabitants had much to learn about Christianity, but
personal contacts between Scandinavians and the greatest Christians of the time demonstrate that the region was now firmly a part

of the European Church. Archbishop Eskil in Lund was a friend and correspondent of the famous theologian and preacher Bernard of Clairvaux, who may well also have been Archbishop Stephen's first abbot. Many of Scandinavia's churchmen and laymen came into contact with Cardinal Nicolaus when he traveled around the North; he would be elected Pope Adrian IV soon after returning to Rome, and he would continue to care deeply about the church he had helped organize in Scandinavia. A network of parish churches was being constructed; it would take some time to be completed. In central Sweden, for example, this happened only in the thirteenth century. At the same time about one thousand churches existed in Norway. The Scandinavian Church had secured a stable economic foundation with its large landholdings and most people paying tithes. Nobody could claim that Scandinavia in the twelfth century was still alien or marginal. Pagan ideas and ritual practices may still have survived here and there, certainly among the Sami of the North into the modern period, but on a small scale and away from the public eye. After centuries of violent as well as peaceful contacts, Scandinavia had become a part of the shared Christian culture of Europe.

CHAPTER 9

ARTS AND LETTERS

Through the centuries, countless throngs have visited Hagia Sophia, the magnificent basilica that Emperor Justinian built in the 530s in his capital, Constantinople (now Istanbul), and dedicated to Holy Wisdom. When new, the building was an architectural wonder of which Justinian was rightly proud; after inspecting the finished building, he is said to have exclaimed, "Solomon, I have outdone you!" (referring to the builder of the Temple in Jerusalem). What continues to amaze visitors to the building is its remarkably large dome, which has withstood the ravages of time for nearly fifteen centuries, a wonder of mathematical calculations and structural engineering in the sixth century.

The building itself, which is no longer a church, has acquired many scars over the centuries. Its walls have graffiti from different periods in different languages, which have only recently been the subject of scholarly study. Among the many words scratched into the marble of Hagia Sophia, one in particular stands out. At some point during the Viking Age a Scandinavian inscribed his name, Halvdan, in runes, in addition to a few more runes that have not yet been persuasively interpreted. It is tempting to speculate about Halvdan, who shared his name not only with the first Norse king of Northumbria and with the first known Danish envoy to the court of Charlemagne, but also with more than two dozen Scandinavians known from runic inscriptions.[1] Why was Halvdan in Hagia Sophia? Was he a Scandinavian pilgrim on his way to the Holy Land? Or was he one of the mercenaries in the emperor's elite

Varangian guard who was commanded to attend mass and, in his boredom, showed off his knowledge of runes? Was he a Christian merchant who celebrated in church the lucky outcome of a business deal? We cannot know the answers to these questions, and until the rest of the runes he inscribed are interpreted, we have no context for his name.

Halvdan was able to read and write the distinctive early medieval script system of northern Europe that we call Scandinavian runes. This was a development of Mediterranean alphabetic scripts that had been adapted to be inscribed, especially in wood but also in stone. Thousands of runic inscriptions have been preserved all around Scandinavia, most famously on the thousands of inscribed stones that dot the Nordic countryside. Most runic inscriptions were, however, made in wood and therefore have perished. We get a hint of what must have once existed through the thousands of pieces of wood with runic inscriptions that were found during archeological excavations in Bergen, Norway, where special circumstances helped the wood survive for centuries underground. The inscriptions here, most of which are from just after the end of the Viking Age, range from simple ownership notes to love poetry, from urgent merchant letters to coarse obscenities. One small piece of wood, for example, contains a small love poem in runes from about 1200: "You love me / I love you / Gunnhild. / Kiss me / I know you."[2]

Inscriptions in Scandinavian granite, rather than in wood, have a much greater chance of surviving to be read today. Thousands have been discovered, and they provide insight into Viking Age society. Most runestones are memorials to the dead, sometimes expressed in very few words—it was, after all, hard work to inscribe stones. For example, the beautiful runestone that is preserved in central Stockholm, inserted into the wall of an early modern building, simply reads: "Thorsten and Frögunn, they [erected] the stone in memory of . . . , their son."[3] The stone is damaged, with the result that the name of the couple's dead son has unfortunately been lost. As is typical of many runic inscriptions, this memorial does not give us any contextual information about either the parents or the son. We do not know what kind of people they were, how the son died, or why the parents chose to memorialize him in this way.

Other runic inscriptions are more informative and thus are a boon to historians. An example is a runestone in Rörbro, outside Ljungby in southern Sweden. Its decoration is much simpler than that of the stone in Stockholm, with the runes applied in a curved band snaking around a cross. The inscription reads:

Özzur made these monuments in memory of Eyndr, his father.
He was the most unvillainous of men,
was liberal with food
and oblivious to hate.
A good thane,
had good faith in God.[4]

Eyndr is portrayed, in neatly crafted verse with good alliteration, as a very good man—what we would expect in this genre. But his goodness is not just generalized; it is of a distinctive kind. Eyndr was a good chieftain; he was generous with food in the way a good chieftain should be (like Hrothgar in *Beowulf* or the leaders praised in skaldic poetry), and he was not one to hold grudges ("oblivious to hate"), again like a good chieftain. His goodness is emphasized in three ways: he was not at all villainous (using understatement in a way that is typical of Nordic literature), he was a good thane (the exact meaning of this term on runestones has attracted a great deal of controversy), and he was a good Christian. These characteristics made him a good chieftain in an age when Christianity was understood as exotic and therefore prestigious. The stone was inscribed after Eyndr had died, and it is likely that his son Özzur commissioned it in an effort to let everyone know that he was the primary heir who should take over his father's position in society; some of his father's good reputation should reflect on him. Another runestone a few hundred meters away memorializes another generation of the same family, but more briefly: "Eyndr and [Sve]in placed these monuments in memory of Özzur."[5] The editor of the inscription believes that Eyndr is the same man as the good chieftain of the other inscription. This Özzur would, then, be the grandfather of the other Özzur.

The Viking Age was the high point of runic inscriptions on stones, but runes were used for two millennia. The oldest examples of Scandinavian runes are from soon after the beginning of the Common Era. They continued to be in use long after the end of the Viking Age. When runes became the object of antiquarian interest in the sixteenth and seventeenth centuries, one of the foremost scholars was Johannes Bureus, reportedly taught by a rune-literate farmer from the Swedish province of Dalarna. Bureus published Swedish primers that also taught runic writing, with the result that some Swedish officers serving on the European continent during the Thirty Years' War (1618–1648) were able to use runes as a readymade code language in their letters to one another. Runes continued to be used even longer in peasant milieus, especially in the province of Dalarna. The last time runes were authentically used was as late as 1900, when the young woman Anna Andersdotter carved into the wall of a shieling (mountain hut) her initials and three runic characters forming the Swedish dialect word meaning that she cared for livestock there: "AAD *gät* 1900."[6]

Knowledge of runes survived in Sweden, and popular books directed at a broad reading public spread this knowledge. This is the background of the hoax runestone that the Swedish immigrant farmer Olof Ohman, in Kensington, Minnesota, fabricated in the late nineteenth century. He pretended that the inscription had been made in 1362. It contains an account of a bloody battle between Scandinavian settlers and American Indians. The "discovery" was a sensation, and to this day many believe in the authenticity of the inscription, despite plentiful evidence that it was made long after the Middle Ages.[7]

Even a quick glance at the *futhark* (the runic alphabet) suggests that it derives from Mediterranean scripts, most likely the Latin script that Westerners still use today. The first rune in the futhark stands for the sound "f." It clearly derives from a capital F; the two cross strokes have simply been turned diagonally, suggesting that the runes were originally designed to be inscribed in wood, where it is hard to cut straight lines across the grain. Other runes remove a stroke or two while still retaining enough for the letter to be recognizable—for example, the к-rune, which rationalizes away one of the two diagonal strokes in a Latin K. Similarly, the two vertical strokes in the Latin letter N are combined into one to form the N-rune.

Each of the runes has a name, typically a common noun beginning with the relevant sound. The F-rune, for example, is called *fehu in Proto-Germanic (fé in Old Norse), which means "cattle," and by extension "wealth." Like any system of writing in older times, runes were sometimes thought to have magical properties, and then their names played a role in whatever potency was ascribed to each rune. For example, the inscription on the Lindholm amulet, a piece of bone that was inscribed at some point in or around the fifth century, is generally agreed to contain invocations of pagan deities. The text begins with a few words that are recognizable, although difficult to interpret exactly: "I, erilaz, am here called wily." Then follows a nonsensical sequence of runes: "AAAAAAAAZZZNN[N]BMUTTT:ALU:" The rune here transcribed as "A" was called *ansuz in Proto-Germanic (ás in Old Norse), which means "god," and the rune transcribed as "T" was called by the name of a god, *Tiwaz. The sequence of runes, thus, seems to begin and end (before "ALU," which may be the word from which English "ale" derives) with divine invocations—in other words, a kind of magic—but there is no agreement on exactly what the runes in the middle mean.

When runes first appeared, the futhark had twenty-four different runes. Inscriptions in this so-called older futhark are typically short and difficult to interpret, especially because the language in which they were written, Proto-Germanic, is incompletely known today. Around the eighth century, Scandinavia went through significant linguistic changes, which resulted in a new, simplified runic alphabet. The younger futhark, which includes only sixteen different runes, was the only alphabet used during the Viking Age. Modern scholars find it much easier to interpret these inscriptions, mostly because the Old Norse language is better known than its Proto-Germanic ancestor. What now sometimes provides a challenge to understanding is that only sixteen different characters are used to represent many more different sounds, meaning that some runes may carry many different phonetic values.

Runic inscriptions often provide insights into the history of Scandinavian society during the Viking Age. Occasionally a rune-stone even tells us about historical events. A stone found at the site of the early medieval trading town Hedeby, now in northwestern Germany, gives much information: "Thorulf, Svein's retainer, raised this stone in memory of Erik, his fellow, who died when men attacked Hedeby. And he was a steersman, a very good man." Erik would have died when the Danish king Svein Forkbeard took back Hedeby from the occupation of the German emperor Otto II in 983. Erik was the "fellow" (*felaga* in the inscription, the Norse word from which the modern English word is derived) of Thorulf, who was a member of King Svein's retinue. Thus, one suspects that Erik also was Svein's retainer. Erik was a *drengr*, like those who "sought" (that is, attacked) Hedeby. A *drengr* is not just any man but a valiant and warlike one. Erik was also the steersman of a ship, implying that he held the rudder when sailing or rowing, and he probably also commanded the people of the ship when they were fighting.[8]

The longest preserved runic inscription on stone is the strikingly elegant runestone in Rök, Sweden, which contains about 750 runes.[9] Parts of the inscription are written in cipher, and some use the older futhark, which was already out of use when the inscription was made. The purpose, clearly, is to make the text difficult to interpret and thus mysterious. Most of the inscription appears in the younger futhark, but even its interpretation is much debated. The meaning of the first few words, however, is clear: "In memory of Vemod stand these runes. And Varin wrote them, the father, in memory of his dead son." Like almost every runestone, the Rök stone is a memorial.

The problems begin with the immediately following rune sequence, made more difficult by the fact that the rune artist who inscribed this stone did not mark where one word ends and the next begins. The following runes literally read: "SAKUMUKMINIÞAT," and this is a formula that returns several times in the inscription. It seems clear that the last three runes represent the conjunction or the pronoun *þat*, "that," but how should one interpret the previous eleven runes? Scholars have understood these words in different ways. Here are a few examples of suggested normalizations into standard Old Norse and translations of the runes:

SAKUMUKMINIÞAT

ságum yggmænni þat	"we saw that terrifying figure"
sagum ungmænni þat	"we say to the young men that" or
	"we say that to the young men"
sagum ungminni þat	"we say that recent memory"
sagum mogminni þat	"we say that folktale" or
	"say to the people that tale"!

Each of these transcriptions (and several others) are possible interpretations of the runes, illustrating how the same rune may reflect several different sounds (the u-rune in this sequence has, for example, been variously read as *y*, *u*, and *o*). The nasal sound before *g* represented in modern print by *n* does not have to be spelled out in runes. Also, according to runic orthography, a sound that appears twice in a row needs to be spelled only once, even when the sounds belong to different words (which explains how scholars have been able, in the last example, to derive two m-sounds from one M-rune). The differing translations also illustrate how ambiguous syntax may be in laconic statements such as these. The interpretations are very different, and our understanding of the rest of the inscription will differ widely depending on how we understand this line.

The basic sense of the sentence that follows the introductory words we just examined is quite clear, and most agree that it should be translated something like this: "which the two war booties were, which twelve times were taken as war booty, both together from different men." When it comes to explaining what this actually means, however, scholars will be influenced by how they interpreted the words at the beginning of the sentence. Scholars who take the beginning to mean "we say that folktale" take what follows as an allusion to a heroic legend, story, or "folktale" about some famous and attractive war booty that changed hands many times. War booty was important to Viking society in Scandinavia, as we have seen in several different contexts, so this interpretation is attractive.

Scholars who, instead, read the first words as "we saw that ter-rifying figure" have associated the Rök text with a riddle in Old English that begins "I saw a creature," especially since that crea-ture carries booty home from war. In the riddle, another figure shows up and "recapture[s] the booty," driving away the previous possessor. Most agree that the riddle is about the moon stealing light (the "booty") from the sun, but having to return it, as hap-pens every month when the moon goes through its phases. There are twelve months in the year, so the Rök stone's words about war booty taken twelve times could be about the moon stealing light from the sun twelve times in a year. This radically different inter-pretation has as much claim to being what Varin intended when he commissioned this magnificent and mysterious monument in memory of his son.

Whichever interpretation one follows, the Rök stone is about the imaginative world of the society where it was inscribed. Varin and his stonecutter were thinking either of a body of legendary sto-ries about heroes and adventures, or about a mysterious cosmologi-cal world of celestial bodies and light coming and going. In a way, the Rök stone is, if not quite a tabula rasa, then at least capable of so many interpretations that we may project our own ideas of what Viking society was like on its malleable sequence of 750 runes. It is a pity that the inscription is so hard to interpret, since it would pro-vide the most detailed insight into the worldview of Scandinavians before their conversion to Christianity if we could be certain how to understand its mystery.

Regardless of which interpretation of the Rök stone one adopts, its contents are literary. The inscription even contains a poetic stanza in the Old Norse meter known as *fornyrðislag*, mean-ing approximately "the meter of ancient words." It is not unusual to find poetry on runestones. Only one inscription, however, contains a complete stanza in *dróttkvætt*, "the meter suitable for a lord's band of retainers," which is the queen of Old Norse meters, the most elegant, difficult, and interesting of them all.

A beautifully shaped piece of granite, partially covered with runes, stands at Karlevi on the long and narrow island of Öland in the Baltic Sea close to the Swedish mainland. Granite is unusual on

FIG. 23. The Karlevi runestone contains a complete stanza in the artful Viking Age meter known as dróttkvætt. The poem praises the martial virtues of the dead chieftain Sibbi; the inscription was made by his retinue. Photo: Bengt A. Lundberg, courtesy of Riksantikvarieämbetet, Stockholm.

this island, which consists almost entirely of limestone. The inscription begins normally enough with a memorial formula: "This stone is set up in memory of Sibbi *goða* [= chieftain], son of Foldar, and his retinue set." The dead man had been a chieftain and the memorial was erected by his loyal retainers.

The standard memorial formula is followed by a complete poetic stanza, which in modern translation reads thus:

> The tree [= a man] of the enemies of Þrúðr [a valkyrie; a man of
>   battle = warrior] whom
> the noblest deeds followed—all men know that—lies
> hidden in this mound; a more righteous wagon-Viðurr
>   [= seafarer]
> upon Endil's broad expanses, one strong in battle,
> will not rule land in Denmark.[10]

The translation demonstrates some of the peculiarities of Old Norse poetry. Key words are replaced by complicated circumlocutions, so-called *kennings*. Thus, the prosaic word "warrior" is replaced by "the tree [trees are typically men in kennings] of the enemies of [the valkyrie = battle goddess] Þrúðr." Similarly, the word "sea" is replaced by "Endil's [= a sea god] broad expanses." In fact, the word translated by "broad expanses," *jǫrmungrundar*, also appears (in Old English, *eormengrund*) in a similar context in the poem *Beowulf*. The hero Beowulf has just injured the monster Grendel, and the warriors celebrate his prowess: "across the wide world, there was none better under the sky's expanse among shield warriors."[11] The similarity of diction and of tone suggests that the poetry and societies of Viking Age England and Scandinavia were closely linked.

But these circumlocutions are not the only features that makes this sequence of words into unusually complex poetry. To explore other characteristics of this kind of verse, we need to quote the stanza in the original Old Norse, and to look a little more closely at some of the words:

> Folginn liggr, hinn's fylgðu
> (flestr vissi þat) mestar
> dæðir, dolga Þrúðar

draugr i þeimsi haugi:
mun't reið-Viðurr ráða
rógstarkr i Danmǫrku
Endils jǫrmungrundar
ørgrandari landi.

The dróttkvætt stanza is typically very regular, consisting of eight lines, each with three stresses, as in the Karlevi poem. Each line has six syllables. There are several patterns of rhyme to explore. Taking the lines two by two, each pair contains three words that alliterate, beginning with the same sound—always two in the first line and the first word of the second line. In the first pair of lines, the words *folginn*, *fylgðu*, and *flestr* alliterate on *f*. In the second pair, the alliterating words are *dæðir*, *dolga*, and *draugr*. All vowels (as well as *j*) alliterate, as in the last pair: *Endils, jǫrmungrundar, ørgrandari*.

Alliteration is a kind of rhyme, known as head rhyme or initial rhyme, but the alliterations just outlined do not exhaust the rhymes of this verse. There is also internal rhyme within each line: the next to last syllable rhymes with another syllable in the same line. In even lines, there is full rhyme: *flest(r)* and *mest(ar)*, *draug(r)* and *haug(i)*, and so on. Odd lines instead sport half-rhyme, where different vowels are followed by the same consonant or consonant cluster, for example *folg(inn)* and *fylg(ðu)*, *dæð(ir)* and *Þrúð(ar)*.

There is even more to the artfulness of this stanza, which is typical of the dróttkvætt meter. The syntax is willfully complicated, with terms belonging together placed as far as possible from each other. The opening words, "he lies hidden" (*folginn ligger*), are left in suspension until the clause is completed in line four: "in this mound" (*i þeimsi haugi*). Similarly, in the second half-stanza: the beginning, "a man will not rule" (*munat reið-Viðurr ráða*), does not get its object (what does he rule?) until the very last word of the verse, "the land" (*landi*).

When Viking Age graves are excavated, they often reveal ingenious stratagems to prevent the dead person from coming back to haunt the living. Sometimes boulders have been placed on top of the corpse; often the dead person's weapons have been made impossible to use. Clearly, Viking Age Scandinavians believed that dead people might come back as ghosts to haunt them unless they took the necessary precautions.[12] In fact, the Karlevi stone, placed on top of a burial mound, screams, "Danger! Ghosts!" Taken by itself, and read as prose rather than poetry, the middle line (which is prominently inscribed at the center of the stone) *draugr i þeimsi haugi* simply and straightforwardly means "ghost in this mound." A casual but rune-literate observer would easily notice and understand this apparent prose line, "ghost in this mound"; it would take more of a concerted effort at deciphering poetry to understand that *draugr* actually does not mean "ghost,"[13] and perhaps the surface message about ghosts would have been sufficient to scare the reader away before he had time to appreciate the subtleties of the poetry.

Once a reader notices a ghost theme, it is easy to find more scary and ghastly details in the inscription. Almost immediately before the words just quoted stands the word *dolga*, which is plural genitive of *dolgr*, "enemy, opponent," although it can also mean "ghost." In the poetry the word is a part of the kenning meaning "warrior": *dolga Þrúðar draugr*, "the tree of Þrúðr's [a battle-goddess] enemies." In the inscription, the word *dolga* is immediately preceded by the word *dæðir*, "deeds"; in the syntax of the skaldic stanza, the two words are far separated from each other. A casual reader easily interprets the runes differently, especially since the same rune may stand for similar but different sounds. We have taken the sequence of runes ᛏᛅᛁᚦᛁᚱ ᛏᚢᛚᚴᛅ TAIÞIR TULKA to be transcribed *dæðir dolga*, but a reader may easily interpret them, instead, as *dauðir dólga(r)*, which means "dead ghosts."[14] If our casual reader has not yet run away screaming from this ghastly place infested with ghosts, he might look around the text a bit more and be struck by the runic sequence ᚢᚱᚴᚱᚬᚾᛏᛅᚱᛁ URKRONTARI. Most experts read this word as *ørgrandari*, which is a hapax legomenon, a word that appears nowhere else in Norse literature. Because we cannot study the word in any other context, it is far from clear exactly what it means, and it can in fact be interpreted in two radically different ways.

We shall try to reconstruct how a Viking Age reader would try to make sense of the unfamiliar word *ørgrandari*, which she would never have encountered before. She would easily recognize the middle syllable *grand* as a common noun meaning "harm, injury" or some form of the verb *granda*, "to do harm, to injure." The meaning of what comes before and what follows is not so obvious. The prefix, UR, here transcribed as ør, carries two separate meanings in Old Norse; it may be taken as either negating the following word ("un-harm"), or intensifying it ("great harm"). The ending -ari can similarly be understood in two different ways. It may be taken as the ending of an adjective in comparative (corresponding to "-er" in modern English "greater"). Or -ari may be understood as the Norse ending making a verb into a noun indicating someone who does something (corresponding to "-er" in modern English "doer" or "destroyer"). Ever since the Swedish runologists Sven Söderberg and Erik Brate interpreted the inscription in 1900, every scholar has taken the prefix as a negation and the ending as the comparative: Sibbi is "more unharmful," which is a typically northern way of saying, with understatement, "more harmless," that is, "more righteous, guileless." But our imagined Viking Age reader, looking at this word out of context, could just as easily interpret it in a different way, understanding the prefix as intensifying and the ending as creating an agent noun, a person who brings great harm, "the utterly-injurer," or "the desolator."[15]

In this way, one may read the inscription on several levels. Even for experts in the field, the skaldic stanza is difficult to interpret. Its meaning would never have been obvious to any Old Norse reader standing there at the stone, perhaps in rain or fog, in snow or midwinter darkness, straining to bend her neck to read the runes, which are set in vertical bands that must be alternately read from the left and from the right. Even experts generally not afraid of ghosts and working in the comfort of their studies with photographs and dictionaries close at hand are still not entirely certain that they have interpreted correctly every word in this mysterious inscription. The stanza has clearly been constructed to contain two messages: its real, deep meaning is lavish praise for the dead chieftain Sibbi, less harmful than whom no one is. The first impression, however, is of ghosts, revenants, and conveyors of death and destruction. Composers of skaldic poetry liked to confuse their readers and listeners, using words that were meant to lead astray until the complete sense of the poem was understood. In the case of the Karlevi stone, the poet wanted to scare passersby who might not have had the time, skill, and nerves required to penetrate the complete meaning of his artfully construed stanza. With the inscription seemingly invoking utterly harmful, desolator ghosts, any intended grave robber might have thought twice before digging into the mound.

With its kennings, misleading word choice, tortured syntax, celebration of warrior prowess, and mystic euphony, the stanza on the Karlevi runestone is typical of its genre, Old Norse court poetry, except for the fact that it is the only piece of dróttkvætt poetry that has survived in a contemporary record. Hundreds of other verses survive because they were quoted in sagas composed, mainly, in Iceland from the twelfth century on. But many more have been lost forever. A medieval list of court poets known as *Skáldatal* lists more than a hundred Icelandic skalds who composed for the halls of Danish, Swedish, and Norwegian kings and chieftains. Many of them are now no more than names, and their poetry is unknown. For example, *Skáldatal* claims that eleven skalds composed for King Sverre of Norway (r. 1177–1202), but not a single poem by any of them has survived.

Skalds composed for kings and chieftains. Their poetry belongs, in the first place, to the great halls of northern Europe, where kings and chieftains inspired their warriors by means of great feasts, with food and mead and recitals of poetry:

> The scop sang
> brightly in Heorot—there was the joy of heroes[16]

The *scop* (pronounced like "shop") was the Anglo-Saxon counterpart of the skald, and this one sang in Heorot, the hall of King Hrothgar of the Danes, when Beowulf and his warriors visited. The quotation is from the Old English poem *Beowulf*. The king had his thane serve "the clear sweet drink" from an "ale-cup," and the warriors ("heroes") were satisfied. The function of parties in the halls was to make the warriors happy and impressed with their chieftains. The richness of the fare impressed, and so did the praise that the poet recited or, possibly, sang. This was poetry for warriors, and the skalds in particular celebrated the martial prowess of the chieftain and his victories in battle.

A skaldic poem consisted of several stanzas that recounted, for example, a victorious battle or a successful raiding career, usually as a series of vignettes, employing the kind of allusive and circumlocutory language that we found on the Karlevi runestone. An example is the poem *Hrynhenda*, recited by the skald Arnorr in the 1040s in front of King Magnus Olavsson (d. 1047) of Norway and Denmark.[17] Twenty stanzas are preserved, partially or entirely, which tell the story of Magnus's career. Since the verses are preserved one by one, we are not certain exactly the order in which they should be read, or even that they all are from the same poem, but the best modern reconstruction at least gives us an impression of what this kind of poetry must have been like.

"Magnus, hear a mighty poem!" Arnorr exclaims emphatically at the beginning of his poem, and for once the skald puts his word in normal prose order, not in the strained syntax typical of skaldic poetry. Everyone was meant immediately to understand this line, and to be silent and pay attention. He demands the undivided attention of the king and his warriors. Then Arnorr continues, now in less obvious syntax, with extravagant praise: "I know no other [prince] more outstanding" and "every prince is far below you." Arnorr declares his intention: "I mean to extol your prowess, prince . . . , in a swift poem." Arnorr goes on to summarize Magnus's life. After the death of his father, Olav Haraldsson, in 1030, Magnus had fled to Russia, and the poem describes how he sailed back on surging warships "with Russian metal [= weapons]" on the Baltic Sea to recruit troops in Sweden. "You did not gain a poor pick of troops," Arnorr says with typical Norse understatement. Magnus then claimed Norway. Later, he attacked and conquered Denmark and fought the Wends. Magnus is always the perfect king and warrior. Arnorr calls him the avenger of his father, a crusher of thieves, a subduer of princes, a generous man. At the helm of his warship *Visundr* (Bison) at the head of his fleet, he is an impressive sight: "Foul surf surged in against the after-deck and the helm of the warship; the red gold shuddered; the powerful hound of the fir-tree [= wind] pitched the rushing ship of fir. You steered sturdy prows from the north; . . . currents shuddered in front." In battle, Magnus is a veritable warrior god—Yggr [= Odin] of battle—who carries red shields, reddens the tongues of wolves, quells the greed of wolves, and reddens the feathers of the gull of Odin [= raven]; in other words, he kills many enemy warriors. His enemy knows he has lost the battle and bolts. Magnus is the perfect warrior king, providing not only dead enemies for carrion eaters, but also plenty of material for Arnorr's poetry:

> Avenger of Olav [Haraldsson = Magnus's father], you furnished matter for the verse; I fashion such [deeds] into words; you allow hawks of [the valkyrie] Hlǫkk [= ravens or eagles] to drink the corpse-sea [= blood]; now the poem will swell. Diminisher of the home of the reed of shields, you have, daring, performed four blizzards of arrows [= battles] in one season; mighty ruler, you are called invincible.

The one season in which Magnus fought four battles was the year 1043, when he defeated both the Wends and the Danes in his successful quest to subdue Denmark to his rule. Such feats were grist for Arnorr's poem, which expanded in length and grew in exalted eloquence until the extravagant and timeless praise of the finish: "King, another lord loftier than you will never be born under the sun."

Arnorr had done his job. He had composed a poem that praised his lord to the skies, thus inspiring those who heard it to follow the gallant king Magnus. We must imagine Arnorr performing the poem at a feast in Magnus's great mead hall, like the scop in *Beowulf*. It is hard to understand how much of the poem, with its broken syntax and enigmatic kennings, was immediately comprehensible to drunken warriors, but surely they would have been able to pick out familiar-sounding kennings and other bits and pieces. They would have been in no doubt that the stanzas were in celebration of their great hero, King Magnus, for they surely understood the purpose of the genre and of this particular poem. Such was the social role of Viking poetry: to build communities of warriors around kings and chieftains. In return, Arnorr would have received generous gifts, for which his poetry was the countergift. He pointed out in typically convoluted formulations that Magnus was a generous king—lines that in themselves were intended to inspire generosity: Magnus was a "terror of seized gold" (in other words, he gives away to his warriors and poets the gold that he conquers) and a "diminisher of surf-fire" (fire in any kind of water is a kenning for gold, so the king, again, diminishes his stores of gold by giving it away).[18]

Skaldic poetry was memorable and some of it was preserved through centuries. Verses from the ninth, tenth, and eleventh centuries are recorded in manuscripts from the thirteenth century and later. Exactly how this poetry survived until then is a much debated issue, with suggestions ranging from the verses being passed on orally from generation to generation, to their being not only written down early on but also at once accompanied by explanatory prose, making it possible for later generations to understand sometimes very far-fetched allusions.

Most of the poetry that survives does not come down to us as the multistanza poems they originally were; rather, they were included piecemeal in prose works, often functioning as evidence to prove the truth of the prose. Most preserved stanzas of Arnorr's *Hrynhenda* have been found in historical sagas telling the story of King Magnus. Typically, the prose narrative is a latter-day retelling and elaboration of what the poetry says, suggesting that the authors of the prose sagas had little or no information about the events they described except for the contemporary poetry that they quoted. For this reason, most historians avoid using the so-called historical sagas as sources for the Viking Age; they prefer to base their reconstructions of events directly on the contemporary poetry— working in parallel with the history writers of the High Middle Ages, not following them. This is why I often use poetry as a source in this book, but sagas almost never. The sagas are, nevertheless, wonderful literary texts in their own right, well worth reading for their creative richness and exciting plots.

With its graphic scenes of battle and battlefields reddened by blood and covered with enemy corpses eaten by wolves and carrion birds, skaldic court poetry was meant for the masculine locale of the mead hall, where women at best had a secondary position, like Hrothgar's queen, Wealhtheow, serving the mead in *Beowulf*. When skalds mention women, they are typically at home in Norway or Iceland, admiring the martial virility of their warrior lovers. Or the soft embrace of a warrior's wife or girlfriend is contrasted with the harsh realities of war: "In battle it was not like kissing a young widow on the high seat," or "in battle it was not at all like when a beautiful [woman] made a bed for the jarl with the curving branches of the shoulders [= arms]."[19] It is typical of the grim humor of skaldic poetry and of Norse understatement to describe the horrors of war and battle by denying that it is at all like a very pleasant situation with erotic overtones. The verses emphasize that women have nothing to do on the battlefield, and that real men are out there fighting and not lolling around at home with the women. Weak men who allow themselves to be seduced— dare one say emasculated?—by their women will lose the battle, as King Harald Hardruler himself is said to have humorously pointed out. "We shall let the anchor hold us in Randersfjord [in Denmark], while the linen-oak [= woman], the Gerðr of incantation [= woman] lulls her husband to sleep." The men of the region are not alert to Harald and his men arriving; instead they stay in bed and they will surely awaken too late, if at all.[20]

The verses about the contrast between the din of battle and the pleasures of a woman's embrace also serve to remind the warriors of victory's rewards. When the victorious warriors finally returned home, women's role was to admire them and their warlike virility. As the skald Thjodolf commented, again with typical understatement, about a victory won by Magnus: "women from Sogn [= Norwegian women, not just those in the Sognefjord region] will not receive such news with sorrow."[21]

Women subdued by virile seducers are common literary and artistic images of conquered lands. Such images show up also in skaldic poetry, as when the poet Eyvind Finnsson imagined Håkon Sigurdsson's seizure of Norway in the late tenth century as "the bride of the battle-god" [= bride of Odin = Norway's land] lying "under the arm" of the conqueror.[22] Women and the pleasures they offered were clearly part of what Norse warriors expected they would get after success in war. It is remarkable, against that background, that no western European narrative source says anything about Vikings raping women during their raids, contrary to popular expectations.[23] The most reasonable conclusion to draw from this silence in the sources is not that rape did not happen but rather that it was so common in war that the chroniclers of the time saw no reason to dwell on it, or even mention it at all. The skalds admitted, at least, that women would attempt to flee from a victorious army, as when Thjodolf Arnorsson praised King Magnus's victories in Zealand in Denmark, which forced women to run: "The maiden in Zealand learned in a single word who carried the standard. . . . For the wealth-pole [= woman] her lot was to dash through the forest."[24]

Beyond fleeing, women had no role on the real-life battlefield, according to the warrior poets of Scandinavia. Still, warlike women appeared in the imagination of Norsemen. Their literature brims with references to valkyries, those "war demons" whose job it was to choose which warriors would die on the battlefield and be taken to Valhalla to become the main god Odin's warriors.[25] One ninth-century poem is framed as a dialogue between a valkyrie and a raven, the archetypical carrion bird of skaldic poetry. The poet Thorbiörn hornklofi begins by calling for the attention of King Harald Fairhair's warriors, whom he addresses by referring to the gifts they received from the king:

Let the ring-bearers listen! . . . I shall recount the words that I heard a white, bright-haired girl [utter], when she spoke with a raven:

—

"How are you doing, ravens? From where have you come with gory beak at break of day? Flesh hangs from your claws; the stench of carrion comes from your mouth. I think you lodged last night near where you knew corpses were lying."[26]

The poem then focuses on King Harald Fairhair, who reputedly unified Norway in the ninth century. The raven claims to have followed Harald since he came out of the egg, and the king was similarly precocious: "[When] young he grew tired of cooking by the fire and sitting indoors, of a warm women's chamber"; he longed to get out on the battlefield and show his mettle as a warrior. The poet here spells out the distinction between "normal" women's indoor existence (as distinct from valkyries), where children also lived, and the glories of the (masculine) battlefield.

When they are not conversing with ravens, valkyries often show up in kennings. The hawks of the valkyrie Hlǫkk [= ravens or eagles] drank the sea of corpses [= blood] after King Magnus killed many in battle; Sibbi was a tree of the enemies of the valkyrie Þrúðr [= a war-like man]. These valkyries are undifferentiated—at least, modern scholars cannot distinguish any individual features that made Þrúðr different from Hlǫkk. The poets chose one valkyrie rather than the other depending on how well her name fit the rhyme patterns of the verse and what her name meant. Þrúðr means "strength," and Hlǫkk means "noise, din [of battle]." In this way, unearthly female beings show up in skaldic poetry, but really mostly to decorate the verse and its kennings, and generally to allude to battle; normally, they do not actually do anything in the narrative.

Skaldic verse is notably silent about romantic love. The proper subject of such poetry was war and battle, not romance. But a few romantic verses do exist, notably inserted into high-medieval sagas about skalds, which typically focus on a love story. Many critics think that these verses were written when the sagas were composed in the High Middle Ages, centuries after the end of the Viking Age.

Romantic ideas do begin to show up in skaldic poetry in the twelfth century, when they probably were influenced by the then new European ideas of courtly love. When the Scandinavian earl of the Orkneys Ragnvald visited Narbonne on his way to participate in a crusade, he was invited to a meal by the viscountess Ermengard, otherwise famous as a patron of troubadours. According to the saga retelling the adventures of the Orkney earls, Ermengard entered the hall with her women, carrying a golden cup to serve Ragnvald, who took the cup as well as her hand and put her in his lap before uttering this verse:

Wise woman, it is certain that your [hair-]growth surpasses in beauty [that of] pretty much most women with locks [like] the meal of Fróði [= gold]. The prop of the hawk-field [= prop of the arm = woman] lets her hair, yellow like silk, fall onto her shoulders; I reddened the claws of the food-hungry eagle.[27]

However romantic, skaldic poetry apparently cannot help itself: the eagle with bloody claws has to be there, even when Ragnvald is addressing in courtly and flattering ways one of Europe's most desirable unattached women. Ermengard was a widow, but she wore her hair down as if she were a young, unmarried women. The romantic praise of a woman is atypical for skaldic verse, so it is tempting to suggest that this stanza was inspired by the courtly troubadour poetry flourishing at Ermengard's court, which Ragnvald may have heard during his travels.

A few poems supposedly written by women skalds survive, but the attribution is in most cases problematic.[28] A two-stanza poem that at least has a fair chance of being authentic was composed by Steinunn Refsdóttir at the end of the tenth century. A die-hard pagan, she wrote a poem to ridicule the Christian god after the Christian missionary Thangbrand had suffered a shipwreck:

> The killer of ogresses' kin [= Thor]
> pulverized fully the mew-perch
> bison [= ship] of the bell's guardian [= priest]
> (the gods chased the steed of the strand [= ship]);
> Christ cared not for a sea-shingle
> stepper [= ship] when cargo-boat crumbled;
> I think that God hardly guarded
> the reindeer of Gylfe [= ship] at all.[29]

This stanza is a typical dróttkvætt stanza, with alliteration and rhyme in the appropriate places, and with the expected kennings, including three different ones meaning "ship." The only thing unusual about it, except for its authorship, is that it is not used for praise.

Although female skalds were unusual, we would expect more visual artists to be women. Almost all Viking Age art is anonymous, however, so it is impossible to prove or disprove this hypothesis. As we saw in chapter 7, women typically worked with textiles— for example, with weaving and embroidery—so it has often been suggested that female artists are behind the examples of textile art that survive. An embroidered tapestry was discovered in the early ninth-century Oseberg burial in Norway, the magnificent ship in which two women were buried with all kinds of luxuries (discussed in detail in chapter 4). The tapestry is poorly preserved, but it is clear that it was a long, narrow (20–23 centimeters wide) strip that probably was meant to hang on a wall. It is made from wool dyed different colors, mainly red, yellow, and black.

The Oseberg tapestry portrays a procession of two rows of horses with knotted tails. Three of the horses pull carts, one of which contains two people, apparently women. Scholars have speculated whether they represent the two women buried in the Oseberg burial (with a cart among their grave goods), and whether the tapestry was specially made to portray the burial procession. The procession in the tapestry also features a large number of men and women walking. The women wear long dresses with trains and cloaks, and some of them carry spears, as do many of the men. Their hair appears to be stuffed into bulging headdresses.[30]

In their attire, the women on the Oseberg tapestry are reminiscent of the valkyries welcoming slain warriors to Valhalla as portrayed on the Gotland picture stones. On these stones, many women do not have their hair hidden by headdresses, but have let it down, as Ermengard is reported to have done when Earl Ragnvald visited her in Narbonne. The valkyries of the picture stones serve food and drink to the dead warriors, and their having let their hair down may suggest sexual availability. Some women portrayed on picture stones hold drinking horns in their hands, as does a small silver figure of a woman found in Birka; they have been interpreted as valkyries serving drink to dead warriors arriving at Valhalla. The warriors typically arrive by horse. Sometimes they ride a horse with eight legs, suggesting that they are so important that the ruler of Valhalla, Odin, has sent his own eight-legged horse, Sleipner, to pick them up. Such picture stones often depict ships. It is at least possible that people of the Viking Age imagined that one had to take a ship to get to Valhalla. Gotland is an island surrounded by water, so one would have needed a ship to go anywhere else. The belief that the way to Valhalla went over the sea would explain why so many Viking Age people were buried in ships, including the two women in Oseberg, the chieftain in Gokstad slain in battle, and many of the warriors in Vendel and Valsgärde.

The picture stones, which are found only in Gotland, contain great series of narrative images. Sometimes, we recognize the stories that are told. Two fragmentarily preserved stones depict, for example, a great snake or dragon, in one case accompanied by a man, suggesting the story of Sigurd "the dragon-slayer," who, according to Eddic poetry and high-medieval texts such as the *Saga of the Volsungs*, fought and killed the dragon Fafnir. Richard Wagner retold this story in his opera *Siegfried*. Other depictions of scenes from the same story appear in connection with two runic inscriptions in Sweden and on a portal in a Norwegian stave church. The inscription on a rock face at Ramsundsberget is famous for its elegantly stylized series of images. The main scene is framed by three snakes, one of which contains the runic text (a rather humdrum memorial formula) of the inscription. Sigurd appears outside the frame, straining as he sticks his sword into the soft underbelly of one of the snakes, Fafnir. Various other figures from the story appear inside the frame. Sigurd roasts the heart of the dragon over a fire and has stuck his thumb into his mouth; according to the story, he burned himself when checking if the heart was done, and when he cooled his finger in his mouth, he accidentally drank dragon blood, thus gaining the ability to understand the language of the birds that are depicted in the inscription sitting in a tree. They promptly inform him that his foster father, the smith Regin, is planning to kill him in order to steal the dragon's treasure. Sigurd therefore kills Regin, who lies headless to the left, surrounded by his smith's tools: hammer, thongs, bellows, and anvil. The picture also shows Sigurd's horse, Grani, loaded with the dragon's treasure.[31]

While Sigurd and his dragon are easily recognizable, other motifs on the picture stones from Gotland are harder to interpret. They are clearly narrative images or series of images, but the stories they tell are otherwise unknown. Who are the three men who appear on a stone from Sanda? They hold different things in their hands: the first clearly carries a spear, another an object that has been interpreted as a sickle or a torch. Are they the three gods Odin, Thor, and Frey? Or are they three men marking out the boundaries of a newly purchased lot of land? And what is the circle just behind them, and what looks like fire below that circle?[32] If we knew more

FIG. 24. A lively inscription on a rock face in Ramsundsberget, Sweden, depicts scenes from the myth of the hero Sigurd. The dragon Fafnir makes up the band in which the runic text was inscribed, and Sigurd can be seen stabbing the animal's soft underbelly. Afterward, he roasted Fafnir's heart, and when he tasted the dragon's blood, he suddenly could understand what the birds said. They warned him of the designs of his foster-father, the smith Regin, whom Sigurd therefore killed while his horse, Grani, was standing by. A masterful artist depicted all this and more with great skill. Photo: Bengt A. Lundberg, courtesy of Riksantikvarieämbetet, Stockholm.

about the stories that were told in Viking Age Scandinavia, we might better understand what this and other picture stones depict.

What the stones prove beyond any doubt is that, like people of every culture and time, Viking Age Scandinavians told stories; we are privileged that we are able to enjoy at least some of those stories because they were written down on parchment in the High Middle Ages. By then, they almost certainly had changed, perhaps especially as they were written down, but pictorial evidence such as the various depictions of Sigurd demonstrates that the main elements of that story at least remained the same.

The images that we have just discussed are narrative and representational. Most art surviving from the Scandinavian Viking Age, however, is decorative and symbolic. The brooches that fastened women's dresses, magnificent bridles and harness-mounts for chieftains' horses, and various other utilitarian objects such as cups, weathervanes, and even ships sport intricate decoration executed in all kinds of techniques by skillful artists and artisans. The keel of the Oseberg ship is entirely covered by carvings; the iron blade of an ax discovered in Mammen, Jutland, is filled with images created by silver-wire inlay; buckles and brooches in cast bronze with rich decoration are common. The Viking Age relished the contrast between different kinds of materials, between different colors, and between empty and decorated fields. The same piece of jewelry, or any other object, may combine materials and techniques to produce many disparate visual effects. Niello, glass, paint, gold, silver, bronze, iron, glass, and much else combined in different constellations to produce the desired play of light and surfaces.

A recurring motif—an animal of some sort—dominates Scandinavian and other northern European decorative art from long before the Viking Age to after its end. What appears to be the same animal appears and reappears everywhere in varying executions and forms. It may originally have been inspired by Roman art; lions or horses come to mind, but for the Viking Age, it might be useful to think of it as a dragon, since it is hard to imagine that the images would have conveyed the idea of any particular real animal to contemporary observers. The image developed over decades and centuries, taking on different characteristics that allow art historians to talk of a succession of styles, each usually given its name from the place where some famous object in that style was discovered: Oseberg, Borre, Jelling, Mammen, Ringerike, Urnes. Distinguishing among styles makes it possible to date objects that carry that style: "the heads and tails of [the snakes on the Ramsundsberget inscription depicting the myth of Sigurd] produce typical Ringerike tendrils," which means that the inscription was probably made during the first half of the eleventh century.[33]

In the development of styles, the animal waxes and wanes; it first becomes stronger, more robust and compact, starting to look like a lion; then it becomes thin, elongated, and sinuous, like a caricatured greyhound; it briefly is filled with speed and movement, only to later return to stasis; the pigtail in its neck grows and shrinks, its lip-lappet likewise; its limbs sprout tendrils that eventually detach and take on a life of their own. Some animals fight one another, while others appear calm and elegant. Thus the typical animal motif of northern decorative art metamorphoses and transforms over the centuries, until it disappears, replaced by new European styles and motifs in and after the twelfth century.[34]

One of the most famous instances of the great animal is on the bow and stern of the Oseberg ship, which are elaborately decorated above the waterline with elegant rows of animals that are shown in sharp relief. The ship was built and the decoration made in around 815–820, and it was buried in 834 in a great burial mound that has preserved it remarkably well. Carved into the oak of the ship, the animals are very similar, even if they differ slightly in the details. They have small heads with large eyes appearing in profile and long, narrow, curved bodies. Their torsos sport two heart-shaped holes, so the entire animal has the form of the number 8, with head (including pigtail), tail, and legs jutting out and interlacing with each other, partially inside the closest heart-shaped hole. The bodies are articulated with lines and other geometrical patterns.

In the tenth century, at some point after 957, a great treasure of about 1.8 kilograms of gold and 2.9 kilograms of silver was buried in the ground in Erikstorp in eastern Sweden. The treasure included 330 coins, mostly Arabic silver dirhams from the period 895–957, allowing the hoard to be dated. Interestingly, the treasure includes a complete set of dress jewelry for a woman. Six of seven golden arm rings consist of two thick threads of gold twisted around each other, the ends narrowing into an elegant knot. The knots are echoed in two dimensions on two rectangular brooches in this treasure, which contain so-called ring chains as well as two depictions each of the usual animal, "with a ribbon-like body, spiral hips, legs which interlace with the body, and a pigtail."[35] Since they are a pair, one assumes that they were intended to fasten a woman's apron dress, although such brooches are usually oval, not rectangular. Art historians have determined the decoration of these brooches to belong to the Jelling style.

The treasure also includes silver chains, some of which may have hung between the two brooches. Many of the Arabic coins have small holes and one even sports a small attached loop; they may have hung from the chains. Alongside them may have hung the hammer pendant found in this treasure. It is made of silver, but it has filigree work in gold forming loops of various kinds. The interplay between the yellow gold and the white silver is typical of Viking Age decoration.

The Erikstorp treasure also contains a round brooch entirely of gold, perhaps intended to fasten an outer cloak. The filigree on this brooch depicts three animals, all biting the ring at the brooch's center, with their limbs intertwined. To make such jewelry, a goldsmith would first mold the basic piece itself, to which he or she would solder the filigree grains (or strings) that he had manufactured. Remarkably, the exact mold used to make this brooch has been discovered in Hedeby, many hundreds of miles to the southwest of Erikstorp. This piece of jewelry was, thus, made in that great town, the home of so many artisans, including goldsmiths. Since the decoration of the other jewelry in this treasure trove is reminiscent of that of the round brooch, it was probably all made in the same place, perhaps in the same workshop. Hedeby was clearly a center for skillful goldsmiths producing exquisite jewelry (and much else) that was exported all over Scandinavia.[36]

On the Erikstorp jewelry, the usual decorative animal is elongated and ribbonlike, although it is robust and appears strong. A hundred years later it had developed an extremely narrow body that looks almost flamboyant surrounded as it is by intertwined limbs and separate tendrils. An example may be found on the runestone that has been moved to the Skansen open-air museum in Stockholm, where it is seen by hundreds of thousands of tourists every year.[37] It originally stood at Ölsta along the ancient main road leading from Uppsala toward the west, the so-called Eriksgata, on which, at least later in the Middle Ages, the Swedish king rode from province to province to be accepted in each. The torso of the animal is draped around the edge of the pleasantly curved stone and contains the runic text. In the middle, its neck loops around its hind parts, and the animal bites its own neck. The head is seen in profile with its elongated eye, small pigtail, and small lip-lappet. The entire animal is intertwined with what looks like many small snakes with tiny heads and small eyes. The whole makes an elegant impression of busyness and movement. This runestone is in the

Urnes style, so called after a carved wooden church portal from Norway that contains several similar animals, even more exuberantly portrayed.

The Ölsta runestone, which has been colored in modern times with what someone guessed were its original colors, is a signed (*"Ásmundr hjó"*) product of the great runemaster Åsmund Kåresson, who is known to have inscribed more than twenty runestones in the Uppland region north of present-day Stockholm. He was a skilled stone-carver, famous for his elegant decorations and well-formulated texts. This stone was commissioned by four siblings, Holmdis and her three brothers, Björn, Gunnar, and Audulf, in memory of their father, Ulf, who was "Ginnlög's husband." We can only speculate about why they chose to commemorate their mother's name in this indirect way, but we must be grateful that they did, since this made it possible for us to know the names of the entire family.

Arts and letters played an important role in Viking Age Scandinavia. The poetry and art that survive were created, in the main, for the upper levels of society, but the same ideas appear in simpler execution for the less well-to-do. What is preserved is certainly only the tip of the iceberg, and much has been lost. We know almost nothing, for example, about Scandinavian music in the Viking Age, although Scandinavians must have enjoyed music a thousand years ago in chieftains' halls and elsewhere. Nonetheless, what survives of poetry, representational and decorative art, and stories teaches us that the Viking Age was not only about raiding, plunder, and warfare. Scandinavians had a sense of beauty and an ear for poetry, and they developed idiosyncratic styles of both art and literature without any close counterparts in the rest of Europe. These were yet other fields of human endeavor in which Scandinavia went its own way during the Viking Age. In the eleventh and twelfth centuries, the old native styles were slowly crowded out by the Romanesque in art and by romance in literature. In these fields as well, Scandinavia opted in to joining Europe.

CHAPTER 10

EPILOGUE

The End of the Viking Age

ON 25 SEPTEMBER 1066, KING HARALD SIGURDSSON HARD-ruler of Norway with his army fought the forces of the English king Harold Godwineson at Stamford Bridge, close to York, England. The battle was not going well for the Norwegians, so the king himself tried to rally his troops by setting a manful example. He "gripped his sword with both hands and hewed it to the left and right. He . . . cleared a way before him, killing many men in the process. . . . Both his arms were bloody, and he went among his enemies almost as if he were cleaving the wind, showing that he feared neither fire nor iron." The old commander of the Byzantine emperor's bodyguard, the hero from the battles of Sicily, the veteran of many a Scandinavian battle on land and at sea was showing his mettle for the last time. Suddenly, an English spear perforated Harald Hardruler's throat; he fell, gurgling and blood gushing, to the ground. "That was his death wound," the Old Norse chronicle *Morkinskinna* drily comments. His warriors valiantly fought on, as they had promised their beloved leader in his mead hall, but in vain. The English won the day, and by the evening the ground was covered with dead Scandinavians.[1]

The battle of Stamford Bridge stands as a fitting epilogue to the Viking Age. Harald Hardruler tried to follow in the footsteps of Svein Forkbeard and Cnut the Great, who had conquered England a half century earlier, but he fell in what would be the last major Viking battle on western European soil. King Harold Godwineson and his army had surprised him by showing up in Yorkshire earlier than expected, after what must have been a forced march from London. Directly after the battle, the English had to march south again, for Duke William of Normandy had invaded with his army. The duke acquired England, and a new nickname, "the Conqueror," by defeating Harold Godwineson and the exhausted English army at Hastings only three weeks later. William counted the Vikings who had settled in Normandy in the early tenth century among his ancestors, but his family had been thoroughly assimilated into French culture after more than a century of living in northwestern France.[2] It was a French ruler, not a Viking, who took over England in 1066.

Vikings stopped attacking western Europe in the late eleventh century for two reasons. Defensive measures had made it more difficult and risky to raid and plunder, and kings at home in Scandinavia no longer tolerated freebooting Vikings, preferring to redirect the aggressive energies of their countrymen elsewhere, particularly toward the east.

Harald Hardruler learned to his regret that it had become too risky to raid in western Europe. After almost three centuries of frequent Viking attacks, the kingdoms of the British Isles and the continent had worked out how to defend themselves. In the eleventh century, each king made sure that he had at his disposal a military apparatus and regular income from taxes, fines, and other fees, as well as feudal services in kind. All these aspects of medieval government had been enhanced at least partially in response to Viking attacks. We can see particularly clearly how it worked in England. Scandinavians continued to threaten William the Conqueror's rule of England after 1066, most seriously when the Danish king Svein Estridsson in alliance with Edgar, a prince of the old Anglo-Saxon royal family, invaded Northumbria in 1069 and succeeded in capturing, if only briefly, the city of York. When William marched in with his army, Svein fled. To be better able to defend his country against foreign attacks, including Viking incursions, William expanded the military and administrative functions of England. Having confiscated, with a victor's right, much land after his triumph at Hastings in 1066, William was able to hand out portions to trusted followers who in return each promised to contribute a certain number of armed knights on horseback if a military need would arise. He also took care to expand the income from his kingdom and to register in detail the resources of the English crown in the so-called *Domesday Book*. William thus managed to build up a defense against all kinds of threats, notably Viking raids, meaning that any potential Scandinavian fighters thought twice about attacking. The risks and the costs had become too great. England in the late eleventh century is probably the best example of a strong European kingdom getting organized and thus capable of defending itself against Vikings, but other states in western Europe experienced similar developments. The Vikings had shrewdly taken advantage of the weak defenses of most European states in the ninth and tenth centuries. They could no longer do so toward the end of the eleventh century.

At home in Scandinavia, meanwhile, other developments prevented Viking expeditions from ever setting sail.[3] As we have seen, the three Scandinavian kingdoms were created around the year 1000, when a king ruled each of them. A king could ill afford competing chieftains. He needed to control violence in his kingdoms, making sure that no competitor was able to gather so much strength that he could contest the power of the king. It would take centuries before any really strong governments existed in Scandinavia, but we may observe the beginnings of the process in the late Viking Age, when King Harald Bluetooth, for example, constructed a network of military camps throughout Denmark. Those camps did not help him hold on to his power when his son Svein rebelled a few years later, but Harald laid the foundations for keeping the regions of Denmark assembled under one ruler. Over the following centuries, that ruler would come from Harald's family, illustrating that royal blood had become more important than military prowess in gaining power.

This is not to say that Scandinavians became peaceful or stopped fighting, raiding, and plundering. They simply directed their energies elsewhere, and they organized such enterprises in new ways. The Scandinavian kings themselves arranged armed attacks against, especially, the peoples living along the southern and eastern coasts of the Baltic Sea. In the centuries after the battle of Stamford Bridge, the kings of Sweden and Denmark attacked

Finland, Estonia, Russia, and the Slavic peoples in what today is northeastern Germany. A Russian chronicle recounts how a Swedish ruler together with a bishop attacked Novgorod with sixty ships in 1142. The Swedes lost the ensuing battle and some 150 men were killed.[4] More successfully, in 1168 King Valdemar I of Denmark conquered the principality of the Wends, a Slavic people who inhabited the southern shore of the Baltic Sea. His son Valdemar II invaded Estonia in 1219. Pope Honorius III supported this military enterprise against the pagans of the eastern Baltic by awarding crusading privileges to Valdemar and his warriors. This kind of warfare produced plunder and booty for Scandinavian kings, who at the same time strove to expand the geographical extent of their kingdoms. Meanwhile, the kings of Norway extended their rule farther and farther north along the Atlantic coast as well as across the sea to the North Atlantic islands. King Magnus Barelegs (r. 1093–1103) seized control of the Isle of Man, the Hebrides, and the Orkneys. In the early 1260s, King Håkon Håkonsson (r. 1217–1263) forced the inhabitants of Greenland and Iceland to recognize him as their ruler, to whom they owed fees and taxes. In this way, Scandinavian kings continued to plunder, collect tribute, and eventually conquer territory, but no longer in western Europe. Scandinavian kings learned to behave more like Charlemagne and less like freebooters and Vikings.[5]

These enterprises brought wealth from outside their kingdoms to the kings of Scandinavia, but those rulers also increasingly relied on income collected from the inhabitants of their kingdoms, especially taxes and fines. Here, the Church, with its demand for tithes, a tenth of all income, showed the way, and it provided the expertise for setting up and managing structures for collecting taxes. Like the English heregeld, taxes from the inhabitants were at first meant for their protection and defense—they were rhetorically framed as replacing everyone's duty of self-defense—but they were soon used to finance all kinds of needs in the emerging kingdoms of Scandinavia, especially the king's need for strong military forces.[6] In this respect, the new kingdoms in the North followed a path parallel to developments in the rest of Europe, where kings during the High Middle Ages (ca. 1000–1300) expanded the financial basis for their kingdoms by creating sophisticated systems for assessing and collecting taxes and other fees.

The medieval kings of Scandinavia reshaped the administration of justice, creating another valuable source of revenue in the form of fines. Whereas justice of old had been a matter of self-help or arbitration through the local community and its assembly, known as a *thing*, kings began to declare certain crimes to be such heinous transgressions against God and society that they must fall under royal justice and punishment. Among such offences were highway robbery, rape and the seduction of women against the wishes of their families, sorcery, and particularly aggravated murders. The culprits were outlawed and could thus be lawfully killed by anyone, but they could also free themselves by paying a hefty fine to the king. These fines became an important source of revenue for Scandinavian kings.

The period from the end of the Viking Age to the late thirteenth century was a politically confused time in all three of Scandinavia's kingdoms, with an almost constant struggle over power, but the struggle mainly played out as a family drama. Five of King Svein Estridsson's sons, for example, became kings of Denmark, and several of them were killed in their fratricidal struggles. One, Cnut, was killed in 1086 inside the church of St. Albans in Odense, where he had taken refuge. After his death, he was promoted as a saint and martyr. Sweden and Norway similarly obtained royal saints who had suffered violent deaths in St. Erik (d. 1160) and St. Olav Haraldsson (d. 1030), reflecting a sacred aura onto their families as well as onto royal power in their countries. Only in the thirteenth century did Scandinavian kings succeed in stabilizing their rule. In 1286, King Erik V of Denmark was killed "by his own men," according to a contemporary chronicle. He was the last medieval Scandinavian king to be murdered, putting an end to a long series of kings who had met violent deaths.[7] Kings became more secure on their thrones.

Changes in the way wars were waged made it more difficult to oppose kings who were ensconced on their thrones. Scandinavian warfare in the Viking Age centered on the longship full of warriors. Many of the famous battles, from Hafrsfjord to Svölðr and elsewhere, took place on ships. In 1134, Erik Emune defeated his uncle, King Niels, in a land battle at Fotevig in Scania. Erik had recruited a contingent of heavy cavalry, which was instrumental in giving him the victory and the royal crown. Cavalry would in the future become the backbone of the armed forces of the Scandinavian kingdoms, alongside military strongholds in the form of castles built from stone. Erik had hired his mounted and armored mercenaries in Germany—an expensive proposition that required the kingdom to have sound finances and steady income from taxes. Tax burdens increased during these centuries, but kings began to offer release from tax payments and other privileges to those of their subjects who instead were able to provide an armed and mounted warrior for the kingdom's cavalry. This laid the foundations for the Scandinavian aristocracy, who traded military service for tax exemptions.

Military forces were but one cornerstone of the medieval Scandinavian kingdoms; another were the national Churches that were in place at least from 1164, when Sweden as the last of the three kingdoms received its own archbishop, with residence in Uppsala. The local churches were closely allied with the kings and provided the administrative skills as well as much of the ideology that underpinned the hereditary monarchies. Kings in turn supported the Church, providing magnificent donations of landed property to cathedrals, churches, and monasteries. The alliance between church and state became visible and ritualized in royal coronations, for the first time in 1163 or 1164 when Archbishop Eystein of Trondheim crowned the boy king Magnus Erlingsson. Unlike his mother, Kristin, Magnus was not the child of a king, which probably explains why he (or rather the real ruler, his father, Earl Erling Skakke) sought ecclesiastical support for his reign. At the ceremony in Bergen, Magnus in return swore an oath to remain faithful and obedient to the pope and the Church, and to be an equitable ruler—in other words, to conform to the current ecclesiastical ideals of just kingship.[8]

A common theme among all these developments is that they served to make Scandinavia into a normal European region that is similar to the rest of the continent, although colder and poorer.

During the Viking Age, Scandinavians developed new military tactics, the surprise attack made possible by their fast ships, which made them infamous and feared. They pioneered new routes for trading and commerce, especially through the interior of eastern Europe, and they settled new lands both there and in the Atlantic west. They developed their own literary and artistic aesthetics as well as a pagan mythology that contrast starkly with contemporary European ideals. Scandinavia followed its own path, distinct from the rest of the continent, as long as it lasted. Perhaps it is too trivial to focus on the macabre spectacle of ravens picking at King Harald's bloodied corpse on the battlefield at Stamford Bridge when dating the end of the Viking Age. A new era truly arrived when the Vikings' unique moment in history had run its course and Scandinavians instead opted to join Europe, embracing Christianity and other ideologies, and adopting European artistic ideals, military tactics, and trading patterns. When Scandinavians became the subjects of kings and the servants of the universal Church, they were no longer Vikings. The Age of the Vikings had come to a close.

FURTHER READING

THE LITERATURE ON THE VIKING AGE IS VAST. A RECENT SURVEY of the state of research is found in Stefan Brink with the collaboration of Neil Price, eds., *The Viking World* (2008), which contains detailed bibliographies and brief thematic essays by some eighty experts. Older, but still very useful, with outstanding essays and attractive illustrations is Peter Sawyer, ed., *The Oxford Illustrated History of the Vikings* (1997). Among the many treatments of the Vikings by a single author stands out Else Roesdahl, *The Vikings* (2nd ed., 1998), a well-conceived survey, particularly good on archeology. Gwyn Jones, *A History of the Vikings* (1968), has aged well thanks to its fully annotated, detailed treatment of raids and settlements; similar in scope is F. Donald Logan, *The Vikings in History* (3rd ed., 2005). The earlier chapters of Knut Helle, ed., *Cambridge History of Scandinavia* (2007), survey the Viking Age from the point of view of Scandinavia. Good general histories of medieval Scandinavia are found in Birgit Sawyer and Peter Sawyer, *Medieval Scandinavia: From Conversion to Reformation, circa 800–1500* (1993), and Sverre Bagge, *Cross and Scepter: The Rise of the Scandinavian Kingdoms from the Vikings to the Reformation* (2014). P. H. Sawyer, *The Age of the Vikings* (1962; 2nd ed. 1971), still eminently readable, brought Viking studies into the modern era by setting raids and settlements in their historical context, and by its careful use of numismatic evidence.

Angus A. Somerville and R. Andrew MacDonald, eds., *The Viking Age: A Reader* (2010), collects relevant sources but makes little distinction between contemporary ones and high-medieval literary treatments. Many sources concerning England (including the *Anglo-Saxon Chronicle* and *The Battle of Maldon*) are available in translation in the first two volumes of *English Historical Documents*, vol. 1, *c. 500–1042*, edited by Dorothy Whitelock (2nd ed., 1979), and vol. 2, *1042–1189*, edited by George W. Greenaway (2nd ed., 1981). Although these collections excerpt many of the European sources for the Viking raids, the most important ones are also available in their entirety in English translation. Particularly useful among year-by-year accounts are Bernhard W. Scholz with Barbara Rogers, *Carolingian Chronicles: Royal Frankish Annals and Nithard's Histories* (1970); Janet Nelson, *The Annals of St-Bertin* (1991); Timothy Reuter, *The Annals of Fulda* (1992); Michael Swanton, *The Anglo-Saxon Chronicle* (1996); Simon Keynes and Michael Lapidge, *Alfred the Great: Asser's "Life of Alfred" and Other Contemporary Sources* (1983); Sean Mac Airt, *The Annals of Innisfallen MS. Rawlinson B 503* (1951); Sean Mac Airt and Gearóid Mac Niocaill, *The Annals of Ulster (to A.D. 1131)* (1983); Samuel Hazzard Cross and Olgerd P. Sherbowitz-Wetzor, *The Russian Primary Chronicle: Laurentian Text* (1973); Adam of Bremen, *History of the Archbishops of Hamburg-Bremen*, trans. Francis J. Tschan and Timothy Reuter (2nd ed., 2002).

Roric in Dorestad and some of his western confrères are treated in Simon Coupland, "From Poachers to Game-Keepers: Scandinavian Warlords and Carolingian Kings," *Early Medieval Europe* 7 (1998): 85–114. A balanced approach to Rurik is taken in Simon Franklin and Jonathan Shepard, *The Emergence of Rus, 750–1200* (1996). Norse settlement in the Danelaw and elsewhere in England is most recently analyzed in D. M. Hadley, *The Vikings in England: Settlement, Society and Culture* (2006). Some of the Scandinavian rulers in the British Isles are treated in Benjamin Hudson, *Viking Pirates and Christian Princes: Dynasty, Religion, and Empire in the North Atlantic* (2005); and King Cnut's most recent biography is Timothy Bolton, *The Empire of Cnut the Great: Conquest and the Consolidation of Power in Northern Europe in the Early Eleventh Century* (2009). The early history of Normandy is ably laid out in David Bates, *Normandy before 1066* (1982). The Scandinavians who emigrated to Greenland and North America are conveniently treated in William W. Fitzhugh and Elizabeth I. Ward, eds., *Vikings: The North Atlantic Saga* (2000). The medieval sagas about them are in

Keneva Kunz, trans., *The Vinland Sagas: The Icelandic Sagas about the First Documented Voyages across the North Atlantic* (2008).

Judith Jesch, *Ships and Men in the Late Viking Age: The Vocabulary of Runic Inscriptions and Skaldic Verse* (2001), systematically explores words relating to ships in Viking Age Scandinavian sources, in the process illuminating the history of Viking ships. The main research institution devoted to Viking ships is the Viking Ship Museum in Roskilde, Denmark. The museum and its staff have published many books and booklets on the subject as well as an abundant website, http://www.vikingeskibsmuseet.dk/en/. Notable is Ole Crumlin-Pedersen, *Viking-Age Ships and Ship-building in Hedeby/ Haithabu and Schleswig* (1997). Ibn Fadlan's account is available in English in Richard N. Frye, *Ibn Fadlan's Journey to Russia: A Tenth-Century Traveler from Baghdad to the Volga River* (2005), and in Paul Lunde and Caroline Stone, trans., *Ibn Fadlan and the Land of Darkness: Arab Travellers in the Far North* (2012), which also includes many other Arabic sources of northern history.

Helen Clarke and Björn Ambrosiani, *Towns in the Viking Age* (1991), surveys the trading centers of northern Europe from an archeological point of view. The fur trade in Russia, in the Viking Age as well as later, is accessibly treated in Janet Martin, *Treasure of the Land of Darkness: The Fur Trade and Its Significance for Medieval Russia* (1986). Adriaan Verhulst, *The Carolingian Economy* (2002), is foundational for the economic history of the Viking period.

Nora Berend, ed., *Christianisation and the Rise of Christian Monarchy: Scandinavia, Central Europe, and Rus', c. 900–1200* (2007), is an important survey of state formation and Christianization on the periphery of Europe. Sverre Bagge, *From Viking Stronghold to Christian Kingdom* (2010), traces state formation in Norway.

Interesting treatments of women in Scandinavian society and literature are two books by Jenny Jochens, *Women in Old Norse Society* (1995), and *Old Norse Images of Women* (1996), as well as Judith Jesch, *Women in the Viking Age* (1991). For insights into the physical characteristics of Viking Age Scandinavians based on examinations of their skeletons, see Kurt Brøste, Jørgen Balslev Jørgensen, Ulla Lund Hansen, and Berit Jansen Sellevold, *Iron Age Man in Denmark* (1984).

Notable among the many surveys of northern mythology is Gabriel Turville-Petre, *Myth and Religion of the North: The Religion of Ancient Scandinavia* (1964). More up-to-date treatments of religions in the North are Thomas A. DuBois, *Nordic Religions in the Viking Age* (1999), and Christopher Abram, *Myths of the Pagan North: The Gods of the Norsemen* (2011). Anders Winroth, *The Conversion of Scandinavia: Vikings, Merchants, and Missionaries in the Remaking of Northern Europe* (2012), focuses on religious change but also treats the society and culture of the Vikings. Carolyne Larrington, *The Poetic Edda: A New Translation* (3rd ed., 2014), is the best translation of this fundamental work for the understanding of Scandinavian religion.

The corpus of skaldic poetry is being edited and translated in a detailed multivolume work under the general editorship of Margaret Clunies Ross in *Skaldic Poetry of the Scandinavian Middle Ages* (2007–). A comprehensive introduction to Scandinavia's medieval literature is found in Carol J. Clover and John Lindow, *Old Norse-Icelandic Literature: A Critical Guide* (2nd ed., 2005). A good presentation of runes and their use is Sven B. F. Jansson, *Runes in Sweden* (1987). All known Scandinavian runic inscriptions, with English translations, are available through the database Samnordisk runtextdatabas, http://www.nordiska.uu.se/forskn/samnord.htm. James Graham Campbell, *Viking Art* (2013), is a well-illustrated survey of Scandinavian art from the early Middle Ages.

ACKNOWLEDGMENTS

DURING THE TIME I HAVE WORKED ON THIS BOOK, I HAVE incurred many debts of gratitude, which I am happy to acknowledge. In the first place, I want to thank my editor Brigitta van Rheinberg, who suggested I write this book and who has supported me with sensitive readings and many valuable suggestions. My agent Lisa Adams of Garamond Agency was, as always, of great help. I want particularly to thank my splendid copyeditor, Madeleine Adams, whose diligent and sensitive work greatly improved the book in many ways. The production editor, Mark Bellis, saw the book through the Press with admirable skill.

I am grateful to many friends and colleagues who have discussed Viking history with me. I want in particular to mention Roberta Frank, whose scholarship I admire and whose friendship I cherish. She has read and commented on parts of the manuscript, and she generously allowed me to publish her paragraph consisting almost entirely of Old Norse loanwords in English. Ray Clemens has been a great friend since we were in graduate school together, and he has continued to put me in his debt through his incisive reading of the manuscript. Janet Nelson, Peter Heather, and Sverre Bagge read the manuscript for the Press and taught me much through their learned and generous comments. I wish especially to thank the much admired Peter Sawyer for gracefully raising no objection to my book adopting the same title as his groundbreaking 1962 work.

My assistant Gina Hurley performed a heroic task in assembling the images and the permissions to publish them. I also want to thank the institutions and persons who permitted me to publish their images, and especially Håkan Svensson, Nicolai Garhøj Larsson, and Raymond Hejdström. Michal Ditzian copyedited several chapters with her impeccable sensitivity to argument, style, and grammar. Alexa Selph compiled the index with, as always, utmost professionalism and skill.

My employer, Yale University, supported the work financially by giving me a sabbatical during which I drafted a large part of the book. The Frederick W. Hilles Fund defrayed some of the costs of finishing the manuscript.

As always, I remain grateful to the libraries and other institutions that assisted me by making books, journals, and electronic resources available. I want to thank, especially, Yale University Library, one of the greatest centers in the world for humanistic research, and Stofnun Árna Magnússonar í íslenskum fræðum, Reykjavik, which with its reference library, rich stores of manuscripts, and expert staff is the ideal place to work on the Scandinavian Middle Ages.

My wife, Jóhanna Katrín Friðriksdóttir, helped me in many ways, read the entire manuscript, and generously shared her expertise. My children, Hjalmar and Elsa, continue to inspire. My parents, Eva Winroth and Hans Erik Johansson, always supported my perhaps eccentric choice of career and I am proud to dedicate this book to them.

ABBREVIATIONS

MGH	Monumenta Germaniae Historica
MGH: SS rer. Germ.	Monumenta Germaniae Historica: Scriptores rerum Germanicarum in usum scholarum separatim editi
RGA	*Reallexikon der germanischen Altertumskunde*
s.a.	*sub anno*, precedes the year under which a notice is found in an annalistic work

NOTES

Since this book is also intended for nonspecialists, I have generally limited the references to available translations when referring to contemporary sources, even though as a rule I have studied them in the original Latin, Old Norse, or Old English. Because I have always included references according to the usual systems (books and chapters, lines, years, etc.), scholars will have little problem finding the appropriate place in the standard editions. Viking studies is a large and lively field; in order not to overload the notes, I have annotated sparingly.

CHAPTER 1: INTRODUCTION

1. R. M. Liuzza, *Beowulf* (2nd ed. Peterborough, Ont., 2013).
2. Tom Christensen, "Lejre and Roskilde," in *The Viking World*, ed. Stefan Brink and Neil Price (Abingdon, 2008), 121–125.
3. Roberta Frank, "The Invention of the Viking Horned Helmet," in *International Scandinavian and Medieval Studies in Memory of Gerd Wolfgang Weber*, ed. Michael Dallapiazza (Trieste, 2000), 199–208.
4. P. H. Sawyer, *Kings and Vikings: Scandinavia and Europe, A.D. 700–1100* (London and New York, 1982).
5. R. I. Page, *"A Most Vile People": Early English Historians on the Vikings* (London, 1987).
6. *Reallexikon des germanischen Altertumskunde* (2nd ed. Berlin, 1967–2007) 35.687–696, s.v. "Wiking," by Thorsten Andersson and Klaus Böldl.

CHAPTER 2: VIOLENCE IN A VIOLENT TIME

1. René Merlet, ed., *La chronique de Nantes* (Paris, 1896).
2. *Annals of St-Bertin*, s.a. 837, trans. Janet Nelson, *The Annals of St-Bertin, Ninth-Century Histories* 1 (Manchester, 1991), 37.

3. *Annals of St-Bertin*, s.a. 843, trans. Nelson, 55.

4. The quoted sources are found in the *Annals of St-Bertin*, s.a. 836, 844, 864, and 873 (kept up by Prudentius 835–861 and by Hincmar 861–882), trans. Nelson, 35, 60, 111, and 183; *Annals of Ulster*, s.a. 844, ed. and trans. Seán Mac Airt and Gearóid Mac Niocaill, *The Annals of Ulster (to A.D. 1131)* ([Dublin], 1983), 302–303; and the D version of the *Anglo-Saxon Chronicle*, trans. Michael Swanton, *The Anglo-Saxon Chronicle* (London, 1996), 111.

5. Anders Winroth, *The Conversion of Scandinavia: Vikings, Merchants, and Missionaries in the Remaking of Northern Europe* (New Haven, 2012), 24.

6. *Alcuini sive Albini epistolae* 20, trans. Paul Edward Dutton, *Carolingian Civilization: A Reader (Peterborough, Ont., 1993)*, 109–110. Alcuin quoted, among other scriptural passages, Isaiah 5:25.

7. [C. Smedt], "Translatio S. Germani Parisiensis anno 846 secundum primævam narrationem e codice Namurcensi," *Analecta Bollandiana* 2 (1883): 69–98.

8. David Morgan, *The Mongols* (2nd ed. Oxford, 2007).

9. Samnordisk runtextdatabas, Uppsala University, U 112. http://www.nordiska.uu.se/forskn/samnord.htm.

10. Samnordisk runtextdatabas, U 374.

11. *Magnúsdrápa* 10, ed. and trans. Diana Whaley in *Skaldic Poetry of the Scandinavian Middle Ages*, edited by Margaret Clunies Ross (Turnhout, 2007–), 2.1.219–220.

12. Halldórr ókristni, *Eiríksflokkr* 7, ed. and trans. Kari Ellen Gade in *Skaldic Poetry of the Scandinavian Middle Ages*, ed. Ross, 1.1.482–483; Haraldr harðráði Sigurðarson, *Lausavísa* 7, ed. and trans. Kari Ellen Gade in *Skaldic Poetry of the Scandinavian Middle Ages*, ed. Ross, 2.1.48–49.

13. *Anglo-Saxon Chronicle*, s.a. 1012, trans. Swanton, 142.

14. *Völuspá* 24, trans. Carolyne Larrington, *The Poetic Edda: A New Translation* (Oxford, 1996), 7 (my adapted translation).

15. *Battle of Maldon*, lines 108–111, 114–119, 134–136, 138–146, 149–153, trans. S.A.J. Bradley, *Anglo-Saxon Poetry* (London, 1982), 518–528 (my translation leaning on published translations).

16. Brian R. Campbell, "The 'superne gar' in 'The Battle of Maldon,'" *Notes and Queries* 16, no. 2 (1969): 45–46.

17. *Battle of Maldon*, lines 160–161.

18. Per Holck, "The Skeleton from the Gokstad Ship: New Evaluation of an Old Find," *Norwegian Archaeological Review* 42, no. 1 (2009): 40–49.

19. Sigvatr Þórðarson, *Víkingarvísur* 6, ed. and trans. Judith Jesch in *Skaldic Poetry of the Scandinavian Middle Ages*, ed. Ross, 1.2.542–545; Hilda Ellis Davidson, *The Sword in Anglo-Saxon England: Its Archaeology and Literature* (Woodbridge, Suffolk, 1998).

20. Alan Williams, "A Metallurgical Study of Some Viking Swords," *Gladius: Estudios sobre armas antiguas, arte militar y vida cultural en oriente y occidente* 29 (2009): 121–184.

21. Winroth, *Conversion of Scandinavia*, 62.

22. Page, "*A Most Vile People.*"

23. Sigvatr, *Knútsdrápa* 1, ed. and trans. Matthew Townend in *Skaldic Poetry of the Scandinavian Middle Ages*, ed. Ross, 1.2.651–652.

24. See chapter 9.

25. Sigvatr, *Erfidrápa Óláfs helga* 27, ed. and trans. Judith Jesch in *Skaldic Poetry of the Scandinavian Middle Ages*, ed. Ross, 1.2.696.

26. Þjódólfr ór Hvíni, *Ynglingatál* 15, ed. Edith Marold in *Skaldic Poetry of the Scandinavian Middle Ages*, ed. Ross, 1.1.34.

27. [Eiríkur Jónsson and Finnur Jónsson, eds.], *Hauksbók udgiven efter de Arnamagnæanske Håndskrifter No. 371, 544 og 675, 40 samt forskellige Papirshåndskrifter af det Kongelige Nordiske Oldskrift-Selskab* (Copenhagen, 1892–1896), 464.

28. My translation, using Saxo Grammaticus, *The Nine Books of the Danish History of Saxo Grammaticus*, trans. Oliver Elton (London, 1905), and Saxo Grammaticus, *The History of the Danes*, trans. Peter Fischer and ed. Hilda Ellis Davidson (Woodbridge, Suffolk, 1979), 1.206.

29. *Ynglingasaga* 6, trans. Lee M. Hollander in Snorri Sturluson, *Heimskringla: History of the Kings of Norway* (Austin, 1964), 10.

30. Britt-Mari Näsström, *Bärsärkarna: Vikingatidens elitsoldater* (Stockholm, 2006); Vincent Samson, *Les Berserkir: Les guerriers-fauves dans la Scandinavie ancienne, de l'âge de Vendel aux Vikings (VIe–XIe siècle)*, Histoire et civilisations: Histoire (Villeneuve d'Ascq, 2011).

31. Þórbjörn hornklofi, *Haraldskvæði* 8, ed. and trans. R. D. Fulk in *Skaldic Poetry of the Scandinavian Middle Ages*, ed. Ross, 1.1.102–103, adapted. See also Klaus von See, "Exkurs zum Haraldskvæði: Berserker," *Zeitschrift für deutsche Wortforschung* 17 (1961): 129–135.

32. Lines 25–26, 29–34.

33. Lines 160–161.

34. *Annals of St-Bertin*, s.a. 852 and 868, trans. Nelson, 74 and 144.

35. *Anglo-Saxon Chronicle*, s.a. 991, trans. Swanton, 126–127.

36. Samnordisk runtextdatabas, U 344.

37. See, e.g., *Annals of St-Bertin*, s.a. 863, 864, 873, trans. Nelson, 105, 118, and 183.

38. *Royal Frankish Annals*, s.a. 774, trans. Bernhard W. Scholz with Barbara Rogers, *Carolingian Chronicles: Royal Frankish Annals and Nithard's Histories* (Ann Arbor, Mich., 1970), 50–51.

39. *Royal Frankish Annals*, s.a. 796, trans. Scholz with Rogers, 74; Einhard, *The Life of Charlemagne* 13, trans. Dutton, *Carolingian Civilization*, 31.

40. *Einhard's Annals*, s.a. 774, ed. Friedrich Kurze, *Annales regni Francorum inde ab a. 741 usque ad a. 829*, MGH: SS rer. Germ. (Hanover, 1895), 41.

41. *Einhard's Annals*, s.a. 785, ed. Kurze, 69.

42. *Royal Frankish Annals*, s.a. 795, trans. Scholz with Rogers, 74.

43. Timothy Reuter, "Plunder and Tribute in the Carolingian Empire," *Transactions of the Royal Historical Society* 35 (1985): 75–94, reprinted in Timothy Reuter and Janet L. Nelson, *Medieval Polities and Modern Mentalities* (Cambridge, 2006), 231–250.

44. H. Schnorr von Carolsfeld, "Das Chronicon Laurissense breve," *Neues Archiv* 36 (1911): 13–39.

CHAPTER 3: RÖRIKS AT HOME AND AWAY

1. As counted by Statistics Sweden: http://www.scb.se/namnsok. The Russian form of the name, Rurik, had 169 carriers.

2. Lena Peterson, *Nordiskt runnamnslexikon med tillägg av frekvenstabeller och finalalfabetisk ordlista* (Uppsala, 2002), 106.

3. Samnordisk runtextdatabas, Ög 153.

4. *Annales Fuldenses*, s.a. 850, trans. Timothy Reuter, *The Annals of Fulda*, Ninth-Century Histories 2 (Manchester, 1992), 30. Roric's story is well told in Simon Coupland, "From Poachers to Game-Keepers: Scandinavian Warlords and Carolingian Kings," *Early Medieval Europe* 7 (1998): 85–114.

5. *Sedulii Scotti carmina* 47.11, ed. Ludwig Traube, MGH: Poetae 3 (Berlin, 1896), 210.

6. Ruotpertus Mediolacensis, *Vita et Miracula S. Adalberti Egmondani*, ed. Oswald Holder-Egger, MGH: Scriptores (Hanover, 1888), 15.2.702.

7. Flodoardus Remensis, *Historia Remensis ecclesiae* 3.23 and 3.26, ed. Martina Stratman, *Historia Remensis ecclesiae*, MGH: Scriptores 36 (Hanover, 1998), 307 and 336.

8. *Russian Primary Chronicle*, s.a. 6368–6370 (860–862), trans. Samuel Hazzard Cross and Olgerd P. Sherbowitz-Wetzor, *The Russian Primary Chronicle: Laurentian Text* (Cambridge, Mass., 1973), 59.

9. Simon Franklin and Jonathan Shepard, *The Emergence of Rus: 750–1200*, Longman History of Russia (London, 1996).

10. *Russian Primary Chronicle*, s.a. 6368–6370 (860–862), trans. Cross and Sherbowitz-Wetzor, 59.

11. Paul the Deacon, *Historia Langobardorum* 1.1, trans. William Dudley Foulke, *History of the Lombards*, Sources of Medieval History (Philadelphia, 1974), 1.

12. Jordanes, *Getica* 4, trans. in Jordanes, *The Gothic History of Jordanes in English Version*, ed. Charles Christopher Mierow (Princeton, N.J., 1915), 57.

13. *Anglo-Saxon Chronicle*, s.a. 876, trans. Swanton, 74–75.

14. D. M. Hadley, *The Vikings in England: Settlement, Society and Culture*, Manchester Medieval Studies (Manchester, 2006); Dawn M. Hadley, "The Creation of the Danelaw," in *The Viking World*, ed. Stefan Brink and Neil Price (Abingdon, 2008), 375–378.

15. Robin Fleming, *Britain after Rome: The Fall and Rise, 400–1070*, Penguin History of Britain (London, 2010).

16. Hadley, *The Vikings in England*, 45–50.

17. Hadley, *The Vikings in England*, 237–264.

18. Hadley, "The Creation of the Danelaw."

19. Benjamin T. Hudson, *Viking Pirates and Christian Princes: Dynasty, Religion, and Empire in the North Atlantic* (Oxford, 2005); Hadley, *The Vikings in England*, 28–71.

20. James Henthorn Todd, ed. and trans., *Cogadh Gaedhel re Gaillaibh: The Wars of the Irish against the Foreigners, or The Invasions of Ireland by the Danes and Other Norsemen*, Rerum Britannicarum medii aevi scriptores [Roll series] 78 (London, 1867), 159.

21. Timothy Bolton, *The Empire of Cnut the Great: Conquest and the Consolidation of Power in Northern Europe in the Early Eleventh Century*, The Northern World: North Europe and the Baltic, c. 400–1700 A.D: Peoples, Economies and Cultures (Leiden, 2009), 128–132.

22. Winroth, *Conversion of Scandinavia*, 56.

23. S. Goodacre et al., "Genetic Evidence for a Family-Based Scandinavian Settlement of Shetland and Orkney during the Viking Periods," *Heredity* 95 (2005): 129–135.

24. Judith Jesch, *Women in the Viking Age* (Woodbridge, Suffolk, 1991), 96–123.

25. Shane McLeod, "Warriors and Women: The Sex Ratio of Norse Immigrants to Eastern England up to 900 AD," *Early Medieval Europe* 19 (2011): 332–353.

26. Matthew Townend, *Language and History in Viking Age England: Linguistic Relations between Speakers of Old Norse and Old English*, Studies in the Early Middle Ages (Turnhout, 2002).

27. I warmly thank my friend and colleague Professor Roberta Frank for permission to reproduce her text, which she composed for teaching purposes when we taught Viking culture together at Yale University.

28. Gillian Fellows-Jenssen, *The Vikings and Their Victims: The Evidence of the Names* (London, 1995); Jesch, *Women in the Viking Age*, 77–78; Gillian Fellows-Jenssen, "Scandinavian Place-Names in the British Isles," in *The Viking World*, ed. Stefan Brink and Neil Price (Abingdon, 2008), 391–400.

29. James H. Barrett, "The Norse in Scotland," in *The Viking World*, ed. Brink and Price, 411–427.

30. Gwyn Jones, *A History of the Vikings* (London, 1968), 289–311; Kirsten A. Seaver, *The Frozen Echo: Greenland and the Exploration of North America, ca. A.D. 1000–1500* (Stanford, 1996); William W. Fitzhugh and Elisabeth I. Ward, eds., *Vikings: The North Atlantic Saga* (Washington, D.C., 2000), 280–349; Jette Arneborg, Georg Nyegaard, and Orri Vésteinsson, eds., *Norse Greenland: Selected Papers from the Hvalsey Conference 2008, Journal of the North Atlantic*, special volume 2 (2012).

31. Niels Lynnerup, "Life and Death in Norse Greenland," in *Vikings: The North Atlantic Saga*, ed. Fitzhugh and Ward, 290–292.

32. Lynnerup, "Life and Death in Norse Greenland," 286–287.

33. Seaver, *The Frozen Echo*.

34. Jette Arneborg and Hans Christian Gulløv, eds., *Man, Culture and Environment in Ancient Greenland: Report on a Research Programme* (Copenhagen, 1998).

35. Joel Berglund, "The Farm beneath the Sand," in *Vikings: The North Atlantic Saga*, ed. Fitzhugh and Ward, 295–303.

36. Ívarr Bárðarson, *Det gamle Grønlands beskrivelse*, ed. Finnur Jónsson (Copenhagen, 1930).

37. Hans Christian Petersen, "The Norse Legacy in Greenland," in *Vikings: The North Atlantic Saga*, ed. Fitzhugh and Ward, 342.

38. Hildur Hermóðsdóttir, *Icelandic Turf Houses*, trans. Anna Yates (Reykjavik, 2012); Jesse L. Byock, *Viking Age Iceland* (London, 2001), 34–42.

CHAPTER 4: SHIPS, BOATS, AND FERRIES TO THE AFTERWORLD

1. *Royal Frankish Annals*, s.a. 810, trans. Scholz with Rogers, 91–92.
2. Max Vinner, *Viking Ship Museum Boats* (Roskilde, 2002), 14–17.
3. *Anglo-Saxon Chronicle*, s.a. 851, trans. Swanton, 64–65; *Annals of St-Bertin*, s.a. 859, trans. Nelson, 90.
4. *Battle of Maldon*, lines 29–41.
5. Erik Nylén, *Bygden, skeppen och havet*, Antikvariskt arkiv 49 (Stockholm, 1973).
6. *Heimskringla*, trans. Hollander in Snorri, *Heimskringla: History of the Kings of Norway*, 221.
7. Judith Jesch, *Ships and Men in the Late Viking Age: The Vocabulary of Runic Inscriptions and Skaldic Verse* (Woodbridge, 2001), 128–132.
8. Sigvatr Þórðarson, *Flokkr about Erlingr Skjálgsson* 1, ed. and trans. Judith Jesch in *Skaldic Poetry of the Scandinavian Middle Ages*, ed. Ross, 1.1.631
9. Vinner, *Viking Ship Museum Boats*, 14–17.
10. Þjóðólfr Arnórsson, *Magnússflokkr* 2 and 4, ed. and trans. Diana Whaley in *Skaldic Poetry of the Scandinavian Middle Ages*, ed. Ross, 2.1.65, 68.
11. "Havhingsten fra Glendalough (Skuldelev 2)," Viking Ship Museum, http://www.vikingeskibsmuseet.dk/en/research/ship-reconstruction/skuldelev-2/.
12. Niels Lund et al., *Two Voyagers at the Court of King Alfred: The Ventures of Ohthere and Wulfstan, Together with the Description of Northern Europe from the Old English Orosius* (York, 1984); Janet Bately and Anton Englert, *Ohthere's Voyages: A Late 9th-Century Account of Voyages along the Coasts of Norway and Denmark and Its Cultural Context* (Roskilde, 2007); Vinner, *Viking Ship Museum Boats*.
13. *Annals of St-Bertin*, s.a. 862 and 866, trans. Nelson, 98 and 131. See also Walther Vogel, *Die Normannen und das fränkische Reich bis zur Gründung der Normandie (799–911)*, Heidelberger Abhandlungen zur mittleren und neueren Geschichte 14 (Heidelberg, 1906), 213–218.
14. Rudolph Keyser et al., *Norges gamle love indtil 1387* (Christiania, 1846), 1.100.
15. Per Lundström, *De kommo vida: Vikingars hamn vid Paviken på Gotland*, Sjöhistoriska museets rapportserie 15 (Stockholm, 1981).
16. Eduard Mühle, "Gnezdovo—das alte Smolensk? Zur Deutung eines Siedlungskomplexes des ausgehenden 9. bis beginnend 11. Jahrhunderts," *Bericht der römisch-germanischen Kommission* 69 (1988): 358–410; Eduard Mühle, *Die städtischen Handelszentren der nordwestlichen Rus: Anfänge und frühe Entwicklung altrussischer Städte (bis gegen Ende des 12. Jahrhunderts)*, Quellen und Studien zur Geschichte des östlichen Europa 32 (Stuttgart, 1991), 239–255; Franklin and Shepard, *Emergence of Rus*, 100–102, 127–128.
17. Samnordisk runtextdatabas, U 778.
18. Samnordisk runtextdatabas, Sö 179.
19. Sigvatr, *Nesjavísur* 5, ed. and trans. R. D. Fulk in *Skaldic Poetry of the Scandinavian Middle Ages*, ed. Ross, 1.2.563–564.
20. *Landnámabók* H2, trans. Jan Bill, "Ships and Seamanship," in *The Oxford Illustrated History of the Vikings*, ed. Peter Sawyer (Oxford, 1997), 198.
21. *Annals of St-Bertin*, s.a. 838, trans. Nelson, 39.

22. *Anglo-Saxon Chronicle*, s.a. 876, trans. Swanton, 74.

23. Samnordisk runtextdatabas, U 258.

24. *Anglo-Saxon Chronicle*, s.a. 882, trans. Swanton, 76–79.

25. Steinn Herdísarson, *Nizarvísur* 1 and 4, ed. and trans. Kari Ellen Gade in *Skaldic Poetry of the Scandinavian Middle Ages*, ed. Ross, 1.2.360–363; Jesch, *Ships and Men*, 209–210.

26. Sigvatr, *Flokkr about Erlingr Skjálgsson* 1, ed. and trans. Judith Jesch in *Skaldic Poetry of the Scandinavian Middle Ages*, ed. Ross, 1.2.631.

27. This and the previous quotation come from *Flokkr about Sveinn Álfifuson*, ed. and trans. Diana Whaley in *Skaldic Poetry of the Scandinavian Middle Ages*, ed. Ross, 2.1.1029–1030. Tying the ships together is also mentioned in Sigvatr, *Nesjavísur* 2, ed. and trans. Russell Poole in *Skaldic Poetry of the Scandinavian Middle Ages*, ed. Ross, 1.2.559–561.

28. Sigvatr, *Flokkr* 2, ed. and trans. Jesch, 632.

29. Sigvatr, *Nesjavísur* 7, ed. and trans. Poole, 1.2.566–568.

30. Arnórr jarlaskáld Þórðarson, *Þórfinnsdrápa* 21, ed. and trans. Diana Whaley in *Skaldic Poetry of the Scandinavian Middle Ages*, ed. Ross, 2.1.254–255.

31. Arnórr, *Þórfinnsdrápa* 6, ed. and trans. Whaley, 236–237; Sigvatr, *Flokkr* 2; Sigvatr, *Nesjavísur* 8, ed. and trans. Poole, 568–569.

32. Þjóðólfr Arnórsson, *Stanzas about Magnús Óláfsson in Danaveldi* 1, ed. Diana Whaley in *Skaldic Poetry of the Scandinavian Middle Ages*, ed. Ross, 2.1.88–89.

33. Arnórr, *Magnússdrápa* 15, ed. and trans. Diana Whaley in *Skaldic Poetry of the Scandinavian Middle Ages*, ed. Ross, 2.1.225.

34. Samnordisk runtextdatabas, Sö 164; Jesch, *Ships and Men*, 120.

35. Torsten Capelle, "Schiffsetzungen," *Praehistorische Zeitschrift* 61 (1986): 1–62.

36. Tove Werner, "Stenskepp i Södermanland: Utbredning och datering," *Fornvännen* 98 (2003): 257–264.

37. *Beowulf* 26–29, 32–42, 47–50, trans. Liuzza, 49–50.

38. *Beowulf* 50–52, trans. Liuzza, 50.

39. Michael Müller-Wille, *Bestattung im Boot. Studien zu einer nordeuropäischen Grabsitte*, Offa 25/26 (Neumünster, 1970); Neil Price, "Dying and the Dead: Viking Age Mortuary Behaviour," in *The Viking World*, ed. Stefan Brink and Neil Price (Abingdon, 2008), 257–273.

40. Þór Magnússon, "Bátkumlið í Vatnsdal í Patreksfirði," *Árbok Hins íslenzka fornleifafélags* 63 (1966): 5–32; Kristján Eldjárn, *Kuml og haugfé úr heiðnum sið á Íslandi*, ed. Adolf Friðriksson (2nd ed. Reykjavik, 2000), 115–119. The grave was reused when, apparently, the bones of several other dead people were moved there. The judgment that it was first constructed for a woman rests on the grave goods found in it.

41. Samnordisk runtextdatabas, N 138, ed. *Norges innskrifter med de yngre runer*, Norges innskrifter indtil reformationen, afd 2 (Oslo, 1941–), 2.165–168.

42. Terje Gansum, "Fra jord till handling," in *Plats och praxis: Arkeologiska och religionshistoriska studier av norrön ritual*, ed. Kristina Jennbert, Anders Andrén, and Catharina Raudvere, Vägar till Midgård 2 (Lund, 2001), 249–286; RGA 22.306–311, s.v. "Oseberg," by E. Nyman, T. Gansum, A. E. Christensen, and K. Düwel.

43. Bengt Schönbäck and Lena Thunmark-Nylén, "De vikingatida båtgravarna i Valsgärde—relativ kronologi," *Fornvännen* 97 (2002): 1–8; RGA 35.375–379, s.v. "Valsgärde," by J. Ljungkvist.

44. The quotations here are chiefly from James E. Montgomery, "Ibn Fadlan and the Russiyah," *Journal of Arabic and Islamic Studies* 3 (2000): 1–25. For clarification I have used Richard N. Frye, *Ibn Fadlan's Journey to Russia: A Tenth-Century Traveler from Baghad to the Volga River* (Princeton, N.J., 2005), and Paul Lunde and Caroline Stone, *Ibn Fadlan and the Land of Darkness: Arab Travellers in the Far North* (London, 2012).

45. Aziz al-Azmeh, "Barbarians in Arab Eyes," *Past and Present* 134 (1992): 3–18.

CHAPTER 5: COINS, SILK, AND HERRING

1. Stavgard is run by Föreningen Stavgard, whose website has more information: http://www.stavgardgotland.com.

2. *Dagens Nyheter*, 19 June 2012, http://www.dn.se/nyheter/sverige/skarpta-straff-for-fornminnesbrott/.

3. Ann-Marie Pettersson, ed., *Spillingsskatten: Gotland i vikingatidens världshandel* (Visby, 2008); RGA 29.366–367, s.v. "Spillings," by Majvor Östergren.

4. Frye, *Ibn Fadlan's Journey to Russia*, 65.

5. Roman K. Kovalev and Alexis C. Kaelin, "Circulation of Arab Silver in Medieval Afro-Eurasia: Preliminary Observations," *History Compass* 5, no. 2 (2007): 560–580, http://www.blackwell-synergy.com/doi/abs/10.1111/j.1478-0542.2006.00376.x.

6. M.A.S. Blackburn and Kenneth Jonsson, "The Anglo-Saxon and Anglo-Norman Element of North European Coin Finds," in *Viking-Age Coinage in the Northern Lands*, ed. M.A.S. Blackburn and M. S. Metcalf, BAR International ser. 122 (Oxford, 1981): 147–255.

7. Dagfinn Skree, ed., *Kaupang in Skiringssal*, Kaupang Excavation Project Publication Series 1 = Norske Oldfunn 22 (Aarhus, 2007).

8. Lund et al., *Two Voyagers at the Court of King Alfred*; Bately and Englert, *Ohthere's Voyages*.

9. P. H. Sawyer, "Kings and Merchants," in *Early Medieval Kingship*, ed. P. H. Sawyer and I. N. Wood (Leeds, 1977), 139–158.

10. RGA 13.584, s.v. "Handel."

11. Lundström, *De kommo vida*.

12. Rimbert, *Life of Ansgar* 24, trans. Charles H. Robinson, *Anskar, the Apostle of the North, 801–865: Translated from the Vita Anskarii by Bishop Rimbert, His Fellow Missionary and Successor* ([London], 1921), 84.

13. Herbert Jankuhn, *Haithabu: Ein Handelsplatz der Wikingerzeit* (3rd ed. Neumünster, 1956).

14. Samnordisk runtextdatabas, DR 1; Wolfgang Laur, *Runendenkmäler in Schleswig-Holstein und in Nordschleswig* (2nd ed. Schleswig, 2009).

15. *Lausavísur from Haralds saga Sigurðsonar* 2, ed. and trans. Kari Ellen Gade in *Skaldic Poetry of the Scandinavian Middle Ages*, ed. Ross, 2.2.816–817.

16. Birgit Maixner, *Haithabu: Fernhandelszentrum zwischen den Welten* (Schleswig, 2010).

17. Lunde and Stone, *Ibn Fadlan and the Land of Darkness*, 163.

18. Rimbert, *Life of Ansgar* 10 and 33, trans. Robinson, 47 and 104.

19. Adam of Bremen, *History of the Archbishops of Hamburg-Bremen* scholion 126, trans. Francis Joseph Tschan and Timothy Reuter, Records of Western Civilization (New York, 2002), 201.

20. Helen Clarke and Björn Ambrosiani, *Towns in the Viking Age* (Leicester, 1991), 73; Adam, *History of the Archbishops of Hamburg-Bremen* scholion 142, trans. Tschan and Reuter, 210.

21. Lund et al., *Two Voyagers at the Court of King Alfred*; Anton Englert and Athena Trakadas, eds., *Wulfstan's Voyage: The Baltic Sea Region in the Early Viking Age as Seen from Shipboard* (Roskilde, 2009).

22. Samnordisk runtextdatabas, U 214–215.

23. Samnordisk runtextdatabas, Sö 198.

24. Jordanes, *Gothic History* 3.21, trans. in Jordanes, *The Gothic History of Jordanes in English Version*, 7.

25. Adam, *History of the Archbishops of Hamburg-Bremen* 4.18, trans. Tschan and Reuter, 199.

26. Lund et al., *Two Voyagers at the Court of King Alfred*; Bately and Englert, *Ohthere's Voyages*.

27. Per G. P. Ericson, Elisabeth Iregren, and Maria Vretemark, "Animal Exploitation at Birka—A Preliminary Report," *Fornvännen* 83 (1988): 81–88.

28. Kovalev and Kaelin, "Circulation of Arab Silver in Medieval Afro-Eurasia."

29. Janet Martin, *Treasure of the Land of Darkness: The Fur Trade and Its Significance for Medieval Russia* (Cambridge, 1986); Christian Lübke, *Fremde im östlichen Europa: Von Gesellschaften ohne Staat zu verstaatlichten Gesellschaften (9.–11. Jahrhundert)*, Ostmitteleuropa in Vergangenheit und Gegenwart (Cologne, 2001).

30. Youval Rotman, *Byzantine Slavery and the Mediterranean World*, trans. Jane Marie Todd (Cambridge, Mass., 2009).

31. Michael McCormick, "New Light on the 'Dark Ages': How the Slave Trade Fuelled the Carolingian Economy," *Past and Present*, no. 177 (2002): 17–54.

32. *Anglo-Saxon Chronicle*, s.a. 1048, trans. Swanton, 166.

33. Flodoard, *Annals*, s.a. 923, trans. in Flodoard, *The Annals of Flodoard of Reims, 919–966*, trans. Bernard S. Bachrach and Steven Fanning, Readings in Medieval Civilizations and Cultures 9 (Peterborough, Ont., 2004), 9.

34. Adam, *History of the Archbishops of Hamburg-Bremen* 4.6, trans. Tschan and Reuter, 190.

35. *Life of Rimbert* 18, ed. Georg Waitz, *Vita Anskarii auctore Rimberti: Accedit Vita Rimberti*, MGH: SS rer. Germ. (Hanover, 1884), 95–96.

36. Fitzhugh and Ward, *Vikings: The North Atlantic Saga*, 312.

37. Richard Abels, "What Has Weland to Do with Christ? The Franks Casket and the Acculturation of Christianity in Early Anglo-Saxon England," *Speculum* 84 (2009): 549–581.

38. Sigvatr, *Lausavísa* 9, ed. and trans. R. D. Fulk in *Skaldic Poetry of the Scandinavian Middle Ages*, ed. Ross, 1.2.710–712. See also Winroth, *Conversion of Scandinavia*, 77–78.

39. Agnes Geijer, *Die Textilfunde aus den Gräbern*, Birka: Untersuchungen und Studien 3 (Stockholm, 1938).

40. Lunde and Stone, *Ibn Fadlan and the Land of Darkness*.

41. Annika Larsson, "Vikingar begravda i kinesiskt siden," *Valör*, no. 3/4 (2008): 33–43.

42. Egon Wamers, "Kristne gjenstander i tidligvikingtidens Danmark," in *Kristendommen i Danmark før 1050*, ed. Niels Lund ([Roskilde], 2004), 43–59; Egon Wamers and Michael Brandt, *Die Macht des Silbers: Karolingische Schätze im Norden* (Regensburg, 2005)

43. Rimbert, *Life of Ansgar* 20 and 24, trans. Robinson, 70–73 and 84.

44. *Annals of St-Bertin*, s.a. 834, 835, 836, and 837, trans. Nelson, 30–37.

45. Peter Spufford, *Money and Its Use in Medieval Europe* (Cambridge and New York, 1988); J. L. Bolton, *Money in the Medieval English Economy, 973–1489* (Manchester, 2012).

46. Spufford, *Money and Its Use in Medieval Europe*, 55–73; Philip Grierson, M.A.S. Blackburn, and Lucia Travaini, *Medieval European Coinage: With a Catalogue of the Coins in the Fitzwilliam Museum, Cambridge* (Cambridge, 1986), 190–266; Adriaan E. Verhulst, *The Carolingian Economy*, Cambridge Medieval Textbooks (New York, 2002), 117–118.

47. *Annals of Ulster*, s.a. 824, ed. and trans. Mac Airt and Mac Niocaill, 281.

48. *Annals of St-Bertin*, s.a. 858, trans. Nelson, 86.

49. Georges Duby, *The Early Growth of the European Economy: Warriors and Peasants from the Seventh to the Twelfth Century*, World Economic History (Ithaca, N.Y., 1974), 118.

50. *Annals of St-Bertin*, s.a. 873, trans. Nelson, 185.

51. Mark Blackburn, "Money and Coinage," in *The New Cambridge Medieval History*, vol. 1, ed. Rosamond McKitterick (Cambridge, 1995), 557.

52. Sture Bolin, "Mohammed, Charlemagne and Rurik," *Scandinavian Economic History Review* 1 (1953): 5–39; Spufford, *Money and Its Use in Medieval Europe*, 68; Michael McCormick, *Origins of the European Economy: Communications and Commerce A.D. 300–900* (Cambridge, 2001); McCormick, "New Light on the 'Dark Ages'"; Kovalev and Kaelin, "Circulation of Arab Silver in Medieval Afro-Eurasia: Preliminary Observations."

53. Heiko Steuer, "Der Handel der Wikingerzeit zwischen Nord- und Westeuropa aufgrund archäologischer Zeugnisse," in *Untersuchungen zu Handel und Verkehr der vor- und frühgeschichtlichen Zeit in Mittel- und Nordeuropa*, vol. 4, *Der Handel der Karolinger- und Wikingerzeit: Bericht über die Kolloquien der Kommission für die Altertumskunde Mittel- und Nordeuropas in den Jahren 1980 bis 1983*, ed. Klaus Düwel et al. (Göttingen, 1987), 113–197; Ingrid Gustin, "Means of Payment and the Use of Coins in the Viking Age Town of Birka in Sweden: Preliminary Results," *Current Swedish Archaeology* 6 (1998): 73–83.

54. See chapter 7.

55. Ola Kyhlberg, "Vågar och viktlod: Diskussion kring frågor om precision och noggrannhet," *Fornvännen* 70 (1975): 156–165; Ola Kyhlberg, *Vikt och värde: Arkeologiska studier i värdemätning, betalningsmedel och metrologi under yngre järnålder: 1. Helgö, 2. Birka*, Stockholm Studies in Archaeology 1 (Stockholm, 1980).

56. James H. Barrett, Alison M. Locker, and Callum M. Roberts, "'Dark Age Economics' Revisited: The English Fish Bone Evidence, AD 600–1600,"

Antiquity 78 (2004): 618–636; James Campbell, "Domesday Herrings," in *East Anglia's History: Studies in Honor of Norman Scarfe*, ed. Christopher Harper-Bill, Carole Rawcliffe, and Richard G. Wilson (Woodbridge, 2002), 5–17.

57. Jan Bill, "Viking Ships and the Sea," in *The Viking World*, ed. Stefan Brink and Neil Price (Abingdon, 2008), 170–180.

58. Adam, *History of the Archbishops of Hamburg-Bremen* scholion 142, , trans. Tschan and Reuter, 210.

59. Brita Malmer, *Den svenska mynthistorien: Vikingatiden ca 995–1030* (Stockholm, 2010).

60. Ildar H. Garipzanov, *The Symbolic Language of Authority in the Carolingian World (c. 751–877)*, Brill's Series on the Early Middle Ages 16 (Leiden, 2008).

CHAPTER 6: FROM CHIEFTAINS TO KINGS

1. Sigvatr Þórðarson, *Erfidrápa Óláfs helga* 2 and 21, ed. Judith Jesch in *Skaldic Poetry of the Scandinavian Middle Ages*, ed. Ross, 1.2.666–668 and 689–691.

2. Einarr skálaglamm Helgason, *Vellekla* 32, ed. and trans. Edith Marold in *Skaldic Poetry of the Scandinavian Middle Ages*, ed. Ross, 1.1.323–324.

3. Peter Sawyer, *Da Danmark blev Danmark: Fra ca. år 700 til ca. 1050*, trans. Marie Hvidt, Gyldendal-Politikens Danmarkshistorie (Copenhagen, 1988), 3.82.

4. Mats Burström, *Arkeologisk samhällsavgränsning: En studie av vikingatida samhällsterritorier i Smålands inland*, Stockholm Studies in Archaeology 9 (Stockholm, 1991); Åke Hyenstrand, *Lejonet, draken och korset: Sverige 500–1000* (Lund, 1996), 21–36. Per H. Ramqvist, "Perspektiv på lokal variation och samhälle i Nordens folkvandringstid," in *Samfundsorganisation og regional variation: Norden i romersk jernålder og folkevandringstid* (Aarhus, 1991), reconstructs fifteen independent "petty kingdoms" in early Scandinavia.

5. Jordanes, *De origine actibusque Getarum*, 19–24, ed. by Francesco Giunta and Antonino Grillone, Fonti per la storia d'Italia 117 (Rome, 1991), 9–11. A detailed discussion of this passage is found in Josef Svennung, *Jordanes und Scandia: Kritisch-exegetische Studien*, Skrifter utgivna av K. Humanistiska vetenskapssamfundet i Uppsala 44:2A (Stockholm, 1967). Cf., e.g., Hyenstrand, *Lejonet, draken och korset: Sverige 500–1000*, 39–40. Procopius, who was a contemporary of Jordanes, stated that thirteen different peoples lived in Scandinavia: *History of the Wars* 6.15.3, trans. H. B. Dewing, The Loeb Classical Library 107 (Cambridge, Mass., 1919), 414–415. Several tenth-century runic inscriptions mention Finnveden; see Sven B. F. Jansson, *The Runes of Sweden* (Stockholm, 1962), 63 and 74–75; and Samnordisk runtextdatabas, Sm 35.

6. Byock, *Viking Age Iceland*.

7. *Royal Frankish Annals*, s.a. 814, trans. Scholz with Rogers, 97–99.

8. Sigvatr Þórðarson, *Bersǫglisvísur* 2, ed. and trans. Kari Ellen Gade in *Skaldic Poetry of the Scandinavian Middle Ages*, ed. Ross, 2.1.14–15.

9. Arnórr jarlaskald, fragment 4, ed. and trans. Diana Whaley, *The Poetry of Arnórr Jarlaskáld: An Edition and Study*, Westfield Publications in Medieval Studies 8 (Turnhout, 1998), 134 and 308–310.

10. Egill Skallagrimsson, *Höfuðlausn* 17, ed. Finnur Jónsson, *Den norsk-islandske skjaldedigtning* (Copenhagen, 1912), B:1, 33.

11. Arnórr jarlaskald, *Haraldsdrápa* 13, ed. and trans. Diana Whaley in *Skaldic Poetry of the Scandinavian Middle Ages*, ed. Ross, 2.1. 274. These lines are capable of several interpretations, as outlined by Whaley, 275.

12. *Beowulf*, lines 2633–2638, trans. Liuzza, 128.

13. *Beowulf*, lines 2847, 2850, 2890–2891, trans. Liuzza, 134–135.

14. Bjarni Einarsson, ed., *Ágrip af Nóregskonunga sǫgum: Fagrskinna—Noregs konunga tal*, Íslenzk fornrit 29 (Reykjavik, 1985), 87; Alison Finlay, *Fagrskinna: A Catalogue of the Kings of Norway* (Leiden, 2004), 67

15. Samnordisk runtextdatabas, DR 291.

16. *Thorfinnsdrápa* 2, ed. and trans. Whaley in *Skaldic Poetry of the Scandinavian Middle Ages*, ed. Ross, 2.1.232.

17. *Beowulf* 1020–1049, trans. Liuzza, 80.

18. *Sigurðardrápa* 6, ed. Finnur, *Den norsk-islandske skjaldedigtning*, B:1, 69–70; Klaus Düwel, *Das Opferfest von Lade: Quellenkritische Untersuchungen zur germanischen Religionsgeschichte*, Wiener Arbeiten zur germanischen Altertumskunde und Philologie 27 (Wien, 1985); Frands Herschend, *Livet i hallen: Tre fallstudier i den yngre järnålderns aristokrati*, Occasional Papers in Archaeology (Uppsala) 14 (Uppsala, 1997), 61–89.

19. Samnordisk runtextdatabas, U 739.

20. Judith Jesch, "In Praise of Ástríðr Óláfsdóttir," *Saga-Book* 24 (1994–1997): 1–18; Jóhanna Katrín Friðriksdóttir, *Women in Old Norse Literature: Bodies, Words, and Power* (New York, 2013), 93–94.

21. Winroth, *Conversion of Scandinavia*, 159.

22. Bjørn Eithun, Magnus Rindal, and Tor Ulset, *Den eldre Gulatingslova*, Norrøne tekster 6 (Oslo, 1994), 32.

23. Steinar Imsen, *Hirdloven til Norges konge og hans håndgangne menn* (Oslo, 2000), 64.

24. Sverre Bagge, *From Viking Stronghold to Christian Kingdom: State Formation in Norway, c. 900–1350* (Copenhagen, 2010); Hans Jacob Orning, *Frem til 1400*, Norvegr: Norges historie (Oslo, 2011).

25. Winroth, *Conversion of Scandinavia*, 13.

26. Generally, see Sawyer, *Da Danmark blev Danmark*; and Ole Fenger, *"Kirker reses alle vegne": 1050–1250*, Gyldendal og Politikens Danmarkshistorie (Copenhagen, 1989).

27. Else Roesdahl, *The Vikings* (2nd ed. London, 1998), 93.

28. H. Hellmuth Andersen, *Til hele rigets værn: Danevirkes arkæologi og historie* (Højbjerg, 2004).

29. Anders Götherström, *Acquired or Inherited Prestige? Molecular Studies of Family Structures and Local Horses in Central Svealand during the Early Medieval Period*, Theses and Papers in Scientific Archaeology 4 (Stockholm, 2001).

30. http://www.bluetooth.com/Pages/Fast-Facts.aspx.

31. A valuable summary of what is known about the burials in Jelling is found in Niels Lund, "Gorm den gamle og Thyre Danebod," in *Danske kongegrave*, ed. Karin Kryger (Copenhagen, 2014). I wish to thank Professor Lund for allowing me to read the typescript of his essay before publication. The theory that Gorm was moved from the mound to the church is presented in Knud J. Krogh, *Gåden om Kong Gorms grav: Historien om Nordhøjen i Jelling*, Vikingekongernes

monumenter i Jelling 1 (Copenhagen, 1993). Preliminary reports from the recent exacavations in Jelling are found in the journal *Skalk: Nyt om gammelt*.

32. Andersen, *Til hele rigets værn: Danevirkes arkæologi og historie*, 53–57.

33. Generally, see Jón Viðar Sigurðsson, *Norsk historie, 800–1300*, Samlagets Norsk historie, 800–2000 (Oslo, 1999); Claus Krag, *Norges historie fram til 1319* (Oslo, 2000); and Orning, *Frem til 1400*.

34. Generally, see Dick Harrison, *600–1350*, Sveriges historia (Stockholm, 2009); and Dick Harrison and Kristina Ekero Svensson, *Vikingaliv* (Stockholm, 2009).

35. Thomas Lindkvist, *Plundring, skatter och den feodala statens framväxt: Organisatoriska tendenser i Sverige under övergången från vikingatid till tidig medeltid*, Opuscula historica Upsaliensia 1 (3rd ed. Uppsala, 1993).

CHAPTER 7: AT HOME ON THE FARM

1. Lars Andersson and Margareta Boije-Backe, *Jarlabankeättens gravplats vid Broby bro: Arkeologisk delundersökning av gravplats med tre skelettgravar vid Broby bro, Täby socken och kommun, Uppland*, Stockholms läns museum: Rapport 1999:4 (Stockholm, 1999).

2. Winroth, *Conversion of Scandinavia*, 110.

3. Rune Edberg, "Spår efter en tidig Jerusalemsfärd," *Fornvännen* 101 (2006): 342–346; Johanne Autenrieth, Dieter Geuenich, and Karl Schmid, eds., *Das Verbrüderungsbuch der Abtei Reichenau*, Monumenta Germaniae Historica: Libri memoriales et necrologia, Nova series 1 (Hanover, 1979), 151.

4. Samnordisk runtextdatabas, U 101, U 136, U 137, U 143, U 310.

5. Winroth, *Conversion of Scandinavia*, 140–144.

6. Ursula Dronke, *The Poetic Edda* (Oxford, 1969–2011), 2.176.

7. Birgit Sawyer, *The Viking-Age Rune-Stones: Custom and Commemoration in Early Medieval Scandinavia* (Oxford, 2000), 112.

8. Kurt Brøste et al., *Prehistoric Man in Denmark: A Study in Physical Anthropology*, vol. 3, *Iron Age Man in Denmark*, Nordiske fortidsminder Serie B—in quarto 8 (Copenhagen, 1984); Peter Bratt, ed., *Forntid i ny dager* (Stockholm, 1998), 168–176; Palle Eriksen et al., eds., *Vikinger i vest: Vikingetiden i Vestjylland* (Højbjerg, 2009).

9. Fredrik Svanberg, *Vikingatiden i Skåne* (Lund, 2000), 28–32.

10. Samnordisk runtextdatabas, N 184.

11. *Anglo-Saxon Chronicle*, s.a. 876, trans. Swanton, 75.

12. Jenny Jochens, *Women in Old Norse Society* (Ithaca, N.Y., 1995); Stig Welinder, Ellen Anne Pedersen, and Mats Widgren, *Jordbrukets första femtusen år*, Det svenska jordbrukets historia (Stockholm, 1998).

13. Samnordisk runtextdatabas, Vs 24.

14. Andrew Dennis, Peter Godfrey Foote, and Richard Perkins, *Laws of Early Iceland: The Codex Regius of Grágás with Material from Other Manuscripts*, University of Manitoba Icelandic Studies 3 and 5 (Winnipeg, 1980–2000), 2.66; Jochens, *Women in Old Norse Society*, 116–118.

15. *Rígsþula* 16, trans. Larrington, *The Poetic Edda: A New Translation*, 248.

16. Óttar svarti, *Hǫfudlausn*, 5, ed. and trans. Matthew Townend in *Skaldic Poetry of the Scandinavian Middle Ages*, ed. Ross, 1.2.747–747; see also Jesch, *Women in the Viking Age*.

17. Roesdahl, *The Vikings*, 34–38.

18. Kent Andersson, *Glas från romare till vikingar* (Uppsala, 2010).

19. *Rígsþula* 15, trans. Larrington, *The Poetic Edda: A New Translation*, 248.

20. Mette Iversen, ed., *Mammen: Grav, kunst og samfund i vikingetid*, Jysk Arkaeologisk Selskabs skrifter 28 (Højbjerg, 1991).

21. Dronke, *The Poetic Edda*, 2.181.

22. James Graham-Campbell and Magdalena Valor, eds., *The Archaeology of Medieval Europe*, Acta Jutlandica 83:1 (Århus, 2007), 192–207

23. Steen Hvass, "The Viking-Age Settlement of Vorbasse, Central Jutland," *Acta Archaeologica* 50 (1979): 137–172.

24. *Beowulf*, lines 81–82, trans. Liuzza, 51.

25. Bratt, *Forntid i ny dager*, 222–230; Cecilia Åqvist, *Sanda—en gård i södra Uppland: Bebyggelse från vendeltid till 1600-tal: Uppland, Fresta socken, Sanda 1:1, RAÄ 147*, UV Mitt Rapport 2004:15 (Hägersten, 2006).

26. *Rígsþula* 8 and 12, trans. Larrington, *The Poetic Edda: A New Translation*, 248.

27. Roy C. Cave and Herbert H. Coulson, *A Sourcebook for Medieval Economic History* (New York, 1936), 46–48, as modernized by Jerome S. Arkenberg at http://www.fordham.edu/halsall/source/1000workers.asp.

28. Michael McCormick, Paul Edward Dutton, and Paul A. Mayewski, "Volcanoes and the Climate Forcing of Carolingian Europe, A.D. 750–950," *Speculum* 82 (2007): 865–895.

29. Rodulfus Glaber, *The Five Books of History* 2.9.17, ed. and trans. John France, Oxford Medieval Texts (Oxford 1989), 81–83.

30. *Beowulf*, lines 3150–3155, trans. Liuzza, 143–144.

CHAPTER 8: THE RELIGIONS OF THE NORTH

1. Einarr skálaglam Helgason, *Vellekla* 14, ed. Edith Marold in *Skaldic Poetry of the Scandinavian Middle Ages*, ed. Ross, 1.1.301–303. See also Christopher Abram, *Myths of the Pagan North: The Gods of the Norsemen* (London, 2011), 130.

2. Einarr, *Vellekla* 14, ed. Marold, 322–323. See also Abram, *Myths of the Pagan North*, 134.

3. *Hávamál* 156, trans. Larrington, *The Poetic Edda: A New Translation*, 36.

4. Winroth, *Conversion of Scandinavia*.

5. Konstantin Reichardt, "Die Thórsdrápa des Eilífr Godrúnarson: Textinterpretation," *Publications of the Modern Language Association of America* 63, no. 2 (1948): 329–391; Roberta Frank, "Hand Tools and Power Tools in Eilífr's Þórsdrápa," in *Structure and Meaning in Old Norse Literature: New Approaches to Textual Analysis and Literary Criticism*, ed. John Lindow, Lars Lönnroth, and Gerd Wolfgang Weber (Odense, 1986), 94–109; Abram, *Myths of the Pagan North*.

6. Stefan Brink, "How Uniform Was the Old Norse Religion?," in *Learning and Understanding in the Old Norse World*, ed. Judith Quinn, Kate Heslop, and Tarrin Wills (Turnhout, 2007), 106–136.

7. John Lindow, "Thor's 'hamarr,'" *Journal of Germanic and English Philology* 93, no. 4 (1994): 485–503; Thomas A. DuBois, *Nordic Religions in the Viking Age* (Philadelphia, 1999), 158–163; Sæbjørg Walaker Nordeide, *The Viking Age as*

a Period of Religious Transformation: The Christianization of Norway from AD 560–1150/1200, Studies in Viking and Medieval Scandinavia 2 (Turnhout, 2011), 235–244.

8. Lilla Kopár, *Gods and Settlers: The Iconography of Norse Mythology in Anglo-Scandinavian Sculpture*, Studies in the Early Middle Ages 25 (Turnhout, 2012), 58–68.

9. Samnordisk runtextdatabas, U 1161.

10. Bragi gamli, *Ragnarsdrápa* 16, ed. Finnur, *Den norsk-islandske skjaldedigtning*, B:1, 4.

11. Úlfr Uggsson, *Húsdrapa* 6, ed. Finnur, *Den norsk-islandske skjaldedigtning*, B:1, 129.

12. Roberta Frank, "Snorri and the Mead of Poetry," in *Speculum norroenum: Norse Studies in Memory of Gabriel Turville-Petre*, ed. Ursula Dronke et al. (Odense, 1981), 155–170.

13. Otto Gschwantler, "Christus, Thor, und die Midgardschlange," in *Festschrift für Otto Höffler zum 65. Geburtstag*, ed. Otto Gschwantler (Vienna, 1968), 145–168; Henrik Janson, "Snorre, Tors fiskafänge och frågan om den religionshistoriska kontexten," in *Hedendomen i historiens spegel: Bilder av det förkristna Norden*, ed. Catharina Raudvere, Anders Andrén, and Kristina Jennbert, Vägar till Midgård 6 (Lund, 2005), 33–55.

14. *Vafthrudnir's Sayings* 35, trans. Larrington, *The Poetic Edda: A New Translation*, 45. About *lúðr*, see Anne Holtsmark, "Det norrøne ord lúðr," *Maal og minne* (1946): 48–65.

15. Snorri Sturluson, *The Prose Edda: Norse Mythology* (London, 2005), 15–16, adapted.

16. Snorri Sturluson, *The Prose Edda*, 33.

17. DuBois, *Nordic Religions in the Viking Age*, 150.

18. Samnordisk runtextdatabas, DR 220.

19. Adam, *History of the Archbishops of Hamburg-Bremen* 4.26–27, trans. Tschan and Reuter, 207–208.

20. Thietmar of Merseburg, *Chronicon* 1.17, trans. David Warner, *Ottonian Germany: The Chronicon of Thietmar of Merseburg*, Manchester Medieval Sources Series (Manchester, 2001), 80.

21. DuBois, *Nordic Religions in the Viking Age*, 48.

22. Olof Sundqvist, Per Vikstrand, and John Ljungkvist, eds., *Gamla Uppsala i ny belysning*, Religionsvetenskapliga studier från Gävle 9 (Uppsala, 2013).

23. Sigvatr Þórðarson, *Austrfararvísur* 4–5, ed. and trans. R. D. Fulk in *Skaldic Poetry of the Scandinavian Middle Ages*, ed. Ross, 1.2.589–591; trans. R. I. Page, *Chronicles of the Vikings: Records, Memorials, and Myths* (Toronto, 1995), 50.

24. Lunde and Stone, *Ibn Fadlan and the Land of Darkness*, 163.

25. *Völuspá* 7, trans. Larrington, *The Poetic Edda: A New Translation*, 5.

26. Olaf Olsen, *Hørg, hov og kirke: Historiske og arkæologiske vikingetidsstudier* (Copenhagen, 1966), 280; Anette Lassen, *Oden på kristent pergament: En teksthistorisk studie* (Copenhagen, 2011).

27. DuBois, *Nordic Religions in the Viking Age*, 153; Michael Müller-Wille, *Das wikingerzeitliche Gräberfeld von Thumby-Bienebek (Kr. Rendsburg-Eckernförde)*, Offa-Bücher 36 (Neumünster, 1976), 1.54–55.

28. *Landnámabók* 218, trans. Herman Pálsson and Paul Edwards, *The Book of Settlements: Landnámabók* (Winnipeg, 1972), 97. About *Landnámabók* as a historical source, see Orri Vésteinsson and Adolf Friðriksson, "Creating a Past: A Historiography of the Settlement of Iceland," in *Contact, Continuity and Collapse: The Norse Colonization of the North Atlantic*, ed. James Barrett, Studies in the Early Middle Ages 5 (Turnhout, 2003), 139–161.

29. Rimbert, *Life of Ansgar* 11, trans. Robinson, 49.

30. Widukind of Corvey, *Res gestae Saxonicae* 3.65, ed. Paul Hirsch and Hans-Eberhard Lohmann, *Die Sachsengeschichte des Widukind von Korvei*, MGH SS rer. Germ. (Hanover, 1935), 140.

31. *Alcuini sive Albini epistolae* 6, ed. Ernst Dümmler, MGH: Epp. 4 (Berlin, 1895), 31.

32. Winroth, *Conversion of Scandinavia*, 12–16.

33. Eric Knibbs, *Ansgar, Rimbert, and the Forged Foundations of Hamburg-Bremen* (Farnham, Surrey, 2011).

34. Winroth, *Conversion of Scandinavia*, 149.

35. *Anglo-Saxon Chronicle*, s.a. 994, trans. Swanton, 126–129.

36. Oddr Snorrason, *The Saga of Olaf Tryggvason*, trans. Theodore M. Andersson (Ithaca, N.Y., 2003).

37. Sigvatr, *Lausavísa* 19, ed. and trans. R. D. Fulk, *Skaldic Poetry of the Scandinavian Middle Ages*, ed. Ross, 1.2.724–725.

38. Samnordisk runtextdatabas, N 210.

39. MGH: Concilia 6.1.140 and 158.

40. MGH: Auctores antiquissimi 9.574.

CHAPTER 9: ARTS AND LETTERS

1. Peterson, *Nordiskt runnamnslexikon med tillägg av frekvenstabeller och finalalfabetisk ordlista.*

2. Klaus Düwel, *Runenkunde* (4th ed. Stuttgart, 2008), 159.

3. Samnordisk runtextdatabas, U 53.

4. Samnordisk runtextdatabas, Sm 37.

5. Samnordisk runtextdatabas, Sm 36.

6. Helmer Gustavson, "Runorna som officerens hemliga skrift och allmogens vardagsvara," in *Gamla och nya runor: Artiklar 1982–2001* (Stockholm, 2003), 113–121; Tore Janson, *Språken och historien* (Stockholm, 1997), 118.

7. Mats G. Larsson, *Kensington 1998: Runfyndet som gäckade världen* (Stockholm, 2012).

8. Samnordisk runtextdatabas, DR 1; see also Düwel, *Runenkunde*, 102.

9. Samnordisk runtextdatabas, Ög 136; see also Erik Brate, *Östergötlands runinskrifter*, Sveriges runinskrifter 2 (Stockholm, 1911), 231–255; Elias Wessén, *Runstenen vid Röks kyrka*, Kungl. Vitterhets-, historie- och antikvitetsakademiens handlingar: Filologisk-filosofiska serien, 5 (Stockholm, 1958); Bo Ralph, "Gåtan som lösning—Ett bidrag till förståelsen av Rökstenens runinskrift," *Maal og minne* (2007): 133–157.

10. Samnordisk runtextdatabas, Öl 1; Roberta Frank, *Old Norse Court Poetry: The Dróttkvætt Stanza*, Islandica 42 (Ithaca, N.Y., 1978); see also Roberta Frank, "Like a Bridge of Stones," *Yale Review* 99, no. 4 (2011), 170–177.

11. *Beowulf,* lines 859–861, trans. Liuzza, 74–75.

12. DuBois, *Nordic Religions in the Viking Age,* 85–91.

13. Sveinbjörn Egilsson and Finnur Jónsson, *Lexicon poeticum antiquæ linguæ Septentrionalis: Ordbog over det norsk-islandske skjaldesprog* (2nd ed. Copenhagen, 1931).

14. Sveinbjörn and Finnur, *Lexicon poeticum.*

15. Sven Söderberg and Erik Brate, *Ölands runinskrifter,* Sveriges runinskrifter 1 (Stockholm, 1900), 14–37; Richard Cleasby, Guðbrandur Vigfússon, and William A. Craigie, *An Icelandic–English Dictionary* (2nd ed. Oxford, 1957), 766.

16. *Beowulf,* 497–498, trans. Liuzza, 64.

17. Arnórr jarlaskáld Þórðarson, *Hrynhenda, Magnússdrápa,* ed. and trans. Diana Whaley in *Skaldic Poetry of the Scandinavian Middle Ages,* ed. Ross, 2.1.181–206.

18. Arnórr, *Hrynhenda, Magnússdrápa* 16, ed. and trans. Whaley, 202; Arnórr, *Magnússdrápa* 2, ed. and trans. Diana Whaley in *Skaldic Poetry of the Scandinavian Middle Ages,* ed. Ross, 2.1.209–210

19. *Krákumál* 14, ed. Finnur, *Den norsk-islandske skjaldedigtning,* B:1, 652; Tindr Hallkelsson, *Hákonardrápa* 1, ed. Russell Poole in *Skaldic Poetry of the Scandinavian Middle Ages,* ed. Ross, 1.1.338–341. See also Roberta Frank, "Quid Hinieldus cum feminis: The Hero and Women at the End of the First Millennium," in *La functione dell'eroe germanico: Storicita, metafora, paradigma,* ed. Teresa Paroli (Rome, 1995), 21.

20. Haraldr harðráði Sigurðarson, *Lausavísur* 4, ed. and trans. Kari Ellen Gade in *Skaldic Poetry of the Scandinavian Middle Ages,* ed. Ross, 2.1.46–47; see also Jesch, *Women in the Viking Age.*

21. Þjóðólfr, Arnórsson, *Stanzas about Magnús Óláfsson in Danaveldi* 1, ed. and trans. Diana Whaley in *Skaldic Poetry of the Scandinavian Middle Ages,* ed. Ross, 2.1.88.

22. Eyvindr skáldaspillir Finnsson, *Háleygjatal* 12, ed. and trans. Russell Poole in *Skaldic Poetry of the Scandinavian Middle Ages,* ed. Ross, 1.1.211–212. See also Roberta Frank, "The Lay of the Land in Skaldic Praise Poetry," in *Myth in Early Northwest Europe,* ed. Stephen O. Glosecki (Tempe, Ariz., 2007), 175–196.

23. Janet Nelson, "The Frankish Empire," in *The Oxford Illustrated History of the Vikings,* ed. Peter Sawyer (Oxford, 1997), 19–47, points out that no Viking rapes are mentioned in the *Annals of St-Bertin,* and I have not seen any such reference in any other of the contemporary year-by-year accounts of Viking attacks, such as the *Anglo-Saxon Chronicle* and the *Annals of Fulda.*

24. Þjóðólfr, *Stanzas* 4, ed. and trans. Whaley, 91.

25. *Kulturhistoriskt lexikon för nordisk medeltid från vikingatid till reformationstid* (Malmö, 1956–1982), 19.468–469, s.v. "Valkyrje," by Anne Holtsmark.

26. Þórbjörn hornklofi, *Haraldskvæði (Hrafnsmál)* 1 and 3, ed. R. D. Fulk in *Skaldic Poetry of the Scandinavian Middle Ages,* ed. Ross, 1.1.94–97. Quotation below is from stanza 6. Unlike Fulk, I have chosen not to emend the text of the manuscripts: "beak" and "mouth" are in the singular, while "ravens" appears in the plural.

27. Rǫgnvaldr jarl Kali Kolsson, *Lausavísa* 15, ed. and trans. Judith Jesch in *Skaldic Poetry of the Scandinavian Middle Ages,* ed. Ross, 2.2.592–593.

28. Sandra Ballif Straubhaar, *Old Norse Women's Poetry: The Voices of Female Skalds* (Rochester, N.Y., 2011).

29. Jesch, *Women in the Viking Age*, 166–167.

30. James Graham-Campbell, *Viking Art* (London, 2013), 58–59.

31. Samnordisk runtextdatabas, Sö 101. See also David M. Wilson, *Vikingatidens konst*, trans. Henrika Ringbom, Signums svenska konsthistoria (Lund, 1995), 166–174; Klaus Düwel, "On the Sigurd Representations in Great Britain and Scandinavia," in *Languages and Cultures: Studies in Honor of Edgar C. Polomé*, ed. Mohammad Ali Jazayery and Werner Winter (Berlin, 1988), 133–156; and Nancy L. Wicker, "The Scandinavian Animal Styles in Response to Mediterranean and Christian Narrative Art," in *The Cross Goes North: Processes of Conversion in Northern Europe, AD 300–1300*, ed. Martin Carver (York, 2003), 531–550.

32. Erik Nylén and Jan Peder Lamm, *Bildstenar* (3rd ed. Stockholm, 2003).

33. David M. Wilson, "The Development of Viking Art," in *The Viking World*, ed. Stefan Brink and Neil Price (Abingdon, 2008), 321–338.

34. Wilson, *Vikingatidens konst*; Graham-Campbell, *Viking Art*.

35. Wilson, "The Development of Viking Art."

36. Mårten Stenberger, "Erikstorpsspännet och Hedeby," *Fornvännen* 45 (1950): 36–40.

37. Samnordisk runtextdatabas, U 871.

CHAPTER 10: EPILOGUE

1. Theodore M. Andersson and Kari Ellen Gade, *Morkinskinna: The Earliest Icelandic Chronicle of the Norwegian Kings (1030–1157)*, Islandica 51 (Ithaca, N.Y., 2000), 271; Kelly DeVries, *The Norwegian Invasion of England in 1066*, Warfare in History (Woodbridge, U.K., 1999), 291.

2. David Bates, *Normandy before 1066* (London, 1982).

3. Good surveys of medieval Scandinavian history in English are Birgit Sawyer and P. H. Sawyer, *Medieval Scandinavia: From Conversion to Reformation, circa 800–1500*, The Nordic Series 17 (Minneapolis, 1993); and Sverre Bagge, *Cross and Scepter: The Rise of the Scandinavian Kingdoms from the Vikings to the Reformation* (Princeton, N.J., 2014).

4. Lindkvist, *Plundring, skatter och den feodala statens framväxt*, 61.

5. Lindkvist, *Plundring, skatter och den feodala statens framväxt*.

6. Niels Lund, *Lið, leding og landeværn: Hær og samfund i Danmark i ældre middelalder* (Roskilde, 1996); Rikke Malmros, *Vikingernes syn på militær og samfund belyst gennem skjaldenes fyrstedigtning* (Århus, 2010); Bagge, *From Viking Stronghold to Christian Kingdom*, 72–79.

7. Bagge, *Cross and Scepter*.

8. Vegard Skånland, *Det eldste norske provinsialstatutt* (Oslo, 1969).

BIBLIOGRAPHY

Abels, Richard. "What Has Weland to Do with Christ? The Franks Casket and the Acculturation of Christianity in Early Anglo-Saxon England." *Speculum* 84 (2009): 549–581.

Abram, Christopher. *Myths of the Pagan North: The Gods of the Norsemen.* London, 2011.

Adam of Bremen. *History of the Archbishops of Hamburg-Bremen.* Translated by Francis Joseph Tschan and Timothy Reuter. Records of Western Civilization. New York, 2002.

Bjarni Einarsson, ed. *Ágrip af Nóregskonunga sǫgum: Fagrskinna—Noregs konunga tal.* Íslenzk fornrit 29. Reykjavik, 1985.

al-Azmeh, Aziz. "Barbarians in Arab Eyes." *Past and Present* 134 (1992): 3–18.

Andersen, H. Hellmuth. *Til hele rigets værn: Danevirkes arkæologi og historie.* Højbjerg, 2004.

Andersson, Kent. *Glas från romare till vikingar.* Uppsala, 2010.

Andersson, Lars, and Margareta Boije-Backe. *Jarlabankeättens gravplats vid Broby bro: Arkeologisk delundersökning av gravplats med tre skelettgravar vid Broby bro, Täby socken och kommun, Uppland.* Stockholms läns museum: Rapport 1999:4. Stockholm, 1999.

Andersson, Theodore M., and Kari Ellen Gade. *Morkinskinna: The Earliest Icelandic Chronicle of the Norwegian Kings (1030–1157).* Islandica 51. Ithaca, N.Y., 2000.

Åqvist, Cecilia. *Sanda—en gård i södra Uppland: Bebyggelse från vendeltid till 1600-tal: Uppland, Fresta socken, Sanda 1:1, RAÄ 147.* UV Mitt Rapport 2004:15. Hägersten, 2006.

Arneborg, Jette, and Hans Christian Gulløv, eds. *Man, Culture and Environment in Ancient Greenland: Report on a Research Programme.* Copenhagen, 1998.

Arneborg, Jette, Georg Nyegaard, and Orri Vésteinsson, eds. *Norse Greenland: Selected Papers from the Hvalsey Conference 2008. Journal of the North Atlantic,* special volume 2 (2012).

Autenrieth, Johanne, Dieter Geuenich, and Karl Schmid, eds. *Das Verbrüderungsbuch der Abtei Reichenau.* Monumenta Germaniae Historica: Libri memoriales et necrologia, Nova series 1. Hanover, 1979.

Bagge, Sverre. *Cross and Scepter: The Rise of the Scandinavian Kingdoms from the Vikings to the Reformation.* Princeton, N.J., 2014.

———. *From Viking Stronghold to Christian Kingdom: State Formation in Norway, c. 900–1350.* Copenhagen, 2010.

Bárðarson, Ívarr. *See* Ívarr Bárðarson.

Barrett, James H. "The Norse in Scotland." In *The Viking World,* edited by Stefan Brink and Neil Price, 411–427. Abingdon, 2008.

Barrett, James H., Alison M. Locker, and Callum M. Roberts. "'Dark Age Economics' Revisited: The English Fish Bone Evidence, AD 600–1600." *Antiquity* 78 (2004): 618–636.

Bately, Janet, and Anton Englert. *Ohthere's Voyages: A Late 9th-Century Account of Voyages along the Coasts of Norway and Denmark and Its Cultural Context.* Roskilde, 2007.

Bates, David. *Normandy before 1066.* London, 1982.

Berglund, Joel. "The Farm beneath the Sand." In *Vikings: The North Atlantic Saga,* edited by William W. Fitzhugh and Elisabeth I. Ward, 295–303. Washington, D.C., 2000.

Bill, Jan. "Ships and Seamanship." In *The Oxford Illustrated History of the Vikings,* edited by Peter Sawyer, 182–201. Oxford, 1997.

———. "Viking Ships and the Sea." In *The Viking World,* edited by Stefan Brink and Neil Price, 170–180. Abingdon, 2008.

Blackburn, M.A.S., and Kenneth Jonsson. "The Anglo-Saxon and Anglo-Norman Element of North European Coin Finds." In *Viking-Age Coinage in the Northern Lands,* edited by M.A.S. Blackburn and M. S. Metcalf, 147–255. BAR International ser. 122. Oxford, 1981.

Blackburn, Mark. "Money and Coinage." In *The New Cambridge Medieval History,* vol. 1, edited by Rosamond McKitterick, 538–560. Cambridge, 1995.

Bolin, Sture. "Mohammed, Charlemagne and Rurik." *Scandinavian Economic History Review* 1 (1953): 5–39.

Bolton, J. L. *Money in the Medieval English Economy, 973–1489.* Manchester, 2012.

Bolton, Timothy. *The Empire of Cnut the Great: Conquest and the Consolidation of Power in Northern Europe in the Early Eleventh Century.* The Northern World: North Europe and the Baltic, c. 400–1700 A.D: Peoples, Economies and Cultures. Leiden, 2009.

Bradley, S.A.J. *Anglo-Saxon Poetry.* London, 1982.

Brate, Erik. *Östergötlands runinskrifter.* Sveriges runinskrifter 2. Stockholm, 1911.

Bratt, Peter, ed. *Forntid i ny dager.* Stockholm, 1998.

Brink, Stefan. "How Uniform Was the Old Norse Religion?" In *Learning and Understanding in the Old Norse World*, edited by Judith Quinn, Kate Heslop, and Tarrin Wills, 106–136. Turnhout, 2007.

Brøste, Kurt, Jørgen Balslev Jørgensen, Ulla Lund Hansen, and Berit Jansen Sellevold. *Prehistoric Man in Denmark: A Study in Physical Anthropology*. Vol. 3, *Iron Age Man in Denmark*. Nordiske fortidsminder Serie B—in quarto 8. Copenhagen, 1984.

Burström, Mats. *Arkeologisk samhällsavgränsning: En studie av vikingatida samhällsterritorier i Smålands inland*. Stockholm Studies in Archaeology 9. Stockholm, 1991.

Byock, Jesse L. *Viking Age Iceland*. London, 2001.

Campbell, Brian R. "The 'suþerne gar' in 'The Battle of Maldon.'" *Notes and Queries* 16, no. 2 (1969): 45–46.

Campbell, James. "Domesday Herrings." In *East Anglia's History: Studies in Honor of Norman Scarfe*, edited by Christopher Harper-Bill, Carole Rawcliffe, and Richard G. Wilson, 5–17. Woodbridge, 2002.

Capelle, Torsten. "Schiffsetzungen." *Praehistorische Zeitschrift* 61 (1986): 1–62.

Cave, Roy C., and Herbert H. Coulson. *A Sourcebook for Medieval Economic History*. New York, 1936.

Christensen, Tom. "Lejre and Roskilde." In *The Viking World*, edited by Stefan Brink and Neil Price, 121–125. Abingdon, 2008.

Clarke, Helen, and Björn Ambrosiani. *Towns in the Viking Age*. Leicester, 1991.

Cleasby, Richard, Guðbrandur Vigfússon, and William A. Craigie. *An Icelandic–English Dictionary*. 2nd ed. Oxford, 1957.

Coupland, Simon. "From Poachers to Game-Keepers: Scandinavian Warlords and Carolingian Kings." *Early Medieval Europe* 7 (1998): 85–114.

Cross, Samuel Hazzard, and Olgerd P. Sherbowitz-Wetzor. *The Russian Primary Chronicle: Laurentian Text*. Cambridge, Mass., 1973.

Deacon, Paul the. *See* Paul the Deacon.

Dennis, Andrew, Peter Godfrey Foote, and Richard Perkins. *Laws of Early Iceland: The Codex Regius of Grágás with Material from Other Manuscripts*. University of Manitoba Icelandic Studies 3 and 5. Winnipeg, 1980–2000.

DeVries, Kelly. *The Norwegian Invasion of England in 1066*. Warfare in History. Woodbridge, U.K., 1999.

Dronke, Ursula. *The Poetic Edda*. Oxford, 1969–2011.

DuBois, Thomas A. *Nordic Religions in the Viking Age*. Philadelphia, 1999.

Duby, Georges. *The Early Growth of the European Economy: Warriors and Peasants from the Seventh to the Twelfth Century*. World Economic History. Ithaca, N.Y., 1974.

Dutton, Paul Edward. *Carolingian Civilization: A Reader.* Peterborough, Ont., 1993.

Düwel, Klaus. *Das Opferfest von Lade: Quellenkritische Untersuchungen zur germanischen Religionsgeschichte.* Wiener Arbeiten zur germanischen Altertumskunde und Philologie 27. Wien, 1985.

———. "On the Sigurd Representations in Great Britain and Scandinavia." In *Languages and Cultures: Studies in Honor of Edgar C. Polomé,* edited by Mohammad Ali Jazayery and Werner Winter, 133–156. Berlin, 1988.

———. *Runenkunde.* 4th ed. Stuttgart, 2008.

Edberg, Rune. "Spår efter en tidig Jerusalemsfärd." *Fornvännen* 101 (2006): 342–346.

Egilsson, Sveinbjörn. *See* Sveinbjörn Egilsson.

Einarsson, Bjarni. *See* Bjarni Einarsson.

[Eiríkur Jónsson and Finnur Jónsson, eds.] *Hauksbók udgiven efter de Arnamagnæanske Håndskrifter No. 371, 544 og 675, 40 samt forskellige Papirshåndskrifter af det Kongelige Nordiske Oldskrift-Selskab.* Copenhagen, 1892–1896.

Eithun, Bjørn, Magnus Rindal, and Tor Ulset. *Den eldre Gulatingslova.* Norrøne tekster 6. Oslo, 1994.

Eldjárn, Kristján. *Kuml og haugfé úr heiðnum sið á Íslandi.* Edited by Adolf Friðriksson. 2nd ed. Reykjavik, 2000.

Ellis Davidson, Hilda. *The Sword in Anglo-Saxon England: Its Archaeology and Literature.* Woodbridge, Suffolk, 1998.

Englert, Anton, and Athena Trakadas, eds. *Wulfstan's Voyage: The Baltic Sea Region in the Early Viking Age as Seen from Shipboard.* Roskilde, 2009.

Ericson, Per G. P., Elisabeth Iregren, and Maria Vretemark. "Animal Exploitation at Birka—A Preliminary Report." *Fornvännen* 83 (1988): 81–88.

Eriksen, Palle, Torben Egeberg, Lis Helles Olesen, and Hans Rostholm, eds. *Vikinger i vest: Vikingetiden i Vestjylland.* Højbjerg, 2009.

Fellows-Jenssen, Gillian. "Scandinavian Place-Names in the British Isles." In *The Viking World,* edited by Stefan Brink and Neil Price, 391–400. Abingdon, 2008.

———. *The Vikings and Their Victims: The Evidence of the Names.* London, 1995.

Fenger, Ole. *"Kirker reses alle vegne": 1050–1250.* Gyldendal og Politikens Danmarkshistorie. Copenhagen, 1989.

Finlay, Alison. *Fagrskinna: A Catalogue of the Kings of Norway.* Leiden, 2004.

Finnur Jónsson. *Den norsk-islandske skjaldedigtning.* Copenhagen, 1912.

Fitzhugh, William W., and Elisabeth I. Ward, eds. *Vikings: The North Atlantic Saga.* Washington, D.C., 2000.

Fleming, Robin. *Britain after Rome: The Fall and Rise, 400–1070.* Penguin History of Britain. London, 2010.

Flodoard. *The Annals of Flodoard of Reims, 919–966.* Translated by Bernard S. Bachrach and Steven Fanning. Readings in Medieval Civilizations and Cultures 9. Peterborough, Ont., 2004.

Frank, Roberta. "Hand Tools and Power Tools in Eilífr's Þórsdrápa." In *Structure and Meaning in Old Norse Literature: New Approaches to Textual Analysis and Literary Criticism,* edited by John Lindow, Lars Lönnroth, and Gerd Wolfgang Weber, 94–109. Odense, 1986.

———. "The Invention of the Viking Horned Helmet." In *International Scandinavian and Medieval Studies in Memory of Gerd Wolfgang Weber,* edited by Michael Dallapiazza, 199–208. Trieste, 2000.

———. "The Lay of the Land in Skaldic Praise Poetry." In *Myth in Early Northwest Europe,* edited by Stephen O. Glosecki, 175–196. Tempe, Ariz., 2007.

———. "Like a Bridge of Stones." *Yale Review* 99, no. 4 (2011): 170–177.

———. *Old Norse Court Poetry: The Dróttkvætt Stanza.* Islandica 42. Ithaca, N.Y., 1978.

———. "Quid Hinieldus cum feminis: The Hero and Women at the End of the First Millennium." In *La functione dell'eroe germanico: Storicita, metafora, paradigma,* edited by Teresa Paroli, 7–25. Rome, 1995.

———. "Snorri and the Mead of Poetry." In *Speculum norroenum: Norse Studies in Memory of Gabriel Turville-Petre,* edited by Ursula Dronke, Gudrun P. Helgadóttir, Gerd Wolfgang Weber, and Hans Bekker-Nielsen, 155–170. Odense, 1981.

Franklin, Simon, and Jonathan Shepard. *The Emergence of Rus: 750–1200.* Longman History of Russia. London, 1996.

Friðriksdóttir, Jóhanna Katrín. *See* Jóhanna Katrín Friðriksdóttir.

Frye, Richard N. *Ibn Fadlan's Journey to Russia: A Tenth-Century Traveler from Baghdad to the Volga River.* Princeton, N.J., 2005.

Gansum, Terje. "Fra jord till handling." In *Plats och praxis: Arkeologiska och religionshistoriska studier av norrön ritual,* edited by Kristina Jennbert, Anders Andrén, and Catharina Raudvere. Vägar till Midgård 2, 249–286. Lund, 2001.

Garipzanov, Ildar H. *The Symbolic Language of Authority in the Carolingian World (c. 751–877).* Brill's Series on the Early Middle Ages 16. Leiden, 2008.

Geijer, Agnes. *Die Textilfunde aus den Gräbern.* Birka: Untersuchungen und Studien 3. Stockholm, 1938.

Glaber, Rodulfus. *See* Rodulfus Glaber.

Goodacre, S., A. Helgason, J. Nicholson, L. Southam, L. Ferguson, E. Hickey, E Vega, et al. "Genetic Evidence for a Family-Based Scandinavian Settlement of Shetland and Orkney during the Viking Periods." *Heredity* 95 (2005): 129–135.

Götherström, Anders. *Acquired or Inherited Prestige? Molecular Studies of Family Structures and Local Horses in Central Sveoland during the Early*

Medieval Period. Theses and Papers in Scientific Archaeology 4. Stockholm, 2001.

Graham-Campbell, James. *Viking Art.* London, 2013.

Graham-Campbell, James, and Magdalena Valor, eds. *The Archaeology of Medieval Europe,* Acta Jutlandica 83:1. Århus, 2007.

Grammaticus, Saxo. *See* Saxo Grammaticus.

Grierson, Philip, M.A.S. Blackburn, and Lucia Travaini. *Medieval European Coinage: With a Catalogue of the Coins in the Fitzwilliam Museum, Cambridge.* Cambridge, 1986.

Gschwantler, Otto. "Christus, Thor, und die Midgardschlange." In *Festschrift für Otto Höffler zum 65. Geburtstag,* edited by Otto Gschwantler, 145–168. Vienna, 1968.

Gustavson, Helmer. "Runorna som officerens hemliga skrift och allmogens vardagsvara." In *Gamla och nya runor: Artiklar 1982–2001,* 113–121. Stockholm, 2003.

Gustin, Ingrid. "Means of Payment and the Use of Coins in the Viking Age Town of Birka in Sweden: Preliminary Results." *Current Swedish Archaeology* 6 (1998): 73–83.

Hadley, D. M. *The Vikings in England: Settlement, Society and Culture.* Manchester Medieval Studies. Manchester, 2006.

Hadley, Dawn M. "The Creation of the Danelaw." In *The Viking World,* edited by Stefan Brink and Neil Price, 375–378. Abingdon, 2008.

Harrison, Dick. *600–1350: Sveriges historia.* Stockholm, 2009.

Harrison, Dick, and Kristina Ekero Svensson. *Vikingaliv.* Stockholm, 2009.

"Havhingsten fra Glendalough (*Skuldelev* 2)." Viking Ship Museum, http://www.vikingeskibsmuseet.dk/en/research/ship-reconstruction/skuldelev-2/.

Herman Pálsson and Paul Edwards. *The Book of Settlements: Landnámabók.* Winnipeg, 1972.

Hermóðsdóttir, Hildur. *See* Hildur Hermóðsdóttir.

Herschend, Frands. *Livet i hallen: Tre fallstudier i den yngre järnålderns aristokrati.* Occasional Papers in Archaeology (Uppsala) 14. Uppsala, 1997.

Hildur Hermóðsdóttir. *Icelandic Turf Houses.* Translated by Anna Yates. Reykjavik, 2012.

Holck, Per. "The Skeleton from the Gokstad Ship: New Evaluation of an Old Find." *Norwegian Archaeological Review* 42, no. 1 (2009): 40–49.

Holtsmark, Anne. "Det norrøne ord lúðr." *Maal og minne* (1946): 48–65.

Hudson, Benjamin T. *Viking Pirates and Christian Princes: Dynasty, Religion, and Empire in the North Atlantic.* Oxford, 2005.

Hvass, Steen. "The Viking-Age Settlement of Vorbasse, Central Jutland." *Acta Archaeologica* 50 (1979): 137–172.

Hyenstrand, Åke. *Lejonet, draken och korset: Sverige, 500–1000.* Lund, 1996.

Imsen, Steinar. *Hirdloven til Norges konge og hans håndgangne menn.* Oslo, 2000.

Ívarr Bárðarson. *Det gamle Grønlands beskrivelse.* Edited by Finnur Jónsson. Copenhagen, 1930.

Iversen, Mette, ed. *Mammen: Grav, kunst og samfund i vikingetid,* Jysk Arkaeologisk Selskabs skrifter 28. Højbjerg: Jysk arkaeologisk selskab, 1991.

Jankuhn, Herbert. *Haithabu: Ein Handelsplatz der Wikingerzeit.* 3rd ed. Neumünster, 1956.

Janson, Henrik. "Snorre, Tors fiskafänge och frågan om den religionshistoriska kontexten." In *Hedendomen i historiens spegel: Bilder av det förkristna Norden,* edited by Catharina Raudvere, Anders Andrén, and Kristina Jennbert. Vägar till Midgård 6, 33–55. Lund, 2005.

Janson, Tore. *Språken och historien.* Stockholm, 1997.

Jansson, Sven B. F. *The Runes of Sweden.* Stockholm, 1962.

Jesch, Judith. "In Praise of Ástríðr Óláfsdóttir." *Saga-Book* 24 (1994–1997): 1–18.

———. *Ships and Men in the Late Viking Age: The Vocabulary of Runic Inscriptions and Skaldic Verse.* Woodbridge, 2001.

———. *Women in the Viking Age.* Woodbridge, Suffolk, 1991.

Jochens, Jenny. *Women in Old Norse Society.* Ithaca, N.Y., 1995.

Jóhanna Katrín Friðriksdóttir. *Women in Old Norse Literature: Bodies, Words, and Power.* New York, 2013.

Jón Viðar Sigurðsson. *Norsk historie, 800–1300.* Samlagets Norsk historie, 800–2000. Oslo, 1999.

Jones, Gwyn. *A History of the Vikings.* London, 1968.

Jónsson, Eiríkur. *See* Eiríkur Jónsson.

Jónsson, Finnur. *See* Finnur Jónsson.

Jordanes. *De origine actibusque Getarum.* Edited by Francesco Giunta and Antonino Grillone. Fonti per la storia d'Italia 117. Rome, 1991.

———. *The Gothic History of Jordanes in English Version.* Translated by Charles Christopher Mierow. Princeton, N.J., 1915.

Keyser, Rudolph, P. A. Munch, Gustav Storm, and Ebbe Hertzberg. *Norges gamle love indtil 1387.* Christiania, 1846.

Knibbs, Eric. *Ansgar, Rimbert, and the Forged Foundations of Hamburg-Bremen.* Farnham, Surrey, 2011.

Kopár, Lilla. *Gods and Settlers: The Iconography of Norse Mythology in Anglo-Scandinavian Sculpture.* Studies in the Early Middle Ages 25. Turnhout, 2012.

Kovalev, Roman K., and Alexis C. Kaelin. "Circulation of Arab Silver in Medieval Afro-Eurasia: Preliminary Observations." *History Compass* 5, no. 2 (2007): 560–580. doi:10.1111/j.1478–0542.2006.00376.x, http://www.blackwell-synergy.com/doi/abs/10.1111/j.1478–0542.2006.00376.x.

Krag, Claus. *Norges historie fram til 1319*. Oslo, 2000.

Krogh, Knud J. *Gåden om Kong Gorms grav: Historien om Nordhøjen i Jelling*. Vikingekongernes monumenter i Jelling 1. Copenhagen, 1993.

Kulturhistoriskt lexikon för nordisk medeltid från vikingatid till reformationstid. 22 vols. Malmö, 1956–1982.

Kurze, Friedrich, ed. *Annales regni Francorum inde ab a. 741 usque ad a. 829*, MGH: SS rer. Germ. Hanover, 1895.

Kyhlberg, Ola. "Vågar och viktlod: Diskussion kring frågor om precision och noggrannhet." *Fornvännen* 70 (1975): 156–165.

———. *Vikt och värde: Arkeologiska studier i värdemätning, betalningsmedel och metrologi under yngre järnålder: 1. Helgö, 2. Birka*. Stockholm studies in archaeology 1. Stockholm, 1980.

Larrington, Carolyne. *The Poetic Edda: A New Translation*. Oxford, 1996.

Larsson, Annika. "Vikingar begravda i kinesiskt siden." *Valör*, no. 3/4 (2008): 33–43.

Larsson, Mats G. *Kensington 1998: Runfyndet som gäckade världen*. Stockholm, 2012.

Lassen, Anette. *Oden på kristent pergament: En teksthistorisk studie*. Copenhagen, 2011.

Laur, Wolfgang. *Runendenkmäler in Schleswig-Holstein und in Nordschleswig*. 2nd ed. Schleswig, 2009.

Lindkvist, Thomas. *Plundring, skatter och den feodala statens framväxt: Organisatoriska tendenser i Sverige under övergången från vikingatid till tidig medeltid*. Opuscula historica Upsaliensia 1. 3rd ed. Uppsala, 1993.

Lindow, John. "Thor's 'hamarr.'" *Journal of Germanic and English Philology* 93, no. 4 (1994): 485–503.

Liuzza, R. M. *Beowulf*. 2nd ed. Peterborough, Ont., 2013.

Lübke, Christian. *Fremde im östlichen Europa: Von Gesellschaften ohne Staat zu verstaatlichten Gesellschaften (9.–11. Jahrhundert)*. Ostmitteleuropa in Vergangenheit und Gegenwart. Cologne, 2001.

Lund, Niels. "Gorm den gamle og Thyre Danebod." In *Danske kongegrave*, edited by Karin Kryger. Copenhagen, 2014.

———. *Lið, leding og landeværn: Hær og samfund i Danmark i ældre middelalder*. Roskilde, 1996.

Lund, Niels, Ole Crumlin-Pedersen, P. H. Sawyer, and Christine E. Fell. *Two Voyagers at the Court of King Alfred: The Ventures of Ohthere and Wulfstan, Together with the Description of Northern Europe from the Old English Orosius*. York, 1984.

Lunde, Paul, and Caroline Stone. *Ibn Fadlan and the Land of Darkness: Arab Travellers in the Far North* London, 2012.

Lundström, Per. *De kommo vida: Vikingars hamn vid Paviken på Gotland*. Sjöhistoriska museets rapportserie 15. Stockholm, 1981.

Lynnerup, Niels. "Life and Death in Norse Greenland." In *Vikings: The North Atlantic Saga*, edited by William W. Fitzhugh and Elisabeth I. Ward, 285–294. Washington, D.C., 2000.

Mac Airt, Seán, and Gearóid Mac Niocaill. *The Annals of Ulster (to A.D. 1131)*. [Dublin], 1983.

Magnússon, Þór. "Bátkumlið í Vatnsdal í Patreksfirði." *Árbok Hins íslenzka fornleifafélags* 63 (1966): 5–32.

Maixner, Birgit. *Haithabu: Fernhandelszentrum zwischen den Welten*. Schleswig, 2010.

Malmer, Brita. *Den svenska mynthistorien: Vikingatiden ca 995–1030*. Stockholm, 2010.

Malmros, Rikke. *Vikingernes syn på militær og samfund belyst gennem skjaldenes fyrstedigtning*. Århus, 2010.

Martin, Janet. *Treasure of the Land of Darkness: The Fur Trade and Its Significance for Medieval Russia*. Cambridge, 1986.

McCormick, Michael. "New Light on the 'Dark Ages': How the Slave Trade Fuelled the Carolingian Economy." *Past and Present*, no. 177 (2002): 17–54.

———. *Origins of the European Economy: Communications and Commerce A.D. 300–900*. Cambridge, 2001.

McCormick, Michael, Paul Edward Dutton, and Paul A. Mayewski. "Volcanoes and the Climate Forcing of Carolingian Europe, A.D. 750–950." *Speculum* 82 (2007): 865–895.

McLeod, Shane. "Warriors and Women: The Sex Ratio of Norse Immigrants to Eastern England up to 900 AD." *Early Medieval Europe* 19 (2011): 332–353.

Merlet, René, ed. *La chronique de Nantes*. Paris, 1896.

Montgomery, James E. "Ibn Fadlan and the Russiyah." *Journal of Arabic and Islamic Studies* 3 (2000): 1–25.

Monumenta Germaniae Historica: Auctores antiquissimi 9. Edited by Theodorus Mommsen. Berlin, 1892.

Monumenta Germaniae Historica: Concilia 6. Edited by Ernst-Dieter Hehl with collaboration by Horst Fuhrmann and Carlo Servatius. Hanover, 1987–2007.

Monumenta Germaniae Historica: Epistulae 4. Berlin, 1895.

Monumenta Germaniae Historica: Poetae 3. Berlin, 1896.

Monumenta Germaniae Historica: Scriptores 15.2. Hanover, 1888.

Morgan, David. *The Mongols*. 2nd ed. Oxford, 2007.

Mühle, Eduard. *Die städtischen Handelszentren der nordwestlichen Rus: Anfänge und frühe Entwicklung altrussischer Städte (bis gegen Ende des 12. Jahrhunderts)*. Quellen und Studien zur Geschichte des östlichen Europa 32. Stuttgart, 1991.

————. "Gnezdovo—das alte Smolensk? Zur Deutung eines Siedlungs-komplexes des ausgehenden 9. bis beginnend 11. Jahrhunderts." *Bericht der römisch-germanischen Kommission* 69 (1988): 358–410.

Müller-Wille, Michael. *Bestattung im Boot. Studien zu einer nordeuropäischen Grabsitte.* Offa 25/26. Neumünster, 1970.

————. *Das wikingerzeitliche Gräberfeld von Thumby-Bienebek (Kr. Rendsburg-Eckernförde)*, vol.1. Offa-Bücher 36. Neumünster, 1976.

Näsström, Britt-Mari. *Bärsärkarna: Vikingatidens elitsoldater.* Stockholm, 2006.

Nelson, Janet. *The Annals of St-Bertin.* Ninth-Century Histories 1. Manchester, 1991.

————. "The Frankish Empire." In *The Oxford Illustrated History of the Vikings*, edited by Peter Sawyer, 19–47. Oxford, 1997.

Nordeide, Sæbjørg Walaker. *The Viking Age as a Period of Religious Transformation: The Christianization of Norway from AD 560–1150/1200.* Studies in Viking and Medieval Scandinavia 2. Turnhout, 2011.

Norges innskrifter med de yngre runer. Norges innskrifter indtil reformationen, afd 2. Oslo, 1941–.

Nylén, Erik. *Bygden, skeppen och havet.* Antikvariskt arkiv 49. Stockholm, 1973.

Nylén, Erik, and Jan Peder Lamm. *Bildstenar.* 3rd ed. Stockholm, 2003.

Oddr Snorrason. *The Saga of Olaf Tryggvason.* Translated by Theodore M. Andersson. Ithaca, N.Y., 2003.

Olsen, Olaf. *Hørg, hov og kirke: Historiske og arkæologiske vikingetidsstudier.* Copenhagen, 1966.

Orning, Hans Jacob. *Frem til 1400.* Norvegr: Norges historie. Oslo, 2011.

Orri Vésteinsson and Adolf Friðriksson. "Creating a Past: A Historiography of the Settlement of Iceland." In *Contact, Continuity and Collapse: The Norse Colonization of the North Atlantic*, edited by James Barrett. Studies in the Early Middle Ages 5, 139–161. Turnhout, 2003.

Page, R. I. *Chronicles of the Vikings: Records, Memorials, and Myths.* Toronto, 1995.

————. *"A Most Vile People": Early English Historians on the Vikings.* London, 1987.

Pálsson, Herman. *See* Herman Pálsson.

Paul the Deacon. *History of the Lombards.* Translated by William Dudley Foulke. Sources of Medieval History. Philadelphia, 1974.

Petersen, Hans Christian. "The Norse Legacy in Greenland." In *Vikings: The North Atlantic Saga*, edited by William W. Fitzhugh and Elisabeth I. Ward, 340–349. Washington, D.C., 2000.

Peterson, Lena. *Nordiskt runnamnslexikon med tillägg av frekvenstabeller och finalalfabetisk ordlista.* Uppsala, 2002.

Pettersson, Ann-Marie, ed. *Spillingsskatten: Gotland i vikingatidens världshandel*. Visby, 2008.

Price, Neil. "Dying and the Dead: Viking Age Mortuary Behaviour." In *The Viking World*, edited by Stefan Brink and Neil Price, 257–273. Abingdon, 2008.

Ralph, Bo. "Gåtan som lösning—Ett bidrag till förståelsen av Rökstenens runinskrift." *Maal og minne* (2007): 133–157.

Procopius. *History of the Wars*. Translated by H. B. Dewing. Loeb Classical Library 107. Cambridge, Mass., 1919.

Ramqvist, Per H. "Perspektiv på lokal variation och samhälle i Nordens folkvandringstid." In *Samfundsorganisation og regional variation: Norden i romersk jernålder og folkevandringstid*. Aarhus, 1991.

Reallexikon der germanischen Altertumskunde. 2nd ed. Berlin, 1967–2007.

Reichardt, Konstantin. "Die Thórsdrápa des Eilífr Godrúnarson: Textinterpretation." *Publications of the Modern Language Association of America* 63, no. 2 (1948): 329–391.

Reuter, Timothy. *The Annals of Fulda*. Ninth-Century Histories 2. Manchester, 1992.

———. "Plunder and Tribute in the Carolingian Empire." *Transactions of the Royal Historical Society* 35 (1985): 75–94.

Reuter, Timothy, and Janet L. Nelson. *Medieval Polities and Modern Mentalities*. Cambridge, 2006.

Robinson, Charles H. *Anskar, the Apostle of the North, 801–865: Translated from the Vita Anskarii by Bishop Rimbert, His Fellow Missionary and Successor*. [London], 1921.

Rodolfus Glaber. *The Five Books of History*. Edited and translated by John France. Oxford Medieval Texts. Oxford, 1989.

Roesdahl, Else. *The Vikings*. 2nd ed. London, 1998.

Ross, Margaret Clunies, ed. *Skaldic Poetry of the Scandinavian Middle Ages*. Turnhout, 2007–.

Rotman, Youval. *Byzantine Slavery and the Mediterranean World*. Translated by Jane Marie Todd. Cambridge, Mass., 2009.

Samnordisk runtextdatabas. Uppsala University. http://www.nordiska .uu.se/forskn/samnord.htm.

Samson, Vincent. *Les Berserkir: Les guerriers-fauves dans la Scandinavie ancienne, de l'âge de Vendel aux Vikings (VIe–XIe siècle)*. Histoire et civilisations: Histoire. Villeneuve d'Ascq, 2011.

Sawyer, Birgit. *The Viking-Age Rune-Stones: Custom and Commemoration in Early Medieval Scandinavia*. Oxford, 2000.

Sawyer, Birgit, and Peter Sawyer. *Medieval Scandinavia: From Conversion to Reformation, circa 800–1500*. The Nordic Series 17. Minneapolis, 1993.

Sawyer, P. H. "Kings and Merchants." In *Early Medieval Kingship*, edited by P. H. Sawyer and I. N. Wood, 139–158. Leeds, 1977.

———. *Kings and Vikings: Scandinavia and Europe, A.D. 700–1100.* London and New York, 1982.

Sawyer, Peter. *Da Danmark blev Danmark: Fra ca. år 700 til ca. 1050.* Translated by Marie Hvidt. Gyldendal-Politikens Danmarkshistorie, vol. 3. Copenhagen, 1988.

Saxo Grammaticus. *The History of the Danes.* Translated by Peter Fischer, edited by Hilda Ellis Davidson. Woodbridge, Suffolk, 1979.

———. *The Nine Books of the Danish History of Saxo Grammaticus.* Translated by Oliver Elton. London, 1905.

Schnorr von Carolsfeld, H. "Das Chronicon Laurissense breve." *Neues Archiv* 36 (1911): 13–39.

Scholz, Bernhard W., with Barbara Rogers. *Carolingian Chronicles: Royal Frankish Annals and Nithard's Histories.* Ann Arbor, Mich., 1970.

Schönbäck, Bengt, and Lena Thunmark-Nylén. "De vikingatida båtgravarna i Valsgärde—relativ kronologi." *Fornvännen* 97 (2002): 1–8.

Seaver, Kirsten A. *The Frozen Echo: Greenland and the Exploration of North America, ca. A.D. 1000–1500.* Stanford, 1996.

See, Klaus von. "Exkurs zum Haraldskvæði: Berserker." *Zeitschrift für deutsche Wortforschung* 17 (1961): 129–135.

Sigurðsson, Jón Viðar. *See* Jón Viðar Sigurðsson.

Skånland, Vegard. *Det eldste norske provinsialstatutt.* Oslo, 1969.

Skree, Dagfinn, ed. *Kaupang in Skiringssal.* Kaupang Excavation Project Publication Series 1 = Norske Oldfunn 22. Aarhus, 2007.

[Smedt, C.] "Translatio S. Germani Parisiensis anno 846 secundum primævam narrationem e codice Namurcensi." *Analecta Bollandiana* 2 (1883): 69–98.

Snorrason, Oddr. *See* Oddr Snorrason.

Snorri Sturluson. *Heimskringla: History of the Kings of Norway.* Translated by Lee M. Hollander. Austin, 1964.

———. *The Prose Edda: Norse Mythology.* London, 2005.

Söderberg, Sven, and Erik Brate. *Ölands runinskrifter.* Sveriges runinskrifter 1. Stockholm, 1900.

Spufford, Peter. *Money and Its Use in Medieval Europe.* Cambridge and New York, 1988.

Stenberger, Mårten. "Erikstorpsspännet och Hedeby." *Fornvännen* 45 (1950): 36–40.

Steuer, Heiko. "Der Handel der Wikingerzeit zwischen Nord- und Westeuropa aufgrund archäologischer Zeugnisse." In *Untersuchungen zu Handel und Verkehr der vor- und frühgeschichtlichen Zeit in Mittel- und Nordeuropa*, vol. 4, *Der Handel der Karolinger- und Wikingerzeit: Bericht über die Kolloquien der Kommission für die Altertumskunde Mittel- und*

Nordeuropas in den Jahren 1980 bis 1983, edited by Klaus Düwel, Herbert Jankuhn, Harald Siems, and Dieter Timpe, 113–197. Göttingen, 1987.

Stratman, Martina, ed. *Historia Remensis ecclesiae*, MGH: Scriptores 36, Hanover, 1998.

Straubhaar, Sandra Ballif. *Old Norse Women's Poetry: The Voices of Female Skalds*. Rochester, N.Y., 2011.

Sturluson, Snorri. *See* Snorri Sturluson.

Sundqvist, Olof, Per Vikstrand, and John Ljungkvist, eds. *Gamla Uppsala i ny belysning*, Religionsvetenskapliga studier från Gävle 9. Uppsala, 2013.

Svanberg, Fredrik. *Vikingatiden i Skåne*. Lund, 2000.

Sveinbjörn Egilsson and Finnur Jónsson. *Lexicon poeticum antiquæ linguæ septentrionalis: Ordbog over det norsk-islandske skjaldesprog*. 2nd ed. Copenhagen, 1931.

Svennung, Josef. *Jordanes und Scandia: Kritisch-exegetische Studien*. Skrifter utgivna av K. Humanistiska vetenskapssamfundet i Uppsala 44:2A. Stockholm, 1967.

Swanton, Michael, trans. *The Anglo-Saxon Chronicle*. London, 1996.

Todd, James Henthorn, ed. and trans. *Cogadh Gaedhel re Gaillaibh: The Wars of the Irish against the Foreigners, or The Invasions of Ireland by the Danes and Other Norsemen*, Rerum Britannicarum medii aevi scriptores [Roll series] 78. London, 1867.

Townend, Matthew. *Language and History in Viking Age England: Linguistic Relations between Speakers of Old Norse and Old English*. Studies in the Early Middle Ages. Turnhout, 2002.

Verhulst, Adriaan E. *The Carolingian Economy*. Cambridge Medieval Textbooks. New York, 2002.

Vésteinsson, Orri. *See* Orri Vésteinsson.

Vinner, Max. *Viking Ship Museum Boats*. Roskilde, 2002.

Vogel, Walther. *Die Normannen und das fränkische Reich bis zur Gründung der Normandie (799–911)*. Heidelberger Abhandlungen zur mittleren und neueren Geschichte 14. Heidelberg, 1906.

Waitz, Georg, ed. *Vita Anskarii auctore Rimberti: Accedit Vita Rimberti*, MGH: SS rer. Germ. Hanover, 1884.

Wamers, Egon. "Kristne gjenstander i tidligvikingtidens Danmark." In *Kristendommen i Danmark før 1050*, edited by Niels Lund, 43–59. [Roskilde], 2004.

Wamers, Egon, and Michael Brandt. *Die Macht des Silbers: Karolingische Schätze im Norden*. Regensburg, 2005.

Warner, David. *Ottonian Germany: The Chronicon of Thietmar of Merseburg*. Manchester Medieval Sources Series. Manchester, 2001.

Welinder, Stig, Ellen Anne Pedersen, and Mats Widgren. *Jordbrukets första femtusen år*. Det svenska jordbrukets historia. Stockholm, 1998.

Werner, Tove. "Stenskepp i Södermanland: Utbredning och datering." *Fornvännen* 98 (2003): 257–264.

Wessén, Elias. *Runstenen vid Röks kyrka.* Kungl. Vitterhets-, historie- och antikvitetsakademiens handlingar: Filologisk-filosofiska serien, 5. Stockholm, 1958.

Whaley, Diana. *The Poetry of Arnórr Jarlaskáld: An Edition and Study.* Westfield Publications in Medieval Studies 8. Turnhout, 1998.

Wicker, Nancy L. "The Scandinavian Animal Styles in Response to Mediterranean and Christian Narrative Art." In *The Cross Goes North: Processes of Conversion in Northern Europe, AD 300–1300*, edited by Martin Carver, 531–550. York, 2003.

Widukind of Corvey. *Die Sachsengeschichte des Widukind von Korvei.* Edited by Paul Hirsch and Hans-Eberhard Lohmann. MGH SS rer. Germ. Hanover, 1935.

Williams, Alan. "A Metallurgical Study of Some Viking Swords." *Gladius: Estudios sobre armas antiquas, arte militar y vida cultural en oriente y occidente* 29 (2009): 121–184.

Wilson, David M. "The Development of Viking Art." In *Viking World*, edited by Stefan Brink and Neil Price, 321–338. Abingdon, 2008.

———. *Vikingatidens konst.* Translated by Henrika Ringbom. Signums svenska konsthistoria. Lund, 1995.

Winroth, Anders. *The Conversion of Scandinavia: Vikings, Merchants, and Missionaries in the Remaking of Northern Europe.* New Haven, 2012.

ILLUSTRATIONS

FIGURES

MAPS

PLATES
(*following page 180*)

INDEX

MAP 2. Northern Europe in the Viking Age. Cartography by Bill Nelson.